ISLAM AND POLITICAL VIOLENCE

ISLAM AND POLITICAL VIOLENCE
Muslim Diaspora and Radicalism in the West

EDITED BY

SHAHRAM AKBARZADEH

& FETHI MANSOURI

Tauris Academic Studies
LONDON • NEW YORK

Published in 2007 by Tauris Academic Studies, an imprint of I.B.Tauris & Co Ltd
6 Salem Road, London W2 4BU
175 Fifth Avenue, New York NY 10010
www.ibtauris.com

In the United States of America and Canada distributed by Palgrave Macmillan
a division of St. Martin's Press, 175 Fifth Avenue, New York NY 10010

Library of International Relations 34

ISBN: 978 1 84511 473 2

A full CIP record for this book is available from the British Library
A full CIP record is available from the Library of Congress

Library of Congress Catalog Card Number: available

Printed and bound in India by Replika Press Pvt. Ltd
From camera-ready copy edited and supplied by the editors

CONTENTS

ACKNOWLEDGMENTS

The editors wish to acknowledge the generous support and assistance of Monash University's School of Political and Social Inquiry, Deakin University's Institute for Citizenship and Globalisation, the Australian Research Council's Asia Pacific Futures Research Network, as well as the Victorian Multicultural Commission and the Centre for Contemporary Islam at Melbourne University. We would like to acknowledge the expert input of Dr Benjamin McQueen of the School of Political & Social Inquiry at Monash University in preparing this refereed collection.

Shahram Akbarzadeh & Fethi Mansouri
Melbourne
March 2007

1

CONTEXTUALISING NEO-ISLAMISM

Shahram Akbarzadeh & Fethi Mansouri

Islamism has been on an evolutionary trajectory. When Osama bin Laden and his band of devotees launched their war on the US under the banner of Islam, they epitomised a metamorphosis that had started at least two decades earlier. Bin Laden's brand stood at the extreme end of Islamism in two key areas. On the national/international and the violence/non-violence matrix, bin Laden's brand of radicalism occupied the extreme internationally violent corner. This new brand was not confined to state-demarcated objectives. Neo-Islamism, as represented by al-Qaeda and the multitude of its affiliates, is global in its strategy and tactics.[1] It is also uninhibited by any sense of common humanity, maintaining a rigidly dichotomous perception of good and evil, where anyone not affiliated with the neo-Islamists would by definition belong to the opposite camp. This binary perspective presents a series of security, social and political challenges.

This brand of neo-Islamism can pose a security threat because it does not seem to conform to the conventional differentiation between civilian and military targets. It views civilian casualties as unavoidable 'collateral damage' in its perspective on grand civilisational conflict. All those working in the Twin Towers, non-Muslims and Muslims alike, were viewed as maintaining the power of the US and the evil West. They were inconsequential in the battle between good and evil. As a result, al-Qaeda affiliates and others inspired by this Manichean view of the world have turned to soft targets in New York, Bali, Madrid and London to inflict pain and uncertainty. The objective of such attacks has been to cause maximum damage and panic. It is impossible to describe such acts as anything but criminal. It is also next to impossible to guard against them. Herein lies the enormous security challenge facing relevant authorities.

The social manifestations of this challenge are multi-faceted. Social liberties have come under threat due to increased security concerns. Whether it is intrusive screening at airports, heightened electronic surveillance, restrictions on purchase of certain chemicals or broader police powers in detaining suspected individuals, Western societies have experienced a growing challenge to individual freedoms that were taken for granted. This challenge grows with every new terrorist attack, or security scare, and has caused uproar among social libertarians who deplore the ease with which social and legal guarantees for our life style are being eroded. The group that feels this the most is the Muslim diaspora.

Europe, North America and Australia are home to substantial Muslim communities.[2] The greatest proportion of these communities moved to the 'West' in search of a better life following the devastation of World War II. These people were welcomed by recipient countries, which benefited from the bolstering of their labour force. Although Muslim social integration in host countries was not always smooth, it was overshadowed by a host of other political issues. Political violence associated with radical Islamists and the sharp turn to the right in the politics of Western liberal democracies have seriously altered the situation, giving rise to a 'Muslim question'. Fundamental questions are now being asked about the capacity of Muslims to live as active citizens in Western democracies. The current 'Muslim question' is another manifestation of the old dichotomous paradigm on Islam and modernity. Just as Islam has been derided by critics like Bernard Lewis and Samuel Huntington as incompatible with modern forms of governance, current critics claim there to be an inherent contradiction between Muslim identity and citizenship in a liberal democracy.[3] The assumed mutual exclusivity of the two has been put on display in the debates surrounding the hijab, most notably in France where the 2004 legislation caused significant unease among Muslims and non-Muslims. The claim that adherence to Islam contradicts commitments and loyalty to the governing values of liberal democracies, and that public display of Muslim faith is an affront to principles of secularism, push Muslims in Europe, the US and Australia into a corner.

The expectation that Muslims need to reiterate their adherence to 'liberal values', be it French, Australian or British, rests on the assumption that Muslim values are at best different and at worst inimical to them. Not only is this assumption disconnected from the reality of Muslim lives, it glosses over the diversity of beliefs and practices that make up the Muslim population. It is an often overlooked fact that

Muslims are divided along ethnic and sectarian lines. They are also divided between those who consciously practice Islam and those who do not.[4] The broad-brush depiction of Muslims as a homogenous entity, paints all Muslims as religiously devout, and (almost naturally) governed by Islamic principles. This simplistic view does not allow for the vast numbers of Muslims who were simply born into a Muslim culture and treat Islam as a pillar of their identity and heritage not the source of a political ideology.

The emergence of the Muslim question in the West has added a worrying dimension to the already vexed relationship between the Muslim world and the West. The recent history of the Middle East is marked by war and bloodshed. Starting with the Arab-Israeli wars, the modern Middle East has witnessed active superpower involvement in inter-state and intra-state conflicts. Afghanistan was a proxy war *par excellence* where the US committed itself to removing the Soviet occupation via support for a range of Islamic militia groups.[5] The Iran-Iraq war was another case where the US threw its weight behind Saddam Hussein's efforts to weaken and undermine the fledgling Islamic regime. The 'War on Terror', however, has introduced a new phase in this relationship as the US now feels justified to take direct action and commit troops to theatres of war. The military operation to eradicate al-Qaeda and topple the Taliban, and the subsequent pre-emptive attack on Iraq, which brought US soldiers in the line of fire, are examples of a new stage in the international affairs of the Middle East. In this stage, the US (with or without the support of the international community) has directly intervened in the region to affect change, giving cause to greater Muslim discontent and antipathy towards Washington and its allies.[6] The complaint that Washington pursues an arrogant policy of domination, marked with double standards – immune to international scrutiny, reverberates far and wide in the Middle East.

The present volume deals with the whole gamut of the above challenges. It explores the changing nature of Islamism and its growing links with indiscriminate acts of violence as well as far-reaching implications of this development for the Muslim diaspora.

Islamism as a National Project

Islamism grew as a response to the failure of the top-down state-building project in the Middle East and the rest of the Muslim world.[7] The modern states of the Middle East and Asia were formally welcomed into the international fold as sovereign polities following Europe's colonial withdrawal. But the colonial past left a lasting legacy. Territorial demarcations drawn up by colonial powers imposed the contours of modern states. This presented a pressing challenge to the legitimacy of the emerging national elites who turned to 'modernisation', whether in the guise of socialism or free market, to justify their claim to the helms of power.[8] Progress became the catch phrase of the leadership in these developing states. Except for the obvious case of Saudi Arabia, which was founded on an alliance of tribal-religious leadership, Islam was not seen as an important parcel of the modernisation drive. Perhaps revealing an intellectual affinity with the colonial powers that viewed Islam as a primitive religion, the national elites did not envisage a place for Islam in the nascent modern states. State policies ranged from active suppression of Islamic manifestations as anti-modern in Turkey and Iran, to ignoring it as irrelevant in Iraq and Jordan, to its public tolerance as politically expedient in Pakistan. The common denominator in all cases, however, was that Islam had nothing to contribute to the modern state.

Islam's exclusion at the top gave it potential for growth in direct correlation with the failure of the modern state project. To a large extent, this failure was a result of uneven socio-economic development in the new sovereign states as national plans were put in place to modernise the economy and train the labour force while retaining ownership and control over economic activities. The rate of growth in the labour force, most markedly signified in the rural-urban migrations which led to the expansion of shantytowns around capital cities, was unmatched by the growth of economic opportunities. Growing unemployment figures and static, if not falling, living standards have fed resentment and disenchantment with the promise of prosperity and modernity.[9] Poverty and unemployment continue to be nagging socio-economic ills confronting the developing world. But what made the states' failure to deliver more pronounced were the institutionalisation of public education and the growing popularity of technical and higher education among the upwardly mobile and, at the same time, the inability of the state-managed economy to absorb them or offer opportunities for their fulfillment. In the 1960s and 1970s, a gap emerged between the expanding expectations of the growing middle class, which was broadening its horizons through education, and contact with the world beyond state boundaries, and the opportunities offered by closed economic and political systems. Such unfulfilled expectations soon evolved into political discontent as the incumbent regimes continued to view their states as their personal fiefdoms and feared the aspirations of the growingly assertive middle class as a threat to their political monopoly.

Discontent in Muslim states gained a new cultural dimension as the socio-economic and political aspirations of the middle class were complemented by the disenchantment of conservative elements of society, often led by Islamic authorities, not comfortable with the Western concepts and images that were permeating Muslim societies. This may have been an unlikely alliance, but secularly educated middle classes proved to be the most articulate and committed proponents of an Islamic critique to the incumbent regimes. Disillusionment with the top-down model of modernisation, which stifled societal initiatives, and the alienation of traditional elements of society who were affronted by what they viewed as moral corruption and 'Westernisation' proved a potent mix. Islamism has drawn from this vast pool of discontent and presented a serious challenge to the authority and legitimacy of incumbent regimes. Islamism in its conventional form, however, has been almost exclusively concerned with state affairs.[10]

The Egyptian Muslim Brotherhood and the Pakistani Jama'ati Islami are two obvious cases in point. The Muslim Brotherhood emerged in the early parts of the 20th century in Egypt and spread to neighbouring states with a heavy emphasis on Islamic education and welfare. The Brotherhood gradually adopted a political tone, largely in response to colonial pressures and the radicalisation of Arab opinion. The Brotherhood had a pan-Arab orientation which endorsed a united Arab front against British and French colonial powers.[11] The end of World War II, which precipitated the decolonisation in the Middle East, and the emergence of the State of Israel underlined the importance of politics for the Brotherhood. The politicisation of the organisation was accelerated by the 1952 coup which led to the presidency of the charismatic Gamal Abdul Nasser. The Brotherhood's political activism was substantiated by Sayyed Qutb who formulated the most coherent ideological position for Islamists. Qutb's rejection of man-made laws as illegitimate and his invocation of divinity to guide the Muslim community (the *umma*) have been among the most erudite expositions of the need for the merger of Islam and politics. This uncompromising Islamist doctrine made Qutb the target of state prosecution and ultimately execution in 1965. The Brotherhood, however, continued on its trajectory of political radicalism as Egypt was defeated in the 1967 and 1973 wars with Israel, and the subsequent peace treaty between Egypt and Israel in 1979. The assassination of Anwar Sadat by Islamists, with assumed links to the Muslim Brotherhood, was a new phase in Egyptian Islamism. Political violence in the form of terrorist attacks on the tourist industry and other soft targets, such as secular literary and public figures or the Coptic community, has grown to become a recurring challenge in Egypt. Such acts present a serious security problem for the state. At the same time, these challenges have been limited to the state of Egypt. Whether in the form of the Muslim Brotherhood or the openly violent fringe groups such as Gama'a al-Islamiyya, Islamism in Egypt has clearly had a national agenda.

Jama'at-i Islami (the Islamic Society) in Pakistan represents another Islamist movement with explicitly nationalist horizons. Although the Jama'at was initially concerned with safeguarding and promoting the Islamic value system for the Muslim population of South Asia, like its counterpart in Egypt, it went through a process of politicisation as a result of the colonial draw-back of post-World War II. One of the significant aspects of this politicisation was the Jama'at's acquiescence to the Pakistani national project at the expense of the idealist notion of transnational *umma*. Despite earlier objections to the geographic partition of South Asia, the Jama'at embraced the new state of Pakistan after its formation and committed itself to its Islamisation.[12] Under the stewardship of Mawlana Maududi, who articulated the Islamist position on the illegitimacy of non-Shari'a-based law and gained great influence over Islamists throughout the Muslim world, the Jama'at transformed itself from a socio-political organisation concerned with the Muslim *umma* to a successful parliamentary party focused on the consolidation of Islam in Pakistan. Maududi was critical of nationalism, which he dismissed as an ideology to divide *dar ul-Islam*, yet his political activism and that of the Jama'at-i Islami were in effect restrained by the boundaries of the nation-state.

Islamism, in its violent or non-violent form, has been a national project. It has been aimed at addressing what the Islamists call 'un-Islamic behaviour' in the community by Islamising it from above. In theory, the Islamist vision is transnational. In reality, however, the Islamist zeal for capturing political power and implementing a thorough legal, social and cultural reformation has worked to lower its horizons. The notion of an Islamic state espoused by Islamists has imposed practical limitations which effectively undercut the ideal of the *umma* as a political entity. Iran and Pakistan represent two examples of the naturalisation of Islamism. In the case of Iran, especially, this process has been remarkable as the Islamic state came into being with salient implications for the international community, most immediately affecting the neighbouring states. Saudi Arabia and Iraq were targeted by the new

Islamist regime in Tehran as the next dominos to fall in the anticipated Islamic revolutions to sweep across the Middle East. Within a decade, however, the rhetoric of cascading Islamic uprisings gave way to measured pronouncements of regional security and collaboration reflecting the very tangible concerns with Iran's national interest among the top echelons of power in Tehran.[13] Iran's rapprochement with the Saudi regime in the 1990s (rejected earlier as corrupt and a barrier to true Islam), and collaboration with the US and the international community against the Taliban (2001), demonstrated the supremacy of national interests over any other idealistic agenda in Tehran's foreign policy thinking.

Hamas and Hizbullah may be added to the long list of Islamist groups that pursue an explicit national objective. Both organisations have gained a stake in the existing political establishment and are at the same time restrained by it. Their violent resistance of Israel is not aimed at awakening a global Islamic movement and the formation of an over-arching Islamic polity, although they make extensive use of the notion of Islamic solidarity and *umma* as sources of external solidarity in their local confrontations with Israel. In this sense, both organisations act within a national mental framework.

International Connection

It is important to note that the national framework of Islamists is not absolute. Islamists and non-Islamists alike have been influenced by and drawn from the international context. Military defeats in Arab-Israeli wars, for example, have left a lasting impression on the Arab public opinion, seriously undermining confidence in Arab leaders' capability and political commitment. Political discontent with incumbent regimes in the Muslim world often gains an international facet as the later are seen to be propped-up by foreign powers. The Iranian revolution was a case in point where a mass protest swelled up against the corruption of the Pahlavi regime and its US backers. The revolution was a national affair, carrying a salient international message – ie. anti-Americanism. In fact, anti-American sentiments have consistently gained a permanent spot in the rhetoric of Islamists. The reason is not difficult to fathom. The US has traditionally favoured preserving the status quo in the Muslim world, first for fear of Soviet advances and later the spread of anti-American Islamism.

Washington's policy towards the Middle East during the Cold War era was governed by its assessment of the Soviet Union as its archrival, which would take advantage of any political opening there to gain a foothold at the expense of US national interests. Evidence of such overtures was present in the military and economic ties between Nasser's Egypt and the Soviet Union, and the growing assertiveness of the Moscow-backed Iranian Communist Party during the short lived Prime Ministership of Mohammad Mossadeq. Further afield, in Vietnam, the US suffered a blow to its image as the Communist led forces marched on Saigon. Fears of Soviet-sponsored insurgencies in South East Asia were ever-present in Washington's policymaking. These concerns were based on the logic of the Cold War, where superpower rivalry and competition were the order of the day. The Soviet invasion of Afghanistan in 1979, in defence of a leftist government in Kabul, set in motion a tragic and overdrawn conflict that reinforced Washington's zero-sum assessment of Cold War dynamics. As far as Washington was concerned, any move that altered the internal dynamics of states in the Middle East offered an unacceptable opportunity to the Soviet Union. Consequently, the US advanced policies that fostered stability and continuity in this oil rich region of the world. For this reason, Washington was very suspicious of political transformations, including democratic change, as demonstrated in its response to Iran under Mosaddeq (1953),[14] or the electoral victory of the Islamic Salvation Front in Algeria and the subsequent coup (1991). Washington was a status quo power. This translated into propping-up unpopular and repressive regimes.

The fall of the Soviet Union did not alter Washington's aversion to change, as Islamism appeared to fill the gap that the Soviet collapse had left behind. The consolidation of the Islamic regime in Iran set a precedent in the region that the US was more than keen to prevent. The US aversion towards Islamists has often resulted in tolerating grossly undemocratic practices targeted at barring Islamists from political power, or simply dismissing the outcome of the ballot boxes as illegitimate. In Egypt, for example, the authorities have systematically excluded the Muslim Brotherhood from parliamentary elections, despite public commitments to opening up the political system. Washington has remained conspicuously silent on Cairo's highly questionable electoral conduct. In the Palestinian Occupied Territories, where Hamas won an unexpected victory at the 2005 polls, the US has withdrawn its diplomatic contacts and aid, refusing to recognise the Hamas-led government, even though the electoral process was internationally endorsed (an endorsement which many other Middle Eastern polls, including the Egyptian, lacked). This pattern, of preserving closed authoritarian regimes to insulate US interests in the region, has meant that anti-establishment Islamists are by necessity anti-American as the US is seen as the external mainstay of local despots.

Anti-American sentiments in the Muslim world, more specifically in the Middle East, were reinforced following the 2006 Israeli incursion into Lebanon to destroy Hizbullah. Much to the palpable frustration of the Lebanese government and international observers, the US refused to endorse a cease-fire plan at the United Nations (UN), giving Israel a free hand to carry out three weeks of air-raids against Lebanon's infrastructure and ground incursions in southern Lebanon. International inaction offered Israel de facto impunity. The same is true of the US. Washington acted with disdain for the international community on the eve of the 2004 invasion of Iraq. The decision to invade Iraq without the explicit sanctions of the UN Security Council was seen in the Muslim world as significant on two counts. First, the US is not accountable to international law and stands above it. Second, the international community is either too powerless to rein in US transgressions or too much under its control to oppose it. In either case, opposing the US, and the international community by extension, has grown to be a fixture of Islamist doctrine.

Widespread disenchantment with the limitations of the international system to address Muslim grievances and deliver justice has further entrenched the alienation of Islamists and given them cause to reject international agencies as illegitimate. The new brand of Islamism that has emerged in the 1980s and 1990s, often linked with the experience of jihad in Afghanistan, makes a direct connection between local and international. Unlike its predecessor, neo-Islamism is not confined within a national mindset. Instead, it regards the 'un-Islamic' behaviour of incumbent regimes in the Muslim world as a manifestation of deeper ills that operate globally. The primary target of neo-Islamists, therefore, is the international system that they view as sustaining injustice, locally and globally. Given the history of the US in the Middle East, it is not surprising that anti-Americanism is a pronounced feature of the neo-Islamist worldview.

Muslim Diaspora

It is ironic that a key aspect of modernity has brought neo-Islamism to the heart of the West. Muslim migration to Europe, America and Australia, and the subsequent natural growth of Muslim populations within these countries, has diluted the binary divide between Islam and the West. The classical division of the world between the land of Islam (*dar ul-Islam*) and the land of disbelief and war (*dar ul-harb*) has become irrelevant as Muslims have made the West their home. By the same token, social discontent among Muslim youth in diaspora due to racial, socio-economic and/or religious discrimination has made them vulnerable to neo-Islamist propositions.

Second and third generation Muslims growing up in Western cities face difficult challenges. The choice of living in the West was not theirs to make but that of their parents – often in response to severe socio-economic or political pressures. Muslim parents see migration to the West as a way of improving the living conditions of their families and offering a better future to the next generation. The strong emphasis on education in Muslim families underlines this desire to see their offspring take advantage of opportunities and excel in their lives. It is not unusual for Muslim parents to seek fulfillment and pride through the achievements of their children. Watching career successes of the second generation makes the pain of dislocation and living away from the home country bearable for Muslim parents. Such successes also compensate in some way for the more difficult experiences of first generation Muslims in securing suitable employment. Against this backdrop of investing in the future of their offspring, while coping with the challenges of living in a socially, religiously and linguistically unfamiliar setting, Muslim migrants retain close links with their country of origin. Through travel, telephone calls to relatives and purchase of imported cultural artifacts (most notably music tapes and CDs), Muslim migrants maintain and regenerate links with their country of origin. This connection offers a degree of cultural continuity and comfort.

However, for Muslim youth in the West, links with the parents' countries of origin start to weaken due to a combination of factors, including the near absence of first-hand experience of living in the 'country of origin', decline of language proficiency in the 'mother tongue' and a sense of disconnectedness. Indeed, for the great majority of Muslim youth in the West, (the lived experiences of Muslims in France, the United Kingdom, the US and Australia, for example), makes these Western states their de facto 'home country' and the state language their 'mother tongue'. The separation of second and third generation migrants from their ancestral land is a natural process and helps them pursue their fortune in their host societies free of nostalgia. This is far from a complete emotional break. References to ancestral origins are not far below the surface, but they are kept in check with a tangible web of connections, loyalties and commitments that are generated in the course of life in the West. For those who have managed to succeed and find fulfillment, it is easy to navigate between emotional connections with their ancestral land and social, economic, political and emotional attachment to the country of residence. For those on the margins of society, however, such navigation may prove hazardous, especially in times of crisis, such as the one we have experienced since the launch of the 'War on Terror'.

Neo-Islamism, therefore, may find a receptive audience among alienated Muslims who feel marginalised and excluded from society. Such individuals are not by necessity economically deprived. Contrary to common wisdom, there is no direct correlation between economic deprivation and political radicalism. The critical factor is the perception of injustice and bridled aspirations. For that reason, the educated middle class youth are at greater risk of radicalisation than the economically underprivileged classes. The July 2005 'home grown' terrorists in the United Kingdom, for example, had typical middle class backgrounds. Yet these individuals maintain a dim view of their chances in society and feel marginalised, even discriminated against – a perception that is often linked to the emergence of Muslim ghettos.[15] Added to this sense of alienation is a grand notion of global injustice meted out to Muslims. Here lies the attraction of neo-Islamism. Not being constrained by a national mind-frame and operating as a transnational force, it appeals to those who have lost their connection to their Muslim ancestral land but find it difficult to be accepted in their country of residence. This dual sense of alienation is often compensated for with idealised notions of Muslim unity and solidarity with global causes.

Neo-Islamism's notion of global jihad feeds on political grievances of Muslims against the global order. The unequal power relations in international affairs represented for example in global inaction in the face of Israel's incursion into Lebanon in August 2006, or growing pressures on the Muslim diaspora reflected in the 2004 French law banning hijab from schools, are noted as evidence of a global conspiracy against Islam. The response, it follows, would need to be global. By virtue of rejecting existing legal and political structures as illegitimate, neo-Islamists are inclined to engage in acts of political violence as the only remaining tool to affect change.

***

This collection of essays is divided into three parts. The first part explores the broad issues of definition, and presents an analysis of the new challenges of trans-national radicalism. Neo-Islamism has operated at a global level and facilitated the rise to widespread apprehension about Islam. The growth of Islamophobic tendencies reflect at once security concerns and fear of the unknown. Islamophobia is the reverse side of the anti-Westernism that is the common currency of Islamism. This discussion by Amin Saikal, James Piscatori and Bassam Tibi is followed by part two, which explores the relevance of Islamophobia to the internal workings of liberal democracies. The Muslim diaspora in the West has attracted significantly negative attention in the mass media and is, at times, treated as the 'fifth column'. The assumed wall that divides Muslims and non-Muslims in the West is the focus of Bryan Turner, Sue Kenny and Michael Humphrey. These authors explore how the notion of difference and the Other has affected the Muslim disapora and brought into question Muslim citizenship. The final part of this book turns to the spread and diversity of radicalism in the Muslim world as well as alternative Muslim responses to neo-Islamism. While Riaz Hassan inquires into how jihadism is understood in key Muslim societies, Greg Fealy presents an assessment of the growing challenge of jihadism in Indonesia. This exposition is followed by a sobering analysis of Sufi spiritualism in Indonesia as it represents a homegrown alternative to political radicalism. The volume is concluded by Lynne Alice's account of a democratic experiment which provides a voice to Muslim identity and sovereignty in the Balkans, a significant enterprise which challenges the neo-Islamists' global conspiracy theory.

2

RADICAL ISLAMISM AND THE 'WAR ON TERROR'

Amin Saikal

Radical political Islamism is not a new phenomenon, but it has certainly gained unprecedented salience in world politics since the tragic events of 11 September 2001. Most prominently, al-Qaeda and its associated groups have deployed an extremist form of it as an ideology to justify violence directed not only at causing structural political and social changes in Muslim societies, but also at combating perceived hostile international forces, especially the US and its closest allies. The actions of the extremist exponents of radical Islamism – activists who are diverse in their ideological intensity and disposition – have generated much terror, fear, bloodshed and insecurity in the world. They have enabled the Bush Administration, or more specifically the neo-conservative, born-again Christian and ultra-nationalist elements within it, supported by many US allies, to declare a war on them for as long as necessary to neutralise radical political Islamism as a force in international politics.

However, the tragedy is that the way this war is being conducted has reinforced rather than marginalised the position of many exponents of radical Islamism, helping them to acquire more resilience and durability than could have been anticipated at the start of this 'War on Terror' in October 2001. Each side in the conflict has benefited enormously from increasing public grievances resulting from the actions of one another, the growing globalisation of technology, mass communications, and movements of people and finances, to hit back at one another. The US and its allies have acted from the level of state dominance, whereas al-Qaeda and its allied organisations have operated from sub-national terrain to achieve their objectives, with the effect of marginalising mainstream Muslims in the conduct of their national and world affairs.

This chapter has three main aims. The first is to highlight the nature of radical Islamism and those forces of political Islam that have deployed it to promote extremist visions, and act, at times violently, in pursuit of those visions. The second aim is to examine the 'War on Terror', and to explore its successes and failures. The third is to look at a way forward in the context of how the rhetoric and actions of the two sides have interacted within a globalised world to generate a durable state of fear and insecurity at the cost of substantially shrinking the space for the mainstream forces of political and ideological moderation.

Islam and Radical Islamism

Islam as a religion, and as an ideology of change and societal living, is akin to the two other main revealed religions: Christianity and Judaism. It came into existence in the early 7th century to complete rather than contradict those religions. It shares much in common with Christianity and for that matter Judaism in terms of both beliefs and values. As monotheistic faiths, all three not only embrace a common concept of God and His attributes, but also give equal weight to the sanctity of life (as a precious gift from God), human dignity, and a moral, ethical and virtuous earthly existence. They are all rich in fundamental moral and social principles from which strong notions of universal ethics, justice and dignified existence can be drawn, and in relation to which a virtuous life can be organised on earth.

In Islam, as in Christianity and Judaism, the notions of the power of God and vulnerability of man and woman as His creatures are combined to caution strongly against an earthly existence which defies God's commands and results in a life contrary to those principles which ensure a pious, truthful, just and communally acceptable living. One of the central elements of Christianity 'is do justly, to love mercy, and to walk humbly with ... God' (Micah 6:8). Christianity has evolved to stress justice, based on the principle that one must not do to others what one would not want others to do to oneself. This is akin to the Islamic principles, as enshrined in the Qur'an, that strongly emphasise the notion of justice as closest to piety, and the value of compassion, forgiveness, mercy, modesty, humility and persuasion as central to earthly existence in order to gain reward in the world hereafter.

Islam is a religion of community, and it emphasises that the rights, freedoms and welfare of the individual should be determined in relation and proportion to the dignity and wellbeing of the community. It attaches high importance to human responsibility, cautioning its followers against unjust rule and arbitrary impositions as well as living in conflict with one another and with the wider world. In essence, Islam is not necessarily incompatible with a pluralist democratic existence.

Like Christianity and Judaism, Islam is rich with principles and practices that call for a humanised and humane world. In Islam, a humane and virtuous existence cannot be fulfilled unless citizens are assured of their common basic rights, freedoms and responsibilities, with access to the necessary opportunities to enable them to fulfil themselves within a community to the best of their abilities. God's will stands supreme, but His creatures are given the faculties of thinking and reasoning to act responsibly on earth in fulfilling God's pleasure in accordance with the changing times and conditions, for Islam is a religion for all times and all peoples.

At the doctrinal level, Islam is monolithic and does not recognise compartmentalisation of life in terms of racial, political, social, cultural and territorial divisions, and essentially calls for the creation of a unified source of earthly power and authority as a reflection of those of God. However, in the course of its historical evolution it has come to accommodate pluralism from within (such as the Sunni–Shi'a sectarian division and sub-divisions within each of these sects) and from outside, as in the case of cultural differences between its followers. It has demonstrated a degree of elasticity in its internal and external dispositions that has ensured its continuity as a dynamic religion and fostered its position as the fastest growing faith even in today's world.

At its inception, Islam stressed to its followers the value of knowledge and education, and placed no barriers to critical thinking, expression and debate. Muslim thinkers have sanctioned consultation, participation and consensus, and emphasised the sanctity of a citizen's privacy against arbitrary actions, and the rule of law with justice as principles to underpin the operation of a Muslim society.[1] Islam has enshrined the value of a participatory system of governance. In other words, it has provided many principles from which the creation of a peaceful democratic way of life can be justified.

Yet Islam – like any other religion or ideology – has been open to a range of interpretations and methods of application in the course of history. Overall, they can be summed up in two approaches – each highly diverse within itself – to the understanding and application of Islam in the Muslim world, and the Muslim Middle East in particular: Jihadi and Ijtihadi.

The jihadi approach calls for strict adherence to fundamentals of Islam as literally pronounced in the Qur'an and Sunna. It presents Islam as highly monolithic, with a firm conviction that there is no separation between religion and politics in Islam and that they are the two sides of the same coin. It contends that there is only one way to build God's government on earth, that is the way God ordained in the Qur'an, and the Prophet Mohammed pursued in creating the original Islamic community. It adheres to the view that the only legitimate form of political system in a predominantly Muslim society is an Islamic government, whose task is to apply Shari'a (Islamic Law) as the law of the land. It postulates that individual and communal rights and freedoms are expendable when it comes to the higher goal of protecting and defending Islam and an Islamic community. It strongly endorses the notion of self-sacrifice and martyrdom, with a proviso to go beyond the limits set in Islam for waging jihad, and if necessary to engage in war without rules or what has widely been viewed by many as 'terrorism' to establish *niazami Islami* (Islamic order) on earth. This approach essentially sets up Islam to justify self-righteousness, combative assertiveness and authoritarian or concealed authoritarian political cultures.

The approach has spawned a doctrine of political jihadism adopted in different ways by a variety of radical Islamists – or those who believe in Islam as an ideology of political and social transformation of their societies, and in the use of violence when needed to achieve their objectives – in the course of history. Some of these Islamists, whether as individuals or groups, have proved to be more puritanical than others, but some have also been reformist in pursuit of re-Islamising their polities and the wider Muslim world. Further, some have been more extreme than others in their attitude to the application of violence as a means to assert, protect and defend their religion and Islamic way of life against outside assaults or perceived threats. Some have invoked religious exclusivity and cultural relativity to oppose Western notions of democracy and human rights, and to adopt modernity in such a way as to conform to their religious and cultural settings.

As such, the phenomenon of radical political Islamism has been embedded in the history of Islam. It has existed in different forms and intensity throughout Islamic history. It has found its doctrinal roots in the birth of Islam as a religion of resistance, reform, renewal and reassertion. Inspired in recent times by the writings of the Egyptian writer and agitator Sayid Qutb, radical political Islamism has come to produce a range of jihadi (or combative) and neo-fundamentalist groups. These include al-Qaeda and many of its associated groups, and more importantly Jama'a Islamiyya and Hezbi Islami Afghanistan (Gulbuddin Hekmatyar) as examples of the jihadi groups, and the Taliban and Lashkar-e Toiba as examples of the neo-fundamentalist variety. These groups have been willing to wage acts of violence without rules and constraints in pursuit of gaols of establishing Islamic order within Muslim countries and beyond.

The Ijtihadi approach, on the other hand, calls for creative interpretation of Islam based on independent human reasoning. In general, it subscribes primarily to the view that Islam does not provide a theory of the state or a blueprint for what exactly should constitute an Islamic government. It maintains that while Prophet Mohammed left behind a powerful and everlasting legacy, he left it to the followers of Islam to apply Islam in the course of history according to changing times and conditions. It argues for a softer relationship between religion and politics in Islam. It claims that Islam is compatible with democracy and what is contained in the Universal Declaration of Human Rights (with the exception of capital punishment, and the right to change religion) and the scientific, technological and economic demands of a modern way of life. Some of the contemporary advocates of the approach have gone so far as to argue that it is even possible to have a secular government in a predominantly Muslim society as long as Islam is respected as the religion of the majority within the state. This approach has produced a variety of liberal Islamists. A prominent living example from the Sunni side is the former Indonesian President Abdurrahman Wahid (1999–2001), and from the Shi'a side is the former Iranian President Mohammed Khatami (1997–2005). Both Wahid and Khatami have strongly argued for compatibility between Islam and democracy, and have rejected any interpretation of Islam presenting it as an impediment to the promotion of democracy, human rights and appropriate modernity.

In many ways, Khatami proved to be a Shi'ite mirror image of Abdurrahman Wahid. Like the Indonesian leader, Khatami set out to argue for Islam's compatibility with democracy and basic human rights and freedoms. While parting with Wahid on the issue of the permissibility of secular politics within a Muslim society, Khatami upheld the need for operating within an Islamic framework, as had been laid down by Ayatullah Khomeini. He called for the creation of what he termed 'Islamic civil society' and 'Islamic democracy', with the principle of 'dialogue of civilisations' governing Iran's foreign relations, even with its arch-enemy, the US. Despite his emphasis on Islam, scrutiny shows that his concepts of Islamic democracy and Islamic civil society came very close in their disposition to embracing most of the values and practices that have underpinned the Western constructs of civil society and liberal democracy.

The 'War on Terror'

In the recent times, it has been Jihadi Islam rather than Ijtihadi Islam that has taken the centre stage in world politics. This has been particularly so since the Islamic takeover of Iranian politics and the consolidation of the Afghan Islamic resistance to the Soviet occupation of Afghanistan nearly three decades ago, and the part played by the US in both of these developments. The first event, which spelt the end of the US influence in Iranian politics, bitterly shaped Washington's view of what it disparagingly called 'Islamic fundamentalism'. Yet, the US backed the second event as an effective means to pursue its long-standing goal of defeating Soviet communism. In Iran, where Islamic politics rapidly assumed an anti-US posture, prompting Washington to denounce it as anomalous and adversarial to its interests, the US set out on a long-term policy of containing the Iranian Islamic regime. In relation to Afghanistan, once the Soviet troop withdrawal was secured by 1989, followed by the collapse of the USSR two and a half years later, Washington left Afghanistan's fate to its Pakistani allies. It supported, if not actively at least passively, Pakistan's orchestration of the Sunni neo-fundamentalist but anti-Iranian regime of the Taliban in Afghanistan. It did so as part of a strategy of enforcing its containment of the Iranian Islamic regime and limiting the space for that regime and other US adversaries in the newly independent but mineral rich region of Muslim Central Asia.[2]

It was primarily in the context of these developments – and the failures of secular and semi-secular regimes that had dominated the Muslim world up to this point, with many of them being supported by the US – that Washington played its part in opening the space more for Jihadi than Ijtihadi Islam. Although representing a minority in the Muslim world, Jihadi Islam was presented with expanding opportunities in the 1990s to widen its impact on the popular politics of Muslim states, affecting their relations with the US and some of its allies.

A situation was created whereby al-Qaeda was able to launch its attacks of September 11 (2001) on the US, and the US to declare in October 2001 a military campaign to punish the perpetrators of the worst terrorist attacks ever on the US. The US campaign, which received widespread international support, marked the start of what President George W. Bush called the 'War on Terror'. Its objectives were to destroy al-Qaeda and its harbourer, the medievalist Islamic government of the Taliban in Afghanistan, with the broader aim of enhancing global security. President Bush warned that the fight was going to be long, but would be directed only against that tiny minority who, as he put it, had 'hijacked' Islam for their extremist and barbaric ends. He expressed his respect for Islam as a religion of peace and tolerance, and assured Muslims, who constitute some 1.3 billion of the world's population, that they had nothing to fear.

Since the start of the 'War on Terror' with 'Operation Enduring Freedom' in Afghanistan, the Taliban regime has been removed and Afghanistan has been put on a path of transformation from a theocratic past to a possibly pluralist future. Al-Qaeda has been dispersed from Afghanistan, with its presence limited largely to the south and southeast of the country. In addition, the US has invaded Iraq on the basis of a claim that Saddam Hussein's regime was linked to international terrorism and possessed weapons of mass destruction (WMD) that threatened the security of the US and its allies. Since 2001, no more terrorist attacks of any significance have occurred on American soil.

Yet no claim of victory can be made in the 'War on Terror'. The respective leaders of the Taliban and al-Qaeda, Mullah Mohammad Omar and Osama Bin Ladin, are still at large. Their networks' opposition activities have continued in Afghanistan at the cost of increasing US and Afghan troop casualties, especially since the start of 2005, although not on a scale seriously to threaten the US-backed government of President Hamid Karzai in Kabul. Al-Qaeda and its associated groups have managed to remain active, with some spectacular operations in different parts of the world, especially the Middle East, Europe and Southeast Asia. Iraq is in a mess, with the credibility of the Bush Administration in tatters as a result of mismanagement of the post-Saddam Hussein situation, and the lack of evidence regarding Iraqi WMD and links with international terrorism.

Many innocent people have been killed, injured, displaced or made destitute, since the tragic events of 11 September 2001. Indeed, the number of civilians who have fallen victim to the 'War on Terror' in one form or another is estimated to be arguably many times more than the 2800 people killed in the terrorist attacks on New York and Washington.[3] Since the start of the Iraq war, the Iraqi civilian casualties alone have been estimated between 100 000 and 650 000.[4] Against this, by 13 March 2007, the US had sustained 3200 troops dead and 24 000 injured, with Iraqi military casualties amounting to many more. The number of American casualties did not include over 21 000 who were listed as 'disease' casualties in the Iraqi theatre of operation.[5] With the Iraq carnage continuing unabated, the usually upbeat former US Secretary of Defence, Donald Rumsfeld, had admitted as early as 12

February 2005 that the US could not win the 'War on Terror' on its own. He had stated:

> By now it must be clear that one nation cannot defeat the extremists alone … It will take the cooperation of many nations to stop the proliferation of dangerous weapons … and it surely takes a community of nations to gather intelligence about extremist networks, to break up financial support lines, or to apprehend suspected terrorists.[6]

Rumsfeld had appealed to America's Europeans allies, many of which have remained highly critical of the US-led invasion of Iraq and the Bush Administration's unilateralist tendencies, to help the US to achieve its objectives in this respect. He had also acknowledged that it might take up to 12 years to defeat the Iraqi insurgency and even then it would be up to the Iraqis to defeat it, not a responsibility of the US and some of its allies who created it in the first place. Yet the Bush Administration has not been able to get any relief and this may remain so for the foreseeable future, for a number of reasons.

One of the most distressing outcomes of US policy behaviour is that many in the Arab/Muslim world have grown convinced that the US and its allies have set out not only to punish al-Qaeda, but also to undermine Islam and penalise its followers in general. President Bush has personally deployed biblical language to define the 'War on Terror' in terms of 'good vs. evil'. He has never failed to mix his personal devotion to Christian evangelism, America's power and the rhetoric of democracy and liberty to convey a belief in the moral force of Christianity and invincibility of the US. The former Italian Prime Minister, Silvio Berlusconi, has gone so far as to declare Western civilisation to be superior to that of Islam, and several political and religious leaders and columnists in the US and elsewhere in the Christian world have made repeated disparaging remarks about Islam, the Prophet Mohammed, and Muslims as linked to terrorism.[7]

Well-known American political and religious figures, such as clerics Pat Robertson and Jerry Falwell, have had no hesitation about taking up the cause. Some American academics, sympathetic to the Bush Administration, have gone as far as to talk about 'the crisis of Islam', postulating that although at one time Muslims created a majestic civilisation, today they have reached a dead end.[8] This approach from the heights of politics to the plains of academia has generated a mindset and a climate in the US that has fanned an unprecedented wave of recrimination and suspicion towards Muslims. The draconian measures adopted by the US and its allies to profile many Arabs and Muslims as potential terrorists have simply reinforced the situation, causing growing anguish among Muslims, and putting them on the defensive about their religion and religious identity.

Yet for Muslims to uphold their religion for the 'common good', and as a base for wider peaceful coexistence in the world, they expect others to accord them the respect that their own religion demands of them in relation to the followers of other faiths. It requires principles of mutual respect and robust reciprocity. Most Muslims believe that the West in general, and the US in particular, have done little in this respect to inspire confidence in Muslims. Starting with the Crusades and European colonialism and finally the rise of US global dominance since World War II, they hold that the Muslim domain has been constantly subjected to suppression and humiliation. In recent times, this has been manifested nowhere more than in relation to Israel's occupation of the Palestinian lands (including Jerusalem – the third holiest city for Muslims), and the US's unqualified commitment to Israel, a commitment which has taken an enhanced dimension since the beginning of the presidency of George W. Bush.

President Bush's description in mid-2002 of the then Israeli Prime Minister Ariel Sharon as a 'man of peace', and his decision to support him in reinvading Palestinian cities, using disproportionate force to pursue his long-standing policy of suppressing the Palestinians, humiliating the Arabs and maintaining Israel's regional supremacy in whatever way necessary, caused outrage in the Arab/Muslim world. Sharon's withdrawal of Israeli troops and settlers from Gaza in September 2005 generated some optimism initially, but it was not linked to an overall negotiated settlement of the Palestinian problem. The Israeli leader's concurrent reinforcement and expansion of larger Israeli settlements in the West Bank did not inspire much confidence about the future. There were 9000 new settlers in the West Bank during the first nine months of 2005: more than the number who were withdrawn from Gaza.[9] Although Sharon was incapacitated as a result of a stroke in January 2005, his legacy of giving the Palestinians as little as possible,and suppressing their resistance in whatever way possible has been pursued vigorously by his successor Prime Minister Ehud Olmert.

Various opinion polls reveal that many Muslims believe that their religion is often misrepresented. They also believe that Washington and some of its allies ignore their grievances for no other reason than to advance certain ideological and geopolitical objectives (such as maintaining control over the oil resources of the Middle East, and ensuring the supremacy of the state of Israel in the region). The predominant view is that – no matter what – the Bush Administration is bent on a hegemonic globalist policy, with the aim of changing the world in the US image, with an emphasis on the moral and civilisational superiority of Christianity in alliance with predominantly religious Zionists. Many Muslims believe, rightly or wrongly, that there is a deliberate attempt, especially from the US and Israeli side, to paint Islam as a religion promoting violence, terrorism and anti-modernity rather than openness to progress, tolerance and peaceful co-existence, which have by and large marked its historical existence.

The invasion of Iraq and the mishandling of its transformation, at the cost of destroying the Iraqi state and inflicting heavy casualties on the Iraqi civilian population, have reinforced a growing view among many of them that the Bush Administration is anti-Arab and anti-Muslim. This has been instrumental in making a growing number of them, including even some moderate Islamists who form the bulk of Muslim intellectuals and professionals – and whose cooperation is needed if the US wishes to rebuild bridges of understanding and trust with Muslims – to become amenable to radical Islamism. By the same token, some have even found it desirable to moderate their view of Bin Laden's extremism and to regard him as a source of dignity and salvation.

Dangerously enough, Bin Laden's opposition to the US and Israel as well as to the US-backed dictatorial regimes in the Muslim world, and his call for the liberation of Muslim people and lands, have increasingly resonated well with many Muslims. It is no wonder that President Bush's repeated assertions in support of morality, liberty and democracy have fallen on deaf ears in the Muslim world. Few Islamists now accord Washington the degree of political and moral respect that is needed to open their hearts and minds to the US. The despicable stories and pictures from Abu Gharib, Guantanamo Bay and Afghan prison camps have had an appallingly lasting impact on the minds of Muslims, as they have also disgusted civilised people everywhere. They have played right into the hands of radical Islamists and neo-fundamentalists in opposition to the US and its allies.

This is not to say that Muslim states do not interact with the US and its allies, but this interaction is largely through state-to-state relations. It is important to be reminded that many governments in Muslim countries are either authoritarian or concealed authoritarian in character. They do not have direct public mandates, and accommodate US power out of political need and fear. In other words, while the US has leverage over most Arab/Muslim regimes, it has not been able to transform this leverage into popular influence in order to win the minds and hearts of their subjects. In addition, while very large numbers of Muslims support democracy, they do not seem to want the US to impose it upon them. They view the Bush Administration's advocacy of democratisation in the Middle East as motivated by a sense of self-righteousness and regional hegemony.

While many Muslim governments have either quietly supported or acquiesced in the US-led occupation of Iraq, a majority of Muslims from Morocco to Indonesia have opposed the occupation, with some of them actively lending financial and human support to the Iraqi resistance and sympathising with the causes and grievances voiced by al-Qaeda and its associated groups. Irrespective of the American view of the Iraqi resistance as 'terrorism', they see the resistance as a defence against what they perceive to be a constant experience of powerlessness and humiliation at the hands of the US and some of its allies.[10]

They have come to view the Iraqi resistance and opposition to the US in the wider Muslim world as an expression of some kind of popular sentiment. From their perspective, this could eventually open the way for the demise of dictatorships and their replacement by popular governments at home, and curtailment of American hegemonic involvement in their countries. They tend to view such an outcome as an important result of the Iraq conflict in shifting the power of action from the authorities to the people for the first time in modern history.

It is evident that the 'War on Terror' has lost its focus, and the relations between the world of Islam and the West – more specifically the US – have grown tense, to say the least. Too many misperceptions and cross-purpose understandings have come to underline this development. Ironically, globalisation (or interdependence) and the technological advances of the last few decades on scales never experienced before have come to play a double-edged role in this respect. On the one hand, they have accelerated and widened the means of mass communications, and the movement of capital, people and technology. This has provided unprecedented means and opportunities, not only for those who could benefit from them for better standards of living and global cooperation, but also for extremist individuals and groups such al-Qaeda, which could engage in relatively cheap, violent actions with relative ease. On the other, by the virtue of the fact that these developments have aided opposition extremists, the US and its allies have found it expedient to adopt such draconian security measures as to promote protectionist policies. While globalisation processes remain a forceful feature of today's world, every conceivable effort is concurrently made to regulate this feature in support of statist interests. Meanwhile, at another level, both state and sub-state actors, most relevantly the US and al-Qaeda, advance poorly defined but nonetheless self-righteous universal goals and ideologies. Thus, what is played out in the current struggle between the US and its allies on one side, and radical Islamists and their sympathisers on the other, is not just the issue of good vs. evil and democracy vs. theocracy, but also isolationist 'self-defence' paralleling globalisation in shaping world politics.

The Way Forward

What is to be done to defuse the situation in support of better understanding and cooperation, and to create a safer and more stable world? It is important that the fate of world politics be wrested from the three minority extremist groups that have interactively emerged to shape the destiny of the mainstream elements of each community: al-Qaeda and its close associates from the Muslim world; elements of neo-conservatives, reborn Christians and ultra naitionalists in the US; and inflexible religious Zionists from Israel. The time has now come for mainstream representatives from all sides to become proactive to reach out to one another for more vigorous and wider dialogue and exchange. This is crucial to restoring trust and to building bridges that have historically been instrumental in generating long periods of peaceful co-existence and cooperation between the West and the domain of Islam. In the West, concerned citizens need to become far more vocal and participatory than they have been to bring about civic pressure on their governments, especially in the US, to recognise the futility of the reckless use of force as a means to solve most international problems. It is important that these authorities be made aware that the use of force against international terrorism can work only up to a point. Beyond that point, the only way to deal with the phenomenon is to delegitimise the causes on which the terrorists draw to justify their actions and widen their circles of recruitment and operations. This can only be done if the root causes are prudently identified and addressed.

First, it is imperative for the Bush Administration to acknowledge the futility of its approach to changing the Middle East according to its vision irrespective of what reality prevails on the ground. It should learn from history that every attempt to force change in the region from outside has ultimately resulted in failure. This was the case with the British efforts in the 1920s, and with the American attempts in the 1950s. The British endeavours came to a crushing end with the post-World War II rise of radical Arab nationalism and the republican coup of 1958 in Iraq. The CIA's overthrow of the elected reformist government of Dr Mohammed Mossadeq in Iran in 1953 and its replacement with the pro-US Shah's dictatorship ended in a serious anti-Shah and anti-US backlash a quarter of century later, resulting in the Iranian revolution of 1978–1979 that brought to power the radical Islamic regime of Ayatullah Khomeini.[11] To the present day, the US continues to suffer from the consequences of this event.

If the US wants to help the people of the region, what it needs to do is to work with reformist, democratic forces to bring about favourable changes. It should give up its long-standing policy of talking about the virtues of democracy and liberty while supporting and protecting dictatorships whenever its suits it. At present, the Bush Administration has more dictatorial regimes as its allies in the region than any of its predecessors. They range from regimes in Egypt and Saudi Arabia to Musharaf's concealed military rule in Pakistan to certain Stalinist cult of personality rule in Central Asia.

With regard to Iraq, the Bush Administration needs to end the occupation of the country using a two-pronged approach. One is to engage in direct negotiation for an end to hostilities with receptive elements of the Iraqi resistance, and open dialogue with Tehran and Damascus, which may have leverage with such elements, in order to entice them to participate in the processes of a political settlement. Another is to promote an internal power-sharing arrangement not within a federalist structure, which is opposed by the Sunni Iraqis who view it as disadvantaging them and carrying the risk of territorial disintegration of Iraq, but rather a unitary consociational democratic structure similar to what long-operated in Lebanon.

The second is to negotiate a clear timetable for troop withdrawal from the country. Under the conditions of occupation, no Iraqi government will be able to achieve the degree of credibility and effectiveness that is necessary for bringing peace and reconstruction to Iraq. Of course, the US can only do this if it is also willing to abandon its long-standing goal of being the dominant power in the Middle East. It should recognise the force of the recent assertion by Secretary of State Condoleezza Rice, that for sixty years the US sacrificed democracy in order to promote stability in the Middle East, but in the end it achieved neither. The time has now come to focus on democracy, and live with the outcomes even if it means Islamic governments. US Iraq policy, and for that matter Middle East policy, suffer from a terrible tension between the US rhetoric in support of democracy and its determination to maintain regional hegemony. As long this remains the case, Washington will not be able to disentangle itself from the Iraqi fiasco with a degree of honour, or help to democratise the Muslim Middle East and empower its peoples to chart their own destiny. The US can no longer afford to be inconsistent in its preaching of moral and ethical values, and application of democracy and liberty as central foreign policy objectives, given the damage that it has caused to America's international credibility.

The third thing that the Bush Administration can do is to promote a viable settlement of the Palestinian problem and accelerate the process of Afghanistan's reconstruction. It needs to act on the principle of what is required to serve the cause of long-term stability and security of the Israelis, Palestinians and Afghans, as well as regional peace, rather than what might enhance short-term American geopolitical preferences. In this respect, it should recognise the democratically-mandated rise to power of the Palestinian radical Islamist group Hamas. It also needs to pressure the Israeli leadership to link Israel's Gaza withdrawal to an overall settlement, and enable the Palestinians to create a viable independent state of their own out of Gaza, the West Bank and East Jerusalem, and President Musharaf of Pakistan to put his house in order as rapidly as possible. While many believe that Afghanistan has been 'terrorism central', to the contrary, it is Pakistan that has been the epicentre of extremism and terrorism. Afghanistan has been the recipient of these phenomena from Pakistan. Despite its public partnership with the US in the 'War on Terror' – which has resulted in massive American economic and military aid to Pakistan and elevation of the country to the status of a major non-NATO ally – elements of the Musharaf Administration continue to help the Taliban and some of their al-Qaeda allies for wider regional strategic interests.[12]

Beyond this, the US should spend a lot more than it has on alleviating poverty and promoting the cause of critical and liberal education, and boosting cross-cultural understanding and inter-faith dialogue. It should devote more energy to building multi-lateral global support for these causes than rely on futile unilateralist efforts to change the world according to Washington's ideological and geopolitical preferences. In other words, it should overhaul American foreign policy to restore its moral and political credibility as a constructive power in world politics, and to reconcile the interests of the US with the expectations of the wider world. These will constitute a badly needed opening if we want to change the world for the better. Otherwise, the prospects for an end to international terrorism and improvement in relations between the West, more importantly the US, and the world of Islam do not look bright in the foreseeable future.

3

IMAGINING PAN-ISLAM

James Piscatori

This chapter aims to outline the story of how an idea – pan-Islam – emerges and takes on a life of its own, with perhaps unanticipated consequences.[1] This discussion is, necessarily, in the nature of an overview. The first part details the emergence of a political symbol, and the second indicates how Muslim politics today is in part, though no by no means wholly, pre-occupied with contestation over this symbol.[2]

Emergence of 'Pan-Islam' as Idea and Symbol

Pan-Islam has its roots in the familiar double assault of imperialism and decentralisation on the Ottomans in the late nineteenth century.[3] Certainly, a broad Islamic sentiment – a pan-Islamic populism of sorts – had begun to emerge from the 1870s in South and South-East Asia and other parts of the Muslim world. The advent of a local press played an important role in stimulating, and giving expression to, this larger concern, at least among the educated classes: 'The more Indian Muslims discovered about the fate of their brethren elsewhere in the Islamic world, the more they wished to know'.[4]

The sultan, Abdulhamid (1842–1918), polemicists such as Jamal al-Din al-Afghani (1838–97), and Western apologists such as Wilfred Blunt were self-interested advocates of a pan-Islamic ideology. But these proponents helped to make a vague idea of unity a symbol of the modern Islamic condition at the same time as they used it to advance partisan political interests. Ethnic, national, and Islamic ideas intermingled in the discord of the early twentieth century. The Young Turks hoped to use a vaguely defined Islam policy to offset imperial losses, such as occurred with Libya, and to rally broad Muslim support. The Treaty of Lausanne (1912) ratified Italian sovereignty over Libya, for instance, but the Turkish sultan was also formally recognised as caliph and provision was made for his name to be mentioned in the Friday sermon (*khutba*) and for the imperial administration to appoint Libya's chief judge (*qadi*). Local newspapers, such as Abul Kalam Azad's *al-Hilal* and Zafar Ali Khan's *Zamindar* in South Asia, closely followed and reported on this drama of a generally ailing empire.[5]

The Turkish Grand National Assembly directly challenged believers and non-believers alike when, in March 1924, it abolished the caliphate, but the consequences were different from what had been anticipated. Kemalists, for their part, assumed it would inevitably lead to the secularisation of Muslim societies; devout followers believed it would further weaken Muslims in their interaction with the West; colonial offices feared that it would stimulate a broad uprising of the worldwide Muslim community. None occurred, but the lingering appeal of Muslim solidarity was significant and assumed its place, ironically, in the formation of modern Muslim states and, more recently, in attempts to undermine them.

Different perspectives emerged between 1923 and 1926. Conservative opinion was represented by Muhammad Rasid Rida (1865–1935), who in his compilation, *al-Khilafa wa'l-imama al-uzma* (The Caliphate or the Greatest Imamate), made the case for a restoration.[6] Radical opinion was represented by 'Ali 'Abd al-Raziq (1888–1966), who, in his *al-Islam wa usul al-hukum* (Islam and the Foundations of Government), expressed doubts about the need for a caliphate.[7] Realist opinion was expressed by 'Abd al-Raziq Sanhoury's *Le Califat: son evolution vers une société des nations orientales*.[8] He advocated a caliphate that would be subject to periodic election at the *hajj*, with the caliph presiding over a loose grouping of Oriental nations in association with the League of Nations – a general argument similar to Muhammd al-Ghazali's early twenty-first century endorsement of a federation or confederation of Muslim states.[9]

The spectrum ranged from those wishing to re-establish a purified religious-political institution (though responding to the distortions of the late Ottoman experience), to those who thought the fusion of religious and political authority was counter-productive or even dangerous, through to accommodationists who saw the best way of adapting to post-war conditions as the creation of an international organisation among sovereign 'Muslim states'. This intellectual diversity merely reflected underlying political differences, despite what was thought to be a common religious sentiment. But, by explicitly placing focus on what the caliphate had meant and the form it should take in the modern world, they each helped to make the post-caliphal community of faith possible. To the question, 'how should the *umma* be constructed now?', little agreement emerged, with, however, the significant exception: the spiritual unity of the *umma* – an unquestioned given – required some form of *political* expression.

Another current was the Muslim international agitation of the period. Few of the associations and individuals attempting to promote pan-Islam in those years refined their thinking into an ideology of pan-Islamism or tried to carry it over into a serious consideration of organisations and plans of action. The pan-Islamic conventions – Mecca in 1924, Cairo in 1926, Mecca in 1926, and Jerusalem in 1931 – grappled with these issues to a degree. While they were clearly less than a success, riven by the competing dynastic rivalries of the Middle East (notably Hashimite, Saudi, and Egyptian), they offered nonetheless a rudimentary form of joint action. Government circles in Europe displayed at times an unwarranted anxiety about these meetings, which, no doubt, refracted on elite sentiment within Muslim societies, encouraging pan-Islamic advocates to redouble their efforts. George Antonius, the great defender of Arab nationalism, had an expansive view of what he thought was emerging: 'I am inclined to believe that for the first time in many years, perhaps in the whole course of history, HMG find themselves faced with the problems of a, if not united, then at any rate uniting, Islam'.[10]

Joining with the Muslim intellectual ferment and the political agitation of the congresses were the influential writings of the Orientalists. These were mostly sympathetic, despite what is often assumed, and largely respected what they saw as the continuities of Islamic thought and history rather than discontinuities. While French observers in the pages of *Revue du monde musulman* and other publications saw the Sufi networks of North and West Africa as potent expressions of an anti-imperial pan-Islam,[11] others tended to look upon the unity of all Muslims as a given and reaffirmed its centrality to Islamic doctrine. For Sir Hamilton Gibb, although 'pan-Islamism', on the one hand, stressed adherence to a broader loyalty, it had in fact promoted allegiance to the Ottoman caliph; it thus advanced a kind of particularised politics. Yet, on the other hand, this very ambivalence highlighted that 'Islamic universalism' was an enduring spiritual and cultural imperative. This universalism was, in fact, in line with 'the broad and deep currents of a people's psychology' and a model of co-operation for the non-Muslim world.[12] With arguments such as these, 'unity' was self-consciously made to become part of the essence of Islam. It was now posited as integral and fundamental, divorced largely from the canonical articulation of concepts like *khilafa, dar al-islam* (the juridical realm of Muslims), and *dhimma* (non-Muslim subjects). Indeed, the scholarly discussions were remarkably thin on these topics.

In addition, the caliphate was presented as at heart a political institution, connected to the law and 'temporal power and sovereignty'.[13] C. A. Nallino in the late 1910s and 1920s with his writings on 'panislamismo' and T.W. Arnold in his magisterial lectures at the University of London, published in 1924 as *The Caliphate*, had helped to suggest – echoed by 'Abd al-Raziq – that, given the functional division of religion and politics in Islamic history, the caliphate was a temporal institution.[14] It had always been such an institution, lacking a strong theoretical basis, bound by history and subject to evolution. The implication was clear: if the institution of the caliphate was temporal and political, it was not permanent and was replaceable. It was but a short step to conclude that what Gibb called a 'spiritual Caliphate' embodying the 'religious conscience of the people as a whole'[15] could become the functional replacement for the caliphate; this, in effect, was pan-Islam.

Although Arnold, writing as the institution disappeared, argued that hope could still be invested in its reconstitution, his larger conclusion points to this broad religious consciousness or what we may call pan-Islamic sentiment:

> A growing number of Muhammadans, now more fully acquainted with modern conditions and more in touch with the aims and ideals of the present day, still cling to the faith of their childhood and the associations that have become dear to them from the Muslim atmosphere in which they grew up. These men likewise cherish an ideal of some form of political and social organisation in which self-realisation may become possible for them in some system of civilisation that is Muslim in character and expression ... Even when the dogmas of their faith have little hold upon them, they are still attracted by the glamour of a distinctively Muslim culture and long to break the chains of an alien civilization.[16]

The conclusion was soon reached that there was no realistic possibility of the caliphate's reinstatement, nor was there a need any longer to re-establish it. *Khilafa* gave way to an idea of 'unity' (*ittihad-i Islam, al-wahda al-islamiyya*).

By mid-twentieth century, then, several broad themes emerged. First, a sense that something had gone wrong – symbolised by the abolition of the caliphate – was all-pervasive, but ultimately incapable of fostering united goals or action. The congresses of the inter-war period were grounded in the belief that the vastness of the Muslim world constituted its natural strength. In their numbers and in their geographic dispersal,

Muslims represented a potentially formidable force. Yet, clearly, this was its failing as well. A sense of subjugation to the West may have been one binding force, yet the political conditions under which Muslims lived varied widely. The dimensions of British, French, Russian, and Dutch rule were very different, and it mattered whether Muslims were subjected directly to foreign rule or lived under informal imperial arrangements. The calculations made separately by Muslims in different circumstances ruled out a simple consensus.

Second, despite the obvious political differences and competing leadership, stirrings of what we now call transnational networks were enhanced and encouraged. Views were exchanged, issues aired, individuals and cultures encountered. Word of events in distant Muslim lands had often reached other Muslim centres through non-Muslim media, censored publications, and rumour. With the international congresses there were more opportunities to forge unmediated and personal linkages.

Third, the symbol of 'unity' was concretised in the idea of pan-Islam, in large part because of the constructions of both Muslim and Orientalist intellectuals. It was a working idea, partial and vague, but, even so, soon few spoke of the essential necessity of the *caliphate* as an institution. No longer present, was it ever necessary? The caliphate's political mission may have passed, but the idea of Islam's political mission had not. The spiritual unity of Muslims was not in question, it must be emphasised; all readily accepted this in line with Qur'anic references to *umma wahida* (one community; e.g., 5:48/53, 16:93/95). But, if the caliphate had been abolished and if Muslims indisputably constitute one religious community, then the political unity of Muslims itself became now, to many, an element of faith regardless of whether the caliph was present or not. Ahmed Ibrahim Abushouk makes this case forcefully in the first article of the first issue of the *International Journal of Muslim Unity*, produced by the International Islamic University in Malaysia: the unity of the *umma* has existed from the time of the Prophet, it is spiritual but also inherently political, and it is not simply synonymous with the caliphate.[17]

Fourth, institutionalised Islamic universalism did not inevitably come about as a result of these connections and new consciousness. Whatever broad awareness was created, it competed with the hesitant but discernible emergence of one-state nationalism (*wataniyya*) in a number of Muslim societies or, at least, the consolidation of dynastic rule and regimes. Individual claims, however obviously promoted by self-interested, would-be caliphs – whether Sharif Husayn of the Hijaz, King Fu'ad of Egypt or the Saudi 'Abd al-'Aziz Ibn Sa'ud – were legitimised by broader notions of solidarity. Particularistic identities were validated, despite the logic of pan-Islamic unity, precisely because they were in part expressed in the universalist language of Islam. Each sought to consolidate his rule by appealing to a larger mission and by encouraging a political identity that intersected with the wider Islamic one. If pan-Islam had been essentialised, then it was also a tool used to legitimise oneself and to devalue competitors.

Reclaiming the Umma

As we have seen, the imagining of pan-Islam occurred over time, but was largely a phenomenon of the late nineteenth and early twentieth century. In the second half of the twentieth century, national elites invoked pan-Islam for everything other than pan-Islamic purposes. With one eye on their domestic publics and the other on rival states, they sought to serve as Islamic patrons, and the rivalry among Saudi Arabia, Iran, and Pakistan was illustrative of this. Counter-elites, including Islamist movements like the Muslim Brotherhood, Hamas, and the Front Islamique du Salut (FIS) largely did the same, seeking not so much to restore the caliphate as to establish themselves in power within familiar political forms. The ability of Muslims to live within national frontiers in the modern world and, at the same time, the presence of Islamic concerns in both domestic and foreign policy suggest that the vast majority of Muslims have been seeking, at most, to create 'Muslim' states, not to supplant the nation-state system. Hence, the prevalence of debates, in some quarters unnuanced ones, over how to Islamise state, society, and economics. The Organisation of the Islamic Conference is regarded by some as the most concrete contemporary institutionalisation of pan-Islam. It is an inter-state organisation based on the principles of 'respect [for] the sovereignty, independence and territorial integrity of each member state' and of 'abstention from the threat or use of force against the territorial integrity, national unity or political independence of any member states'.[18]

In reality, ambivalence is embedded in Muslim self-understandings of Muslim political solidarity. On the one hand, as we have seen, the political unity of all Muslims acquires the force of dogma in some circles, even though it is not clear how to attain or organise it. On the other hand, the political mission of Islam is best represented in the national enterprise, even though the national guardians routinely invoke wider standards of legitimacy. As the pan-Islamic dimension has appeared to recede, some 'radicals', if you will, have sought to fill the void. They seek, in their view, to reclaim the *umma* from the nation-state and dynastic regimes. They seek to reconstruct modern Islam along the lines of an alternative interpretation, one which places the community of faith above individual states and governments. What they lack in coherence they make up in fervour. Examples are obvious: Hizb al-Tahrir al-Islami (the Islamic Liberation Party), the Muhajirun (an offshoot of the Hizb al-Tahrir in the UK), Usama Bin Ladin and Ayman al-Zawahiri (leaders of al-Qaeda). In effect, pan-Islam went underground, re-emerged spectacularly, and attacks the status quo in the name of a 'tradition' that has only relatively recently appeared.

Bin Ladin's statement of 7 October 2001 dated the current troubles of the Muslim world to eighty years before.[19] Although he did not directly say what the benchmark was, it likely refers to the demise of the caliphate in 1924. This interpretation is consistent with general Islamist accounts that link European, specifically British, intervention with local secularising regimes – here Atatürk – to explain the collapse of Muslim unity. Today it is the American presence in the Middle East and elsewhere that is particularly harmful because it is both economic and ideological; its attempt to attain market domination is dependent on the curtailing of Islam to a kind of safe, conservative, and largely privatised Islam such as the ruling elites of the Muslim world practise.[20]

The juridical bifurcation of the world into Islamic and non-Islamic realms has gained new currency as purportedly Muslim states fall into the non-Islamic category. In the medieval period, 'Abbasid jurists had established a clear frontier between the land of unbelievers (*dar al-harb*) and the land of believers (*dar al-islam*); the former was the realm of war and the latter of peace. This distinction grew fuzzy over time, and virtually disappeared as the state system crystallised in the Muslim world. But this manner of thinking has reappeared, predictably directed against Western enemies but also directed against nominally Muslim regimes. States like Saudi Arabia or Pakistan may proclaim themselves to be Islamic, but they are actually 'allies of Satan' (*a'wan al-shaytan*).[21] The old Muhajirun went so far as to say that because no regimes could be considered Islamic today, there is no such thing as *dar al-islam*. Some medieval scholars had argued that there was an intermediary realm of lands in a truce with the Islamic world (*dar al-sulh*). This concept underpins Bin Ladin's offer of a cessation of hostilities to European states in April 2004. Further, one suspects that this is the normative context in which, in his intervention prior to the American election of November 2004 and wanting to counter President Bush's argument that al-Qaeda hates Western freedoms,[22] he singled out Sweden as an example of a freedom-loving state that did not merit attack.[23]

Nevertheless, not all who invoke traditional frameworks of international analysis are committed to the path of violence. To the contrary, a number of intellectuals, among them the former Egyptian Muslim Brother Yusuf al-Qaradawi, now in Qatar and popular on al-Jazeera television, and Taha Jabir al-Alwani, an Iraqi who moved to the US in the mid-1980s, have been concerned with the situation of Muslims living outside the majority Muslim world. *Fiqh* or jurisprudence has covered Muslims in a personal capacity but has always had a territorial dimension built into it as well. The development of a permanent Muslim minority presence in Western and other societies has seemed to call for clearer guidance on modern conditions, such as military service, participation in elections, and contracting home mortgages. In various rulings and opinions, this jurisprudence of the minorities (*fiqh al-aqalliyat*)[24] effectively makes the division between majority and minority the critical demarcation of the modern world. Al-Qaradawi, for instance, gave contradictory *fatwas* concerning the obligation of Muslim soldiers in the war against the Taliban in Afghanistan, but the initial ruling largely rested on the national obligations of American Muslims in the American military.[25] The rationale for this kind of judgement involves an acceptance, at times explicit, at others tacit, that Western societies are tantamount to *dar al-islam* if they allow Muslims to practise their faith openly and without interference.

The pan-Islamic dimension is an important part of the logic of today's evolving jurisprudence since, it is argued, minority Muslims, no matter where they reside, are still members of the larger *umma* and have obligations as members of that community. But they owe, and are clearly expected to give, obedience to the laws of the land in which they reside, unless, naturally, those contravene God's law. The redrawing of the internal borders, to the extent that it has in fact occurred, has wider implications.

In an important way, these concerns are helping to subvert the internal/external bifurcation of conventional international relations thinking. On one level, it is recognised that Muslims are increasingly living in an 'external', predominantly non-Muslim domain. Yet, on another level, the defence of and care for these same Muslims is regarded as an 'internal' Muslim prerogative – that is, a matter for the *umma*, no matter how elusive the notion may seem. The territorial and the universal – 'traditional' frameworks and new ones – thus meet, in a hybrid way, on the common ground of religious obligation and political expectation. Nevertheless, guidance as to how to negotiate between these levels of obligation is far from final and is best viewed as a work in progress.

Differentiation

There is one further dimension to this story, however. Summarising complex debates, we know that the early expectations of transnational theories have not come to fruition. One expectation centred on the undermining of the state. Whilst this point is not developed here, it is clear that the subverting of the state has not happened even though alternative institutional ideas have emerged. Another expectation was that transnational links would encourage new communities or establish new identities. As has been suggested, there is increasingly something to this aspect: largely due to the crises of failed regimes, if not failed states, and to the power of globalised communications media both to familiarise and to objectify, the *umma* has gained some social weight as an alternative form of affiliation. This accounts, in part, for the widespread Muslim discontent over the perceived injustices of Palestine, Kashmir, and Chechnya among others. It perhaps also accounts for the current exaggerated fear of Islamist networks – an echo of nineteenth century European anxiety over pan-Islamic anti-colonialism.

To the extent that a transnational, pan-Islamic, identity is emerging, it has been valorised not only by understanding what Islam is not, but also by self-understanding – tacit, now increasingly explicit, notions of how Muslims view themselves. We have already seen this in the self-consciousness of 'minority' Islam. It must also be seen in an increasing concretisation of what can only be called sectarianism. While confessional animosity was vehemently expressed in earlier periods, such as Ibn al-Jawzi's anti Shi'i and anti-Sufi tract, *Talbis Iblis* (The Devil's Deception), in the twelfth century, one immediately thinks more recently of Abu Musab al-Zarqawi's fetid diatribe against the Shi'a of Iraq.[26] But more than this has occurred.

In a very real way, the entire thrust of modern Islamic political thought has been trans-sectarian, preferring attractively vague notions like *shura* (consultation), *ijma'* (consensus) and *al-dawla al-islamiyya* (Islamic state) to the more contentious debates over precise authority of religious leaders or shrine-centred ritual. In Persia in the eighteenth century, Nader Shah famously tried to induce the Ottoman Sultan to recognise Twelver Shi'ism as the fifth orthodox school of law and, in 1743, convened a grand conference of religious officials to reconcile the two major sects.[27] The Egyptian Mahmud Shaltut, Shaykh al-Azhar in the Nasserist period, issued a *fatwa* in 1959 that authorised Shi'i instruction at al-Azhar for the first time in 900 years and directly referred with approval to Shi'i legal ideas. He described Islam as the 'religion of unity' (al-islam din al-wahda).[28] A new institution and journal (Risalat al-islam) was created to promote convergence of legal thought – taqrib al-madhahib – and for a while, the Islamic revolutionary state of Iran produced a journal, Risalat al-taqrib, to promote the same goal. [29]

What is more, it is clear that self-professed reformers have long preferred an eclecticism (takhayyur) and synthesis (talfiq) to strict adherence to distinctive schools of thought. This was the impulse behind the law reforms of the early to mid-twentieth century, but also currently of the popular website, 'Islamonline'. The arguments of Shaykh Qaradawi – in print, on al-Jazeera, or on Islamonline – are madhhab-lite, speaking of general principles and common concerns, rather than making specific reference to the principles of the Hanafi, Maliki, Shafi'i or Hanbali schools of law (madhhabs) and citing few of the classical works of jurisprudence. The consequence of such a modern approach is subject to debate, however. Wael Hallaq has argued that, over time, the strategy has been 'arbitrary' and driven by the demands of political centralisation and modernisation, in the process leading to the 'demise of the shari'a'.[30] Others have argued that it meshes with the modern emphasis on Muslim commonality and thereby creates a virtual pan-Islam at the same time as it establishes pan-Islamic authority – in the words of Peter Mandaville, a 'virtual caliphate'.[31]

While many jurists continue to promote synthesis in the hope of greater harmony, another distinctive feature of the modern landscape is an accentuation of difference: the pronouncing of takfir (excommunication) on fellow Muslims, for example, but also the self- and cross-identification of Muslims as Salafis, Shi'a, Wahhabis, Shafi'is, Mourides, Nursis, and the many variations on these identities. Salafi tracts, purportedly aimed at mu'amalat, the practice of the faith, often denounce Shi'i deviations in such emotive terms that the sense of the umma seems to vanish into the ether.[32]

The questioning of synthetic or eclectic reasoning in modern Islam does not have to be radical or confrontational, however. Indeed, there are many Muslim intellectuals who are critical of this approach, fearing that the loss of strict methodology associated with a distinct school of interpretation creates aimlessness at best, Mawdudian and Qutbian politicisation at worst. A distinguished scholar of Islam, Hamid Algar, has argued, for example, that the Wahhabis, by their beliefs and practices, are outside Sunni Islam. According to him, his intention in saying so is not polemical, but to set the historical record straight and to maintain intellectual integrity:

> That Wahhabis are now counted as Sunni is one indication that the term 'Sunni' has come to acquire an extraordinarily loose meaning …; it fact, [in this usage] it signifies little more than 'non- Shi'i'.[33]

Just as many are promoting a kind of generic Islam and undifferentiated notions of unity, sectarian and theological differences have also hardened. This may reflect the general interaction between globalisation and localisation or the natural tension between unity and diversity. But the competing ideas and identities that have historically existed across and within Muslim societies and that are being reified anew today complicate the pan-Islamic project. To the extent that the *umma* is being imagined, which it doubtless is to some extent, it may also be a fractured imagination.[34]

Conclusion

Awareness of these differences undermines simple ideas of universal community and the centrality of doctrine, but it also reminds us of the deep structures that underpin Muslim societies. There are lines of division among Muslims, now seen mainly but not only in nation-state terms; there are also mobile communities that escape easy categorisation, now especially seen in Muslims of the West who undermine a strict divide between an Islamic 'here' and a non-Islamic 'there'. Muslim transnational networks are well-financed organised additions to the scene, but they could not exist without underlying strata of affiliation and support, however unformulated and inarticulate they may at times be. And, it must be acknowledged, there is also a more sharply delineated sense of inclusion and exclusion among some Muslims – one that aspires to redraw the internal borders of Islam if not more urgently than, then contemporaneously with, reconfiguring the balance of power between Muslims and non-Muslims. Many of these speak in the name of a fictive, capital E 'Islamic Empire'; to invoke Homi Bhahba, these radical Islamists deploy the 'language of archaic belonging'.[35]

Pan-Islam has always been the source of outside anxiety. Further, to the extent that the notion of the *umma* is becoming formalised, it may well sharpen the sense of victimisation and injustice among Muslims and criticisms of Western policy. This may especially be so if, unlike the past, pan-Islamic identity reaches beyond the elite level. This consciousness may be deeper and broader now, but to the extent that faultlines exist, they are not dynastic and perhaps not even national or ethnic as in the past, but theological and ideological. In the end, the construction of the *umma* will continue to depend in no small way on the possibilities, and indeed the limits, of the intra-Islamic conversation.

4

JIHADISM AND INTERCIVILISATIONAL CONFLICT

CONFLICTING IMAGES
OF THE SELF AND OF THE OTHER

Bassam Tibi

In discussing the issue of xenophobia and human security in relation to the place of Islam in contemporary world affairs, there is a need to determine and clear up the subject matter to ensure an unbiased in-depth analysis. Islam is a religion, a cultural system and a worldview that unites its believers in one *umma* (Islamic community). At present, there are transnational Islamic and Islamist efforts at 'reimagining the umma'.[1] In spite of shared values and other commonalities among Muslims, there exists no single monolithic Islam. One encounters this preoccupation and essentialisation in the work of both Western Orientalism and Islamist internationalism. However, despite the existing diversity, Islam as a transnational religion is nevertheless a civilisational unity.[2] This is the point of departure for dealing with the topic placed at the center of the present analysis, namely xenophobia and human security.

In the age of the 'cultural turn'[3] and the religionisation of politics,[4] the notion of an Islamist internationalism creates a security concern in view of assaults carried out by a jihadist minority in the name of Islam. These events have been contributing worldwide to unfavorable attitudes towards Islam and Muslims. To avert this, it has been asked whether a development 'from Islamist jihadism to democratic peace'[5] could be launched. At issue in this context is security and xenophobia becoming intertwined.

Introduction

In the international press coverage, one finds contradictory views concerning Islam and terrorism. In considering the diversity within Islam, one finds a peaceful love-preaching Islam as much as another militant hatred-spreading Islam taught in Salafist and Islamist madrassas in the pursuit of 'jihad without borders', as for example in Pakistan.[6] Talking about Islam in general, I dissociate myself from the claim of one essential Islam, be it in the positive sense (religion of peace and tolerance) or in the negative sense (religion of jihadism, as understood by jihadist Islamists). In social and historical realities, Islam is reflected by Muslim societies as taking different shapes on all levels. In this study of Islam, the point of departure therefore is to address the two pending issues of security and xenophobia in terms of facts, not within the framework of religious texts. As an Arab Muslim human rights activist, who was among the co-founders of the Arab organisation for human rights, I share the view that 'the right to security' – expressed in article 2 of the French Revolution's *Déclaration des Droits de l'Homme et du Citoyen*: 'ces droits sont de la liberté et sûreté' – is to be seen among the basic human rights. In contrast to this view, political Islam in its direction of *jihadiyya* (jihadism) denies Muslim non-combatants as well as non-Muslims the right to security. Given this fact, and the related ideology of Islamist jihadism used by some Westerners as an excuse for demonising all Muslims as a threat to human security, this chapter focuses on jihadism as a reality, as a case of othering non-jihadist Muslims as 'un-Islamic' and non-Muslims as *kafirun* (infidels).

In the context of the present analysis two forms of xenophobia complementary to one another are at issue: the use and abuse of jihadist terrorism by non-Muslims for advancing an Islamophobia; and the preaching of hatred by Islamist Imams directed against non-Muslims viewed as *kafirun*. The remedy is not the prevailing Muslim culture of self-victimisation, nor accusing the West or what is viewed to be 'Islam' in a general sense. The remedy is justice, enlightenment and proper education. One step in this direction is an understanding of the issue itself. This is the spirit of the present analysis and the task ahead.

In addressing the pending issues, I dissociate myself from the rhetoric of a clash of civilisations. I am one of the co-authors of a book written against the spirit of Huntington, published under the title *Preventing the Clash of Civilizations*. The shared sentiment alternative to Huntington's scenario is phrased in my contribution as 'cross-cultural morality'.[7] To ensure human security, we need an Islamic contribution that contradicts the mind leading to hatred and assaults legitimated with Islamic references. To combat xenophobia, we not only need a critique of Islamophobia, but also of the othering of non-Muslims by Muslims themselves. Ibn Arabi's concept of belief as *mahabba* (love) and the rationalism of Ibn Rushd are among the Islamic sources of my thinking for a Muslim contribution to human security and against xenophobia. For the sake of honesty and integrity one needs to enhance the criticism against xenophobia by including the Islamic othering of non-Muslims as well as the anti-Western ideology of jihadist Islamism. Muslims are a part of humanity, which should be safe and free of all kinds of xenophobia. Therefore, a Muslim contribution to human security and to the fight against xenophobia is also needed, it is more promising than an exclusive Islamic sense of victimhood, or the other extreme of an Islamic superiority. Muslims rightly contest their inferiorisation by some Westerners, but they ought not reverse this in looking at themselves as superior to non-Muslims. There is no credibility if a balance between the self and the other is not achieved.

The chapter focuses on jihadism as a religious legitimisation of terrorism. Jihadism is defined as an irregular war posing a threat to post-bipolar security. It is argued that jihadism constitutes one dimension of Islamism, also addressed as political Islam.[8] It emerges from the contemporary politicisation of religion in the countries of Islamic civilisation undergoing a crisis. The same phenomenon can be observed in other world religions of which the result is a variety of contemporary religious fundamentalisms.[9] In political Islam this phenomenon is represented by two major streams: institutional Islamism and jihadism. Unlike institutional Islamists, who seek to achieve their goal (i.e. the Islamic shari'a state) through participation in political institutions, the jihadists subscribe to violent direct action believed to be fought as 'terror in the mind of God'.[10] This politicised religion touches upon the security of people in general, and of Muslims in Algeria, Egypt, Pakistan and many other Islamic countries in particular.

Muslims have been exposed to the security threat of these 'warriors of God' since the 1980s. It is expressed in two ways, one is local and the other is global. There is locally the call for toppling the existing order and the resort to terror being a practice addressed in this chapter as 'irregular war'. Clearly, jihadist Islamism poses a threat to the existing state order, but it is also an issue that touches on international security. Above that, it is also one of the sources of xenophobia. The call of Sayyid Qutb, the *spiritus rector* of Islamism, for a *Pax Islamica* (an Islamic world order) precedes al-Qaeda and its internationalism by several decades and refers to the global level. However, post-Cold War developments paved the way for jihadist terrorism to move to the fore. In this context there is a shift from Clausewitzian inter-state war to the new one of irregular warriors fighting a neo-jihad. Based on this observation, it is argued that jihadism is a challenge that requires the unfolding of adjusted patterns for countering terrorism to ensure human security.[11] To be sure, while jihadism is a variety of terrorism, it is not classical jihad.[12] At issue is how to respond, first to 'terror in the mind of God' being the new post-bipolar irregular war, and second, to the call for toppling the international order of secular states and the will to replace it by a global Islamicate (a *dar al-Islam*) mapping the entire globe.

After having outlined the interrelation between xenophobia and human security in world politics in its present post-bipolar development, and after having pointed to the shift in focus away from the state towards dealing with the jihadism of emerging non-state actors, the ensuing study of terrorism in international affairs is the major concern. Jihadism is a terrorist branch of contemporary political Islam. Within the new environment of international affairs, jihadism has affected recent patterns of interaction between world cultures at this crisis-ridden time. The study of terrorism predates jihadism,[13] related in this study to the occurring changes in international politics in general and political Islam in particular.

In the world of Islam, Islamism and its jihadist terrorism are not totally new phenomena, even though their incorporation into world politics – within the framework of the ascendancy of non-state actors[14] – is recent; their move to the fore is a compelling issue and thus there is a need for including their investigation into international studies. This change in international politics is also compelling to the extent that many approaches of International Relations (IR), as well as the related traditional wisdoms, need to be questioned and subjected to a new reasoning. Among the pertinent changes to be taken into account is the rise of politicised religion becoming an issue of international affairs.[15] The matter is not restricted to looking at concrete cases of terror legitimated as jihad in the path of God, but the political discourse related to it needs to be included. This consideration leads to the insight that neo-jihad is not a goal in itself, but rather just a means in the pursuit of a new order in line with this discourse. The use of religion in politics underpinning the legitimisation of irregular war is not a pretext and it matters to post-bipolar security not only in terms of incorporating terrorism in military studies, but also for dealing with the new phenomenon within the scope of 'order'. In the tradition of Hedley Bull, order is viewed to be the pivotal subject of world politics.[16] In this regard, we need to take a glimpse at the discipline itself for grasping the issue and for incorporating jihadism as a new issue in the respective studies.

At their heights, IR were, as Stanley Hoffmann once noted, an 'American discipline'. I hasten to add, a discipline 'of the Cold War era'. All major schools of the discipline concurred on sharing the view of the state as the basic actor. Long before Samuel P. Huntington coined the term 'clash of civilizations', Raymond Aron, who was the mentor of Stanley Hoffmann in Paris, turned our attention to the fact that bipolarity has been the 'veil' concealing the real source of conflicts in international politics. Aron points at 'the heterogeneity of civilizations'.[17] People belong by nature and by their socialisation in family and society to cultures and civilisations, and only formally to existing states. In real states, citizenship constitutes a part of the identity of the people. In the world of Islam, states are 'quasi-states', i.e. nominal states,[18] and citizenship does not provide 'identity'. In this context, Islamism revives the collective identity of the imagined community of the *umma* in Islam.

The ideology of jihadism challenges these states. In Qutb's vision of an Islamic peace, the jihad determined by the worldview of acting *fi sabil Allah* (in the path of God) for expanding the abode of Islam within an alleged order of the Islamicate to the entire world is directed against both, the West and Islamic Westernised elites, which are othered equally. In short, there are conflicting visions. The Kantian views on world peace based on the existing Westphalian order are challenged by the call for a *Pax Islamica* being the vision of the jihadism of political Islam.[19] The addressed conflict in world affairs on a non-state level is grounded on the current politicisation of religion, a phenomenon that is clearly not restricted to Islam. Basically, it results in a variety of religious fundamentalisms. Every variety of this phenomenon includes in its centerpiece a concept of order for remaking the world.[20] In their own variety, Islamic fundamentalists believe that *hakimiyyat Allah* (God's rule)[21] is the ultimate divine political order, first to be established in the world of Islam and then enhanced to an Islamic world order mapping the entire globe. This order is meant to facilitate ruling along the Islamic vision of a global *Pax Islamica*. It is unfortunate to see that not only Islamists – one is asked to be aware of the distinction between Islam and Islamism[22] – subscribe to the view that *dar al-Islam* ought to comprise all of humanity. The orthodox-Salafist worldview of Islam also claims universality. This worldview becomes a world-political problem through the politicisation of Islam.

Within Islamism itself, we need to distinguish between those committed to political Islam in an institutional framework (e.g. the Islamist AKP in Turkey) and others, who present their new interpretation of the classical Islamic jihad as the new *action directe* of terror believed to be in the mind of God. This jihadist political Islam lies at the center of the present chapter. The major argument is that jihadist Islamism in the understanding of a pattern of irregular war is a basic issue area of post-bipolar international security. Based on the foregoing introductory remarks, the following analysis is pursued in three steps. First, the subject matter will be established. Next, light will be shed on the politicisation of religion underpinning the worldview of the jihadists. Finally, it will be outlined what I term as 'irregular war' being the instrument of jihadism for establishing the new divine order they envision.

The Subject Matter and the Scope of the Analysis

From the outset, it is important to note that any dealing with these issues is difficult as it involves breaking taboos and challenging prevailing understandings. Nevertheless, after 11 September 2001 it has become easier to speak of jihadist Islamism as a security threat. From an enlightened point of view however, it has equally become a requirement to combat spreading Islamophobia. Yet, one needs to be aware that Islamists themselves are exploiting the suspicion of Islamophobia attached to constructed images of Islam for associating any pointing at the Islamist activities in security studies with an alleged demonisation of Islam. In the aftermath of September 11, the situation has improved and worsened at the same time. The assaults of September 11 made clear that Islamists are in action, but unfortunately, they also paved the way to revive established clichés about Islam in relating this religion without distinction to terrorism. Among the extremes we find, on the one hand, the well-known accusation of Orientalism reaching new heights by also hitting scholars who do not share the view that terrorists were no more than a 'crazed gang' (E. Said) acting for their own. On the other hand, we face the extreme of imputing all evils to 'militant Islam', equating it with Islam itself. This chapter aims at enlightening against both extremes while endeavoring to introduce the jihadism of political Islam into security studies.

In fact, Islamist terrorists refer to themselves as people fulfilling the religious duty to jihad being an obligation for every Muslim. A closer look at the phenomenon shows that we are dealing with a new pattern of jihad that can be described as an 'invention of tradition',[23] for it is not the classical Islamic jihad. Nevertheless, and despite clarification, we need to take the Islamic self-reference of these jihadists seriously. The religious image of the jihadists of themselves, to be 'the true believers',[24] is not an expression of cynicism, but rather sincere true belief, even though their action might contradict orthodox religious doctrines. Understanding this is pertinent, because it is a basic effort to enable ourselves to grasp the current historical phenomenon of religiously legitimated terrorism. The religious legitimisation is neither instrumental nor does it serve as a camouflage for covering otherwise criminal acts. The Islamist terrorists do not perceive their action to be *irhab* (terrorism), but rather *jihadiyya* (jihadism) – a new interpretation of religious jihad being a *farida* (duty). To reiterate, in the claimed capacity of being jihadists, these Islamists believe themselves to be acting as the 'true believers'. I shall take pains to shed light on religious-fundamentalist terrorism in an effort at explaining Islamic-fundamentalist jihadism, while firstly placing this terrorism in the debate on warfare in terms of a new pattern of irregular war. Then, secondly, we need to relate the purpose of 'remaking the world' to jihadism as a means for achieving the goal. This creates the background for a security approach needed to guide a policy required for coming to terms with the challenge of jihadism on two counts: first, as terrorism and second, as a threat to the existing order of the state as well as to world order itself.

Among the methodological grounds required for the analysis of jihadism as a security concern, we fulfill the already addressed need of introducing the study of religion into the discipline of IR. In addition to this condition, the study of war needs to go beyond legalistic constraints attached to an inter-state war (e.g. declaration of war by a state) to consider non-state violent action as war. To be sure, traditional wisdoms no longer help in grasping the recent current of irregular war of which jihadism is a case in point. In general, we are challenged to rethink the discipline of IR and to introduce to it many innovations. There were times in the past age of bipolarity when scholars in 'the dividing discipline'[25] of IR were not only separated through schools of thought, but were equally divided along ideological lines and boundaries. Those among them who dealt with security were disparaged as 'right wingers', in contrast to the left wing IR-scholars, who focused on political economy. Apart from the political differences between these ideologies, there existed a methodological distinction: students of international security focused on state actors and on their military capacities, whereas political economists in political science only believed in the relevance and priority of economic structures. The school of thought of the global system reduces the latter approach to absurdity. As can be demonstrated on our case: we cannot explain jihadism with a reference to the 'global system', unless we – as some do in an absurd manner – view terrorism as a protest movement directed against economic 'globalisation' run by the US, and thus unwittingly justify both jihadism and anti-Americanism.

Not only in the light of post-bipolarity, but also of September 11, we may discern new challenges on the rise that compels us to question both approaches of the phased out 'left and right' scheme. This would enable us to consider new perspectives for grasping changed international relations in general, and international security in particular. Among these challenges we see the civilisational self-assertive 'revolt against the West'[26] directed towards secular Western values. In considering this revolt, new areas are to be brought into the study of IR. As already mentioned, Raymond Aron addressed this subject in terms of 'heterogeneity of civilizations'. Without a reference to Aron or his work, Huntington speaks of a 'clash between civilizations'. In putting the work of both scholars aside, we find an appropriate explanation of the pending issue in the work of Hedley Bull, who unravels the fallacy of the so-called global village in stating that

> it is also clear that the shrinking of the globe, while it has brought societies to a degree of mutual awareness and interaction they have not had before, does not in itself create a unity of outlook and has not in fact done so ... Humanity is becoming simultaneously more unified and more fragmented.[27]

Based on this observation I developed my concept of a simultaneity of structural globalisation and cultural fragmentation.[28] This divergence has been generated by European expansion, which has contributed to the structural mapping of the entire world along the lines of standards designed by Western civilisation.[29] However, there was no successful overall universalisation of Western values that matches the current degree of globalisation. In short: I distinguish between the *globalisation* of structures and the *universalisation* of values. Thus, the globalisation of structures coexists with cultural fragmentation (with the lack of universally valid and accepted norms and values). The new challenges are related to new challengers, who are non-state actors. Their addressed revolt against Western values has – more or less successfully – launched a process of de-Westernisation[30] that starts with knowledge, values, and worldviews and then moves to political order itself. If we stubbornly insist on the validity of the realist model in simply reducing jihadist terrorism to a problem of 'rough states' while overlooking the cultural roots of the phenomenon, then we deprive ourselves of the ability to grasp the issue and thus of developing proper responses to the new security threat.

In the first place, we need to understand in what way politicised religion in our post-bipolar time serves as a tool for the articulation of the 'revolt against the West' (norms and values). Political Islam is the frame of reference for developing the idea of classical jihad to a new concept of terrorist jihadism against the West. This new interpretation of jihad understood as a pattern of an irregular war is related to an action that can be – in a way – addressed in the Georges Sorelian term of '*action directe*' against the existing order. It is a form of terrorism that heralds an end to the classical Clausewitzian inter-state war. Then, neither al-Qaeda nor any similar group has an army that can be combated by regular armed forces. To threaten the states that 'harbor' jihad-terrorists with military intervention is therefore utterly meaningless. In particular, democratic Western states are part of the global networking of terrorism that uses migration and the related diaspora culture for providing jihadism with a 'Hinterland'. The German logistic base related to the cell of al-Qaeda in Hamburg is a case in point.

In dealing with Islamism as an issue of national and international security in the light of September 11, we need to look at Islamic civilisation, out of which the jihadist groups – being inventors of tradition, and also non-state actors – are emerging. In international politics, this civilisation consists of states, being members of the international community. Even though the Islamic civilisation is often described as the 'world of Islam', it does not constitute a world of its own in that its states are part of the international system. Only in one sense Islamic states exist of their own, namely as a grouping of states of a distinct civilisation. These states have their own international organisation of the Islamic conference, the OIC. Since the rise of political Islam[31] in that part of the world, any dealing with Islamist movements has also become a policy issue on international grounds and it is no longer merely an academic concern for the students of Islam. Neither the work of oriental philologists nor the study of cultural anthropologists can be helpful for dealing with the pending issues. In contrast, an IR-oriented approach, placing Islamism in security studies, is more promising. This view is supported by the fact that Islamists unequivocally make clear the target of their call, namely to topple the existing order of the nation-state to be replaced by what they envisage to be a *hakimiyyat Allah* (rule of God) as the substance of an Islamic state and a new world order. Here again, we do not face a simple cultural attitude, but rather the vision of an alternative political order. The issue of *nizam Islami* (Islamic order) ranks as a top priority on the agenda of Islamism.

In contemporary history, the very first Islamist movement, the movement of the Muslim Brothers,[32] was founded in Egypt in 1928 by Hasan al-Banna. It was al-Banna himself who reinterpreted the doctrine of jihad[33] to lay grounds for jihadism in the understanding of terrorism. In this tradition, Islamists envision an international order designed by the shari'a. The outcome is the current competition between a *Pax Islamica* and the *Pax Americana* of the West. This is the substance of the challenge of Islamic fundamentalism as related to the claim to replace the Westphalian order in world politics. The repeatedly mentioned 'revolt against the West' is also characterised by an effort at de-secularisation. Thus, Islamism is directed against the secular character of world politics.[34] Therefore, at issue is a civilisational conflict in world politics, because secularisation and de-secularisation are related to rival civilisational worldviews and thus to conflicting world political visions.

As already indicated, the 57 nation-states of Islamic civilisation are grouped in the OIC (the sole regional organisation in world politics established on the civilisational grounds of a religion). Among these states we find only very few that can be qualified – of course only in a very limited sense – as democracies. It follows that in most of these states there exists no opening for a political opposition. Thus, the rise of political Islam is not, and cannot be, expressed through institutional channels (Turkey is an exception). Islamist movements are however the basic political opposition in the world of Islam, but they are denied a realm for activities in the pursuit of their political goals in their own Islamic countries. For this reason, they act in the underground and move their followers to the West for establishing a *Hinterland* for their activities of opposing superficially secular regimes at home.

The major aim of Islamist movements is at present to topple existing regimes at home. This leads to the question: can one exclusively locate Islamism in the world of Islam itself? In a widely received essay by Michael Doran, on 'other people's war',[35] we find the argument that in September 2001 al-Qaeda primarily wanted to hit its enemies in the world of Islam via the US. Doran's essay overlooks or even confuses the two levels of order targeted in the strategy of Islamism: first, the replacement of the governmental establishments in the world of Islam itself by the *nizam* (system) of *hakimiyyat Allah* (God's rule), and on these grounds; second, the creation of a global *Pax Islamica* via an Islamic *'thawra al-alamiyya* (world revolution)[36] carried out by political Islam.

Thus, on September 11 these levels were both confused and intermingled. It is only in this sense that one may speak of 'somebody else's war' when addressing the assaults of September 11. Jihadist Islamism is both a domestic (the world of Islam) and an international (world politics) phenomenon. Internationalism is intrinsic to Islamism, which uses the Islamic diaspora in the West, yet, to achieve both goals.

Jihadism, the Politicisation of Religion and the Othering of the Foes

The politicisation of religion underpins the justification of the call for a new Islamic order to be achieved by the irregular war of jihadism. These issues are at the center of the present analysis. The jihadist threat to security in world politics has been illustrated by September 11 as an act of irregular war viewed as 'terror in the mind of God', thus using a religious legitimisation.[37] Is this 'Islamic world revolution' contributing to a 'clash of civilizations'?[38] Is this threat to security the source of the emerging 'new world disorder'?

The claim of Islamism gives expression to a civilisational competition between two concepts of order. This is the background of the statement that politicised religion leads to an international conflict. Huntington created a landslide among scholars of IR in addressing this conflict in terms of 'clash of civilizations'. A year ahead of Huntington's book, I dealt with competing civilisational concepts of order in my book *Krieg der Zivilisationen* of 1995. I acknowledge my failure to introduce the concept of civilisation to the discipline of IR. That has been the accomplishment of Samuel P. Huntington. In my book on civilisational conflicts in world politics, I – despite disagreement – acknowledge Huntington's *Foreign Affairs* article of 1993 and discuss it at length. The major points of disagreement were elaborated upon in my contribution to the already mentioned book of the former President of Germany (see endnote 7). In this contribution not only the seniority of Huntington in the debate, but also his success are acknowledged, however, while corrections regarding his views on Islam and its civilisation in the study of IR are also made. Furthermore, I argue that social scientists who, in the wake of the topical and increasingly important role of Islam, deal with these issues not only need to introduce social science to Islamic studies,[39] but equally have to know more about Islam.

This scholarly debate touches upon the present topic. I refer to it to dissociate myself from Huntington's rhetoric of a clash, and to make clear that I refuse to join the club of those politically correct scholars who demonise Huntington. I believe his work has contributed to the debate and I find it sad to see how Huntington has been defamed as a 'Cold War warrior' and even been accused of Islamophobia for pointing at political Islam as a security issue. The security threat of jihadism is a matter of fact, it is neither a view of, nor a distortion by the media or by scholars seeking a 'substitute for the Soviet Union'. Yet, the traditional students of Islam are reluctant to deal with this issue in their academic Islamic studies. They are Orientalists who are philologists, historians or simply students of religion, thus they have no authority to judge about international security. Their disciplines, as well as cultural anthropological studies, have succumbed to Edward Said's conviction of 'Orientalism'. Neither the scholars of these disciplines nor the late Said himself have a professional competence to deal with international affairs. We rarely find scholars among Western Orientalists who have a professional social-scientific background. Nevertheless, these scholars were called upon to review as authoritative 'readers' submitted project proposals for the study of fundamentalism in Islam as an issue of international security.[40] In most cases known to me, the Orientalists in point turned these research proposals down with the pseudo-scholarly argument, the issue is not serious and does not deserve funding, or simply said: 'There exists no fundamentalism; it is a construction'. This was belied by the event of September 11. In a case known to me in Switzerland, those philologist readers argued that 'fundamentalism' is a product of Western media and not a reality. Certainly, it is not a digression in this chapter to refer to this kind of handling of the study of political Islam and security in established scholarship. The reference merely serves to show the grave obstacles standing in the way of the research on the addressed subject matter of this chapter. The curtailment of the right of free speech in research is a troubling disservice to scholarship in contemporary Western institutions.

Despite all odds, I find it, as a Muslim scholar living in Europe, but scholarly acting in the US, easier to address the jihadist security threat at the American academe than at the European. In the US, it was possible to carry out a major project for the study of fundamentalism that led to the publication of seminal five volumes on this subject. After September 11, it has become more than clear to what great extent we need to pursue further the study of Islamism and international security. The inquiry into the linkages between religion and international politics highlighted the links between Islamism and world politics. In the light of the impact of September 11, it is pertinent to draw on some existing approaches to the study of politicised religion as well as international security and to link them to one another. As the case of jihadism suggests, there is a need to establish these new approaches in IR. This need is emphasised by the fact that politicised religion is among the major issues of the political crisis of order in international politics after the end of the Cold War.

In considering the post-bipolar 'cultural turn' in our world, one can state a crisis of meaning growing from the crisis of modernity itself. The already mentioned lack of a universalisation of Western values along with intensifying globalisation continues to generate this crisis of meaning with global political ramifications. Globalisation, but not a successful Westernisation[41] has been taking place worldwide. The phenomenon of the return of the sacred in a political shape, being an effort at de-Westernisation, is not properly understood in the West. The formula of Jürgen Habermas of a 'post-secular society'[42] is nothing else than a poor approach for dealing with a real phenomenon with quasi post-modern concepts that fail to explain the resort to religion in non-Western civilisations. Habermas does not understand that the competition between a secular and a divine order goes along with two worldviews opposed to one another: neo-absolutisms and relativism,[43] arising from the very same context. We see, on the one hand, the politicisation of religion, as demonstrated by Islam, assuming the shape of a neo-absolutism challenging the contemporary world order. On the other hand, we see post-Christian developments emerging in Western Europe ensued by a crisis of identity. Westernisation in the world of Islam is receding for the benefit of a drive at de-Westernisation being promoted by Islamic revival. At issue are the effects of this process on a changing world order.

The contemporary neo-absolutism of political Islam claims to decenter the West and to replace its Westphalian secular order through a divine Islamic one. Jihadism is among the means for reaching this end. In this context, it is possible to understand the reference in the introductory remarks to the French social scientist Raymond Aron, who addresses the 'heterogeneity of civilizations'. The pertinence of this issue to IR revolves around the existence of different worldviews and – along these lines – of different concepts of order. While one of them is secular, the others (e.g. the Islamic) are based on the politicisation of religion. With the exception of Western civilisation, almost all other world civilisations are related to and determined by a religion and the related worldview.[44] In the case of Islam, an Islamist concept of order is becoming a broadly accepted public choice. This concept of *din-wa-dawla* (unity of religion and state) challenges the validity of the secular nation-state in the world of Islam and goes further beyond by enhancing its claim to an Islamic order to cover world politics altogether.

Again, in the intellectual tradition of the philosophical approach to IR presented in the work of Raymond Aron and Hedley Bull, I relate my study of religion to their study of values in international affairs. In this context, Islamism is interpreted as an expression of Islamic revival being equally political, cultural and religious. To reiterate the major findings of this inquiry: the outcome of Islamism is a civilisational challenge to the world order. The Islamist othering of non-Muslims is based on an alleged 'Judeo–Christian conspiracy'[45] believed to be directed against Islam, therefore it is bound to a 'revolt against the West'. In this regard I draw on Bull's essay, explaining the resort to religion as a cultural-political articulation in the pursuit of de-Westernisation. For unfolding a world political perspective for understanding jihadism, we need to go 'beyond left and right'[46] and equally overcome in the study of IR the burden of the traditional boundaries of a dividing discipline. For reaching this end, I operate in my work on the following two methodological assumptions:

First, we need a serious IR-oriented study of religion, considering how its politicisation leads to religious fundamentalism. Of course, the prevailing clichés and catchwords transmitted in the media, which convey the phenomenon under issue in terms of 'fanatism, terrorism and extremism' ought to be contradicted, but this is not the business of IR-discipline. It is dishonest to refer to this deplorable image of Islam in the West in order to turn down the study of the jihadist threat of Islamism to world order as an expression of 'Islamophobia'. Jihadism and not Islam is under issue, although this threat emerges from the politicisation of Islam.

Second, the addressed politicisation reaches its height when it embraces Islamic universalism. The result is a concept of world order designed and articulated in divine Islamic terms. This is unique to Islam because of its universalism. For instance, the politicisation of religion in Hinduism only leads to a concept of order restricted to the envisaged Hindu nation of Hindustan. It follows, a Hindu-fundamentalist threat to security is confined to the territoriality of Hindu civilisation, i.e. it is exclusively regional and only pertinent to South Asia. In contrast, Islam is a universalistic religion and its politicisation touches upon the international order. As the intellectual precursor of political Islam, Sayyid Qutb, proposed international peace can only be achieved by spreading *hakimiyyat Allah* on global grounds. The implication of this view is that there can be no world peace without the global domination of Islam.[47]

This is an articulation of an Islamist internationalism in a civilisational conflict with the bid for a related international order. This is the ideological background of persons like bin Laden and of globally networked movements like al-Qaeda, which provide the internationalist model for all of the contemporary jihadist movements acting *fi sabil Allah* (in the path of God) for establishing the Islamist order of *Pax Islamica*. It can be safely stated that jihadist internationalism is a security concern. To enlighten about this threat has nothing to do with Islamophobia.

Cultural diversity is natural and it could be enriching for humanity. However, the politicisation of the already addressed heterogeneity of civilisations results in raising claims – as is the case in political Islam – for a political order. It does not only create herewith a challenge to the existing world order, but also leads to dividing lines that separate humanity. One should have been alerted in the 1950s, when the precursor and foremost thinker of contemporary political Islam, Sayyid Qutb, challenged the existing world order; he maintained a deep civilisational crisis of the West to be resolved by Islamic dominance. In his pamphlets, in particular in his *Signs along the Road* and in his *World Peace and Islam*, he proposed that only Islam is in a position to overcome this crisis and to save humanity.[48] To be sure and to reiterate, this is the very source of the worldview of bin Laden and of all of al-Qaeda's jihad fighters. Clearly, this is not the view of a 'crazed gang', but rather the authoritative expression of a mainstream of jihadist Islamism in the world of Islam. Is it desirable that the Westphalian order in world politics[49] will be replaced by an Islamic order?

Hedley Bull did not know of Qutb and of his views, but he was aware of the fact that the stated civilisational 'revolt against the West' is best 'exemplified in Islamic fundamentalism'.[50] In the course of the post-bipolar crisis of international order, these ideas (e.g. Qutb's) have become more topical, enjoying a mobilising function in the world of Islam. The reference to these ideas reinforces Islam's new role as well as its appeal as a public choice as seen by the Islamists. The fact that political Islam can be traced back to the year 1928, when the Society of Muslim Brothers was founded, provides evidence that Islamism predates the demise of the Cold War. Yet, political Islam and its ideology did not get its current mobilising appeal before the end of bipolarity. The heterogeneity of civilisations then came to the fore in the shape of politicised religions. The concept of order in Islam has been given the name of *al-dawla al-Islamiyya* (the Islamic State). The reader is asked to recall that the Islamist neo-jihad in the 21st century is an effort – at times with the means of irregular war – to reach this end of materialising the new order, which political Islam claims at home as well as internationally.

In summing up the preceding analysis, one is able to state that the foremost issue related to the pertinence of the politicised religion of Islam to IR, being an expression of 'the revolt against the West', is its rejection of the existing secular order of Westphalian origin. One may ask, are we heading in a direction 'beyond Westphalia'?[51] There is no doubt, the Westphalian order is not a sacred cow and therefore it is fully legitimate to question its existence in a changed world. However, neither the violent jihadist means of Islamism nor the *hakimiyyat Allah* concept of order seem to be the appropriate alternative humanity is looking for to overcome the crisis of the secular nation-state. For a religiously diverse humanity, no alternative political concept of order grounded on religion can be accepted. Why? On the state level, the *nizam Islami* (Islamic system)[52] is a totalitarian political pronouncement of Islamism not even acceptable to all Muslims, in particular not to those committed to freedom and democracy. Some jihadists yearn for the traditional order of the caliphate of the sunna which is not acceptable to the shi'a. The exponents of political Islam believe that in the long run they will prevail in being in a position to materialise Qutb's vision of world peace under the banner of Islam. This kind of peace is a threat to non-Muslims, who according to the shari'a would be discriminated as subdued *dhimmi*.[53]

To put minds at ease, of course, we are not heading towards a new political order pertinent to IR based on the politicised rules of the Islamic shari'a. Clearly, on grounds of feasibility this Islamist goal will continue to be difficult to achieve in the foreseeable future. Nevertheless, if the conclusion out of this statement were that the jihadist call for an Islamic world order is practically irrelevant and meaningless, then it would be premature and wrong. On domestic and regional grounds the call for an Islamic shari'a state serves as a mobilising device with great appeal to deprived Muslims. The result would be to destabilise and to undermine the legitimacy of the existing order. The political terrorist *'action directe'* of jihad in the path of God aims at establishing a *hakimiyyat Allah*. This is much more than the rhetoric of a romantic order because it contributes to generating real disorder. One needs to keep in mind that this action is carried out by a movement based in transnational religion and its global networks.

The provided assessment of jihadism needs to be placed in the broader debate within the study of religion and politics. Therefore, a reference to the inquiry into religion in social-scientific terms is a part of this summing up. Let me first mention the two approaches employed in the academic literature on political Islam. We first find the approach applied by political scientists interested in religion and politics. Some focus on country studies, others on the study of Islamist movements[54], which are viewed as an indication of dissent and an expression of political opposition. Some scholars operate on the assumption of an instrumental use of religion by Islamists for giving their movements a religious legitimacy. I disagree with this approach on the basis of my empirical survey completed among Islamists. It leads exactly to the opposite assumption: an Islamist is a political man of action, this is true, but he is also a 'true believer'. Jansen addresses this fact appropriately as 'the dual nature of Islamic fundamentalism'.[55]

There is also another approach, recently introduced to IR, which looks at civilisations in history.[56] These efforts are pursued without overlooking the fact that international actions and international behavior are related to states, not to civilisational entities. However, civilisations have their own distinct worldviews and provide substance for the understanding of order, war and peace, being pivotal for the study of international affairs. Along civilisational patterns not only local cultures (e.g. Indonesia and Senegal), but also states (e.g. OIC) can group to form entities in world politics. Therefore, the studies of world civilisations and of world politics can be linked to one another. Now, what approach proves more promising for studying the rise of jihadism and of its impact on international affairs in a changed world after the demise of bipolarity? Of course, this question does not overlook the focus of this inquiry, namely the politicisation of religion by Islamist movements being an issue of security. There are different levels of the analysis to which the study of political religion, understood as an element of potential conflict, can be related. It is of prime importance to deal with the significance of religion, ethnicity, culture, and other sources of conflict. Previously they were ignored by subsuming them beneath the East–West rivalry. Since the demise of bipolarity and of the bisected world of the Cold War, hitherto suppressed conflicts related to these factors are now on the rise. Islamist movements are among the new forces related to politicised religion. In fact, emerging religious fundamentalism and ethnicity cannot be properly understood without studying religion and its links to culture as well as to ethnic identity politics, and, of course, the mapping of civilisations.

In addition, neither Islamic fundamentalism nor its jihadism can be viewed as passing phenomena; it is wrong to reduce them to topicalities of current events. Doing so is based on a mistaken view.[57] Currently, all regional conflicts around the world are related either to fundamentalism or to ethnicity. In some cases, like in the Balkans, Chechnya, and Kashmir, we even find a mixture of both, merging to a kind of ethno-fundamentalism. In short, understanding the background of jihadism demands a comprehensive security analysis and requires a new approach that is open to drawing on the scholarly findings of a variety of disciplines. In this regard, religion, ethnicity, culture and civilisation are the issues that need to be studied in order to be understood.

Jihadism and Security: The Challenge of Irregular War

The narrow mind of traditional security studies no longer provides adequate perspectives for studying the new challenges. In view of the necessity for a new approach, there has been a few promising revisionist approaches, like the one presented by Barry Buzan,[58] but we are still at the beginning of the road. It was a step forward when Buzan carried security beyond the conventional military issues. However, September 11 was a case in point for supporting the idea that security studies still have to continue to deal with issues related to violence and force, but from a new perspective and no longer within the traditional boundaries and constraints of the organised military force of the state.

It was a serious challenge to security studies when asked to explain how on September 11 irregular jihad warriors as non-state actors declared war on Western civilisation. The declaration of jihad-war by the private actor bin Laden and his al-Qaeda questioned the basic assumptions of traditional security studies. There is a need to deal with jihad as an Islamic concept of a religion whose followers number one quarter of the world population (1.5 billion Muslims of 6 billion people worldwide). All Muslims together constitute a community, which Islam addresses as *umma*. In their name, al-Qaeda declared jihad as war on the West. Can political Islam succeed in the political mobilisation of the Islamic *umma* led by Islamist and jihadist groups? Well, we have learned how Islamists refer to religion in the pursuit of non-religious ends. It is true, these groups constitute only a minority in the Islamic *umma*, but they (e.g. al-Qaeda) are well organised and well equipped and therefore they cannot be ignored or belittled. Their number matters little, for such groups are very capable of destabilising and creating disorder through their means of irregular war. In what way is the new jihad an irregular war? And how can it be contained?

To be sure, jihadism in the shape of terrorism is no longer the classical jihad of Islam;[59] it is the outcome of the politicisation of Islam. It follows the earlier introduced need for a differentiation between Islam and Islamism. The latter includes jihadist fundamentalism, which creates a security concern. We should recall that Islam is a religion and that it builds up the framework for the respective civilisation,[60] which, however, manifests great cultural and religious diversity in itself. The differences between Sunnite and Shi'ite Muslims in addition to the ones between a variety of religious denominations and numerous sects are great. Islam is characterised by great cultural diversity. For example, African Islam is entirely different from the Islam of South-East Asia, or that of the Indian subcontinent. All of these varieties differ from the original Arab pattern. The addressed religious and cultural diversity is also reflected in Islamic fundamentalism throughout the world of Islam. There is, thus, a weakness in those security studies (e.g. Huntington's 'clash of civilisations') which claim the existence of a collective acting as a monolith called Islam. Given all of these distinctions, and in view of the fact that there are multiple political Islamist movements that seek to legitimise themselves through religion for toppling existing orders, how could the international approach of jihadist Islamism become a threat to security? How consistent is the internationalism of al-Qaeda?

To begin with, despite the existing great diversity, all Islamist groups adhere to similar concepts of political order as based on religion and shari'a -divine law, as well as to the new interpretation of jihad discussed earlier. Thus, the argument for including jihadism in security studies and for unfolding a new security approach is based on solid grounds. Some of those who refuse to include Islamism in security studies confuse Islam and Islamism. In our age of the 'cultural turn', it is clear that cultures and civilisations play an increasingly important role in international politics, but they cannot act, because they are not actors. Huntington aims to find a way out of this impasse in that each civilisation is seen to be led by a 'core state'. In the case of Islam, this construct does not work for the simple reason that none of the fifty-seven existing Islamic nation-states is in a position to lead the entire Islamic *umma* and its civilisation. In addition, even though there are many rough states among these Islamic entities, none of them causes the real problem of jihadism and its new irregular warfare. That was the greatest flaw in the planning of the Iraq war, which was based on a 'security threat' believed to be posed by Saddam Hussein.[61] This was wrong and the Iraq war has diverted the needed efforts to face the jihadist threat in the 'War on Terror'. The focus on the state in terms of security proved to be utterly wrong, because it overlooked the real issue. The threat is related to the jihadist movements, which are all non-state actors, not to Iraq. Therefore, the de-Saddamisation of Iraq did not affect these groups at all, let alone weakened them. In contrast, the Iraq war unwittingly strengthened the irregular war of jihadism.

The interpretation of jihadism as an Islamist 'revolt against the West' is a notion that refers to a civilisational conflict being an international conflict. This is the issue that makes abundantly clear to what extent the worldviews of civilisations play a vital role in world politics. In Iraq for instance, the US views the de-Saddamisation as liberation, while the Iraqis condemn the US presence as a military occupation of crusaders. These are different worldviews. In considering this fact and in continuing this line of reasoning, war is not simply understood as a military conflict between states. In my earlier book *The War of Civilizations*, I consider the conflict over different worldviews, which are a particular set of norms and values, in the analysis of security. After all, the idea of order is always based on civilisational values. In the analysis presented in that book, conflict is seen to revolve around the normatively different understanding of five issue areas: 1) the state, 2) law, 3) religion, 4) war/peace and 5) knowledge. Civilisations differ in these issue areas and therefore there are conflicting concepts of world order. One may argue, value-related conflicts have nothing to do with military capabilities, but they could nevertheless contribute to the emergence of real conflicts. At the beginning, the 'war of civilisations' could be looked at as a war of values and worldviews that directly creates conflict on all three levels: the domestic, the regional, and the international. On September 11, and in the ensuing assaults, this kind of war undeniably assumed a military shape. It follows that Jihadism contributes to the militarisation of conflicts between civilisations. This supports the idea that differences in worldviews, if they cannot be negotiated, could lead to an armed conflict. Now, the West is strong, but the irregular war of terrorism is the weapon of the weak, unable to be defeated by conventional military force. The irregular war of the Islamist Intifada is a convincing case in point. Israel won all Arab–Israeli inter-state wars within a short time, but it is incapable of winning this irregular war. This happened again in the Lebanon war against Hezbollah. The Israeli Defense Force (IDF) failed again.

In the light of the presented distinctions, the needed new security approach has to deal with the pending issue on two levels. First, the level of conflicts over values, which have political implications, but cannot be settled by military means. Second, the level of the irregular use of force by the fundamentalists believed to be pursued in the 'mind of God'. It is extremely important to distinguish between these two levels at this stage of the analysis for shedding light on the military dimension of the politicisation of religion. Nevertheless, the events of September 11, as well as the ensuing jihadist attacks, have revealed how interrelated these levels are. I have already maintained that the jihad-terrorists of al-Qaeda have militarised value conflicts concerning 'order' that exist between the Islamic and the Western civilisation. The assaults on New York and Washington were not an action by a 'crazed gang', but an act of irregular war through jihadism, which is a stream within Islamic fundamentalism. This resort to terrorism was an actualisation of the conflict related to civilisational worldviews. In short, the values related fight over 'what world order' assumes a military form. 'Gangs' do not involve themselves in this business of international affairs.

The irregular war at issue is an indication for the combination of the dissent over worldviews with incalculable and unpredictable use of force. In this interpretation, jihadism is the Islamic variety of contemporary terrorism being the current shape of the use of force by irregular warriors in a new pattern of war. To this pattern belongs the use of bodies by jihadists to assail persons and buildings of the 'enemy' in their *action directe*. The major target is political: it is the order of the secular nation-state. The enemy should be demoralised and made uncertain about what lies ahead. The rejection of the secular state applies to fundamentalists in all religions. It is, however, unique to Islamic fundamentalists to go beyond the level of the nation-state in embracing the universalism of Islam and to call, in the course of the politicisation of this universalism, for the establishing of an Islamic world order. On these grounds, a conflict emerges between two competing concepts of world order, the prevailing secular Western and the Islamic one of God's rule envisaged for the future. The jihadist terrorism of the Islamists is an irregular war for this end. John Kelsay, scholar of Islam, states, 'in encounters between the West and Islam, the struggle is over who will provide the primary definition of the world order'. He then asks who will lead the world in the future:

> Will it be the West, with its notions of territorial boundaries, market economies, private religiosity, and the priority of individual rights? Or will it be Islam, with its emphasis on the universal mission of a transtribal community called to build a social order founded on pure monotheism natural to humanity?[62]

For Islamic fundamentalists, Sayyid Qutb, the quoted spiritual father of their ideology, has already provided the answer to this question. In his *Signs along the Road*, he states that only Islam is designed to lead the entire humanity in the world of the future. It is clear that these questions and given answers indicate a competition between Western and Islamic concepts of world order. At issue are normatively different understandings of the notions of war and peace, as well as of law and justice. Again, this is the content of the values related to 'war of civilisations'. It follows that we are confronted not only with a new era for the study of security but also with new substance. At issue is a jihad against the West in a 'new Cold War' confrontation. Jihadism serves to escalate the conflict over worldviews through militarisation to an irregular war. Thus, the politicisation of religion is not simply a state of mind or a dispute over difference. If it were, one may prescribe 'tolerance'. Nevertheless, this prescription does not work when violence as terror is involved. What we have here is a great security problem. Long before the world was confronted with the case of September 11, there were the earlier cases of Kosovo, Macedonia, Chechnya, Kashmir and, of course, the al-Aqsa Intifada in the Middle East, in which jihadism is involved. The fight over Erez Israel versus Islamic Palestine is related to religion and to conflicting civilisational worldviews, in this exceptional case both are based on religion. Even the secular Arafat declared, on 26 January 2002, the Islamic jihad when Israeli tanks encircled his residence. One could see him on BBC-World shouting in a row five times: 'My answer is *jihad* ...'. This declaration of an irregular war is equally most appealing and most difficult to respond to with conventional means.

To be sure, the irregular war is not exclusively based on terrorist acts committed by Islamic fundamentalists. It is a general phenomenon, regardless of the substance of conflict and can be stated without referring to related cases. Not only in Kashmir, but also on the soil of India, Muslims and Hindus fight over their political beliefs in religious disguise. The known reports about the destruction of the Ayodhya Mosque in India through terrorist acts back in December 1992 were followed by terror of the jihadists. Similarly, the actions by the Jewish settlers in the occupied territories of Palestine (e.g. the Hebron massacre, February 1994) are revenged by Hamas and Jihad Islami. It does not help to belittle the threats of Islamic jihadists posed to international security in view of the terror of the others. When referring to these actions, my intention is merely to support the following three central observations related to the security-oriented study of jihadism:

First, there is the problem of political order. Islamic fundamentalism, as a powerful variety of the politicisation of religion does not only give expression to existing cultural differences. In this regard, the revived worldviews touch upon a concept of order with the implication of creating a gap between existing civilisations. Whereas religious fundamentalism is a global phenomenon that can be found in almost all world religions, all of them share, despite whatever variations a certain kind of family resemblance, which allows generalisation. However, Islamism is a very specific variety when it comes to the issue of international order. In terms of security, jihadists mobilise on religious grounds and they are in this pursuit most appealing and subsequently successful. Despite the need for military security measures to face their irregular war, we have to acknowledge that fundamentalists cannot only be fought with armies to undermine their appeal and their call for an Islamic order. For dealing with these issues, we need a security approach, which is neither fixated on the state nor on the predominance of conventional military thinking and its traditional wisdoms.

Second, there is holy terror and irregular war. Not all fundamentalists fight for their goals within the framework of institutions, thus with political means. Among them, we also find those who resort to violence in the form of terrorism to enforce their concept of order. Jihadism is a variety of 'terror in the mind of God', which combines fundamentalism and the related worldviews about order with terrorism (i.e. 'holy terror'[63]) with irregular war.

Third, there is the question of whether Islamism is different from Islamic fundamentalism. In this contribution, the terms political Islam, Islamism, and Islamic fundamentalism are used interchangeably. This is not common, because some dispute the application of the fundamentalism-concept to Islam with the intent to combat spreading prejudices. However, this is utterly misleading. It is true, the term 'fundamentalism' has been ill-handled as a cliché, but it is – despite all odds – a scholarly and analytical concept for studying the politicisation of religion. By using the term Islamism as an alternative to the one that refers to the global phenomenon of fundamentalism, the respective scholars are unwittingly contributing to the stereotyping of Islam by implicitly restricting the politicisation of religion to it. In contrast, I argue that 'Islamism' is only a depiction of a specific variety of the phenomenon of political religion addressed as a religious fundamentalism. This phenomenon does not only occur in Islam. However, jihadism as the military dimension of this phenomenon is specifically Islamic. It compels for including the inquiry into Islamism in the field of security studies. The new reasoning in this field has to be addressed as 'new frontiers of security'.[64] The new approach set out from a demand to go beyond the traditional concept of security dominated by military thinking in order to smooth the way for broadening the scope and deepening the insights to enable oneself to deal with the new pattern of irregular war.

The introduction of the concept of 'irregular war' for conceptualising and understanding the jihadism of the Islamists is based on the assumption that with the end of the East–West confrontation conventional Clausewitzian wars are less likely. Wars between states and between organised, institutionalised armies have almost disappeared thus wars waged by non-state actors as irregulars would prevail in the future.[65] Therefore, most of the issues must be thought through anew. Security experts have been arguing for a long time that this change has to be taken into consideration and have underscored the need for a new security approach. Scholars like Barry Buzan, and later Martin van Creveld and Kalevi Holsti, have ventured into a groundbreaking study of security and war going beyond the fixation with institutionalised armies. Both the changed character of wars and non-military aspects are to be emphasised more and more strongly and need to become central subjects of security studies. In this sense, and in this sense only, I argue that religious fundamentalism in Islam and its jihadism are to be dealt with in the framework of a new security approach. Jihadism is both a propaganda fight for a new order and an irregular war, which on September 11 and in following events has proved to be powerful. Organised armies are helpless against the terrorist acts of violent jihadists, in particular suicide bombers. Prior to these recent developments, earlier events in Algeria, Egypt, Israel, Afghanistan, as well as in Xinjiang, Kashmir, Kosovo, and Macedonia demonstrated this issue.

One can take it for granted that the West will not be able to cope with jihadism and the related challenges for security within the old state-centered approach. The North Atlantic Treaty Organization (NATO) was able to overpower the Serbian army with its regular armed forces in 1999. The same applies to the effort to oust Saddam Hussein in the Iraq war in March–April 2003. However, neither the religious-ethnic UÇK irregulars' acts of revenge against the Christian Serbs and Macedonians, nor the irregular war against the coalition troops in Iraq could be contained. Another example is the already mentioned inability of the Israeli Defense Force (IDF) to cope with the Intifada 'against the infidels'. This understanding is currently gaining topicality for the response to the irregular war of jihadism as practiced on September 11. This jihadist threat continues. The victory over the Taliban and over Saddam Hussein cannot be repeated against the jihadists in both countries.

In being confronted by jihadist Islamism we find ourselves exposed to parts of the Islamic diaspora in the West, hijacked by the Islamists, who claim to be its representatives as the 'true voice of Islam'. Jihadists of the diaspora abuse basic democratic rights and demonise their critics as the 'voice of Islamophobia', for camouflaging their activities to establish their logistic base in the West. Important components of Islamic jihadism exist for instance in Germany being a case in point.[66] With these facts in mind, the study of security must cover an inquiry into the networking between the region of conflict itself, in this case, the world of Islam, and its extension through global migration abroad for which the term 'gated diaspora',[67] i.e. Islam in the West, has been coined. The denunciation of references to the conflict between political Islam and the West as an indication of Islamophobia in an effort to obscure these issues is utterly misleading and detrimental, both for the integration of Muslims and for Western security itself. As an alternative to this in Europe, I have presented the concept of Euro-Islam[68] based on the Europeanisation of Islam being the alternative to the envisioned Islamisation of Europe.[69]

Conclusions

In my view, Islamic fundamentalism, in contrast to an open and enlightened Islam, is an ideology of a new totalitarianism.[70] Humanity needs a security approach against jihadism. The 'open society'[71] is the bedrock of human security. For me, security strategies are not merely means for preserving the status quo, but for defending freedom and democracy. How can we prevent the enemies of the 'open society' from abusing its freedom and from making democracy act against itself.[72] Fundamentalists have been successful in establishing themselves within the Islamic diaspora of Europe on the level of civil society applied to Islamic communitarism. My alternative is a European Islam.[73]

In concluding the analysis presented in this chapter, I restate that jihadism has grown from Islamic fundamentalism, which is itself the result of the politicisation of Islam. Jihadism is a pattern of irregular war. In instrumentalising democratic freedoms, but also in abusing the weakness of the awareness of European values, the exponents of jihadist Islamism succeeded in finding safe heaven in Europe. Fundamentalists, who are against the political integration of Muslim migrants as citizens, were able to hijack parts of the Islamic diaspora. Integrated Muslims would be true European citizens, whereas Muslims at the fringe of society can be mobilised as ethnic-religious minorities for the political ends of fundamentalism. In order to curb the security threat of jihadist

Islamism, we need a new approach for dealing with the addressed triangle: the world of Islam, the West and the Islamic diaspora in Europe. Jihad terrorism as irregular war is to be located in this triangle. The war against jihad terrorism should neither be restricted to military means nor to the legal understanding that it cannot be declared, because one cannot declare war on a non-state actor. The instruments needed for stopping Islamic fundamentalism in the world of Islam and in Europe are multifaceted. In this contribution, I have been at pains to analyze and to shed light on the challenge of jihadist Islamic fundamentalism to Western, Islamic and international security. Political Islam is primarily a challenge to Muslims themselves in their dealing with the predicament of modernity.

The solution for Europe lies in Europeanising Islam for countering the efforts at an Islamisation of Europe. In the world of Islam itself, the option is either to accept the subjection to the new totalitarianism or to smooth the way through reforms embracing secular democracy[74] within an open liberal Islam. This would open the way for Muslims to join the rest of the world within the framework of democratic peace. Democracy in Islam would help Muslims to come to terms with the rest of the world and to give up the illusion of Islamisation. The jihadist-terrorist internationalism of political Islam is not a contribution to world peace. Terrorism[75] alienates Muslims from the rest of humanity; therefore, Muslim politicians are best advised to join the countering of terrorism and to dissociate themselves in concrete politics, not in a simple lip-service from global jihad.

5

NEW AND OLD XENOPHOBIA
THE CRISIS OF LIBERAL MULTICULTURALISM
Bryan S. Turner

Introduction : The Stranger

This discussion of xenophobia can be put into an appropriate social context in terms of a quotation from the black sociologist Paul Gilroy:

> New hatreds and violence arise not, as they did in the past, from supposedly reliable anthropological knowledge of the identity of the Other, but from the novel problem of not being able to locate the Other's difference in the commonsense lexicon of alterity. Different people are certainly hated and feared, but the timely antipathy against them is nothing compared to the hatreds turned towards the greater menace of the half-different and the partially familiar.[1]

We live in an environment where the traditional norms of hospitality towards strangers are breaking down, and in which the social character of outsiders is changing. These changes are part of the growing liberal sense of a crisis in multiculturalism. Although this problem is essentially political, it has an important ethical underpinning. Jacques Derrida has in written eloquently and convincingly about the rights of the stranger, arguing that ethics is in fact hospitality.[2] If we cannot treat guests with hospitality, they will become aliens. If they are aliens, we have no particular responsibility towards them, because they are not fully rights-bearing individuals. If we have no social responsibility for them, they remain outsiders. Our relationship is one of estrangement.

Derrida's account of hospitality is highly dependent on the work of Emile Benveniste who demonstrated the ambiguous and contradictory nature of a cluster of concepts: host, guest, and stranger.[3] In Latin a guest is called *hostis* and *hospes*. Whereas *hospes* is the etymological root of 'hospitality' and 'hospital', *hostis* is an 'enemy'. Benveniste argued that both 'guest' and 'enemy' derive from 'stranger', and the notion of 'favourable stranger' evolved eventually into 'guest', but 'hostile stranger' became the enemy.[4] More precisely, the idea of a stranger in Latin is closely related to debates about rights and membership of the household. Whereas *peregrinus* was a category of person living or peregrinating outside the boundaries of a political territory, *hostis* was a stranger in the midst of the city who was recognised nevertheless as enjoying equal rights with Roman citizens. In Latin, *hostis* is always bound into a set of exchanges or gifts that create mutual obligations through reciprocity, but the problem is that gifts can also be competitive and aggressive, indeed poisonous. They compel as well as oblige, but the point of this argument is that *hostis* unlike *peregrinus* is a near, not distant relationship. In the ancient world, a stranger is a person who lives in the neighbourhood, and who can be bound to us by shared ritual activity.

The same type of argument is presented by Benveniste in his analysis of the Greek *xenos* (stranger) from which we derive 'xenophobia'.[5] The term *xenos* indicated a kind of pact involving definite obligations, which can be inherited by subsequent generations. These *xenia* or social contracts came under the protection of Zeus Xenios, and consisted of an exchange of gifts between the contracting parties, who also bound their descendants to the agreement. In ancient Greece, both kings and commoners could be bound by these pacts with (friendly) strangers. However, with the growth of the state and the decline of the ancient world, these ritualised relationships between men – I use the gendered noun deliberately – and between clans were replaced by a classification of what is inside and what is outside the *civitas*. In the terminology of modern political philosophy, these ritualised relationships were replaced by secular citizenship, which is a system of contributory rights, namely rights and duties, that bind people to the nation state, and taxation replaces a system of gift-enforced relationships. Citizenship builds nations on the basis of mutually agreed rights and duties.

In European languages, we do not, as far as I am aware, possess a word parallel to xenophobia, namely 'xenophilia'. Benveniste's study embraced a range of languages (Latin, Greek, Germanic, Indo-Iranian and Hittite), but in these languages there is no trace of 'xenophilia'. This absence is telling. It appears that there is little linguistic possibility for the love of strangers; there is simply no social role for a stranger who is an object of genuine friendship. We have 'xenogamy' or 'cross-fertilisation' in the natural world, but no love of strangers in the social world. We might conclude therefore that xenophobia is the normal state of affairs in the competitive relationship between social groups.

Benveniste's analysis is perhaps less pessimistic than this conclusion suggests. His research shows the presence of respect for the friendly stranger who lives in our midst and shares our rights. But the pessimistic sociological and political conclusion may be more compelling. From classical sociology, we can derive the case for a more generic form of xenophobia from arguments that are implicit in Emile Durkheim's *The Elementary Forms of the Religious Life*.[6] Durkheim's theory of religion concentrates on how social groups classify objects, and he famously proposed that religion involves a classification of the world into the sacred and the profane. We might argue that in Durkheim's terms the contrast between the stranger and the host society is fundamental to all social groups. No society can exist, from this Durkheimian perspective, without a concept of an Other. Since 'hostile' is also derived from *hostis*, there are again classificatory reasons for defining the outside world as estranged. The sense of an inside community requires a xenophobic classificatory scheme that regards outsiders as at least potentially dangerous. Now modern political philosophy has been profoundly influenced by the work of Carl Schmitt who defined 'the political' as the struggle between friend and foe, in which the state is, following Max Weber, that institution which can exercise sovereign power over this relationship.[7] A sovereign is some person who can declare a state of emergency, exercise political will, and give a clear definition to the enemy.

On the basis of this argument, I propose a distinction between 'old xenophobia' and 'new xenophobia'. The former refers to a set of social circumstances that existed in what Benveniste called 'ancient society', that is before the rise of the modern state.[8] In old xenophobia, the stranger/enemy is a clearly recognised person or social group, who lives proximately, that is in our midst, or adjacent to our community. The traditional stranger is a palpable and recognised figure, with whom we can exchange gifts. He can be welcomed to the fireplace, the foundation of the classical city, and he can recognise with us the authority of the fireside gods. In particular, the stranger is somebody whom we can marry, or with whom we might exchange women. The relationships with this stranger are regulated by ritual customs and practices. The exchange of gifts is typically institutionalised by strictly defined activities of gift giving. This reciprocal relationship is always ambiguous – a mixture of co-operative and threatening behaviour, that is only partially regulated by rituals. It can always break down into a hostile relationship, or periodically into war. However, warfare in ancient society was typically ritualised behaviour, not leading necessarily to extermination of the enemy. The stranger might be converted into a domestic slave as a result of warfare, or after a series of skirmishes more peaceful relations could be re-established.[9] Ethnic cleansing was not common in ancient societies, because as Zygmunt Baumann makes clear such forms of extermination require considerable planning and co-ordination, namely the involvement of state and its administration.[10] Holocaust is a modern strategy to eliminate a whole population, and not a military strategy of warring bands.

Benveniste now compares these ancient relationships with *xenia* under modern circumstances, namely where citizens establish legal relationships with strangers by creating criteria of membership through various forms of naturalisation.[11] With the growth of states, there emerges a complex web of classificatory niches including stateless person, refugee, asylum-seeker, and migrant. Some states also recognise dual citizenship, or classificatory schemes that in effect create 'quasi-citizens'. The logic of this political development is described by Saskia Sassen, where she argues that the rise of the modern state closed down the traditional migratory routes of informal workers who moved around Europe on a seasonal basis in search of casual employment.[12] These migrations typically followed for example the migration of herring around northern Europe or corresponded with harvest time. Modern states by creating passports and strict membership based on citizenship converted such seasonal workers (or guests) into aliens who require passports or work permits to enter a national territory. While the transition from the ancient world to the nation state created major changes in identity, there were continuities with the old world. Modern citizenship also implicitly involves a system of exchange, or what I shall called 'contributory rights'. The citizen is somebody, who, through a series of contributions that are associated with work, public service (such as war) or parenting, enjoys a set of corresponding entitlements (to vote or to receive welfare benefits or social security). Strangers can become part of this network of rights and duties, if they also begin to participate in the host society.

However, these relationships between host and stranger, or between citizen and guest-worker have been transformed by globalisation, and a new type of xenophobia is emerging. With globalisation, and especially the globalisation of labour markets, modern societies have all become in some sense multicultural societies. Nathan Glazer comments ironically on this state of affairs in the title of his book *We Are All Multiculturalists Now*.[13] With the global development of diasporic communities, the stranger is both proximate and distant, because he is involved in a global network of communities extending around the world. Migrant labour is typically connected to economically marginal societies or communities, and their remittances are often necessary to support distant relatives. Where migrant labour does not become integrated into the host community through marriage, work or citizenship, they can remain isolated from the mainstream. Indeed with some forms of multiculturalism, cultural differences become institutionalised and produce fragmented, isolated, and underprivileged social groups. Their children become part of a diversified, marginalised, urban underclass.

These migrant communities have been increasingly augmented by a flow of stateless people, refugees, asylum seekers, boat people, victims of failed states and civil wars. The growth of global cities has also therefore been accompanied by a global underclass of illegal or semi-legal migrants and refugees who work in the informal economy, and come to constitute a disprivileged 'weight of the world'.[14] The stranger becomes an anonymous and placeless person without citizenship or rights, and a member of an underclass that is seen by the state to be the recruiting ground for criminals and terrorists. The stranger is somebody who is recruited to service in prisons, detention camps, inter-state zones, departure areas, and a variety of other intermediate, quasi-legal zones.

The stranger has become increasingly an international rather than merely a national problem. According to the UNHCR, the number of refugees who cross international borders has risen from 2.4 million in 1975 to 10.5 million in 1985 and to 14.4 million in 1995, but if we include internally displaced persons, then the total refugee figure is more like 38 million people.[15] The number of displaced persons per conflict has risen from 40 000 per conflict in 1969 to 857 000 per conflict in 1992.[16] The stranger who is the target of new xenophobia is a displaced person, typically a woman and her children, who are seen to be a burden on the local economy, and indeed they may ultimately contribute to the collapse of local economies. They do not bear gifts, only burdens.

During the Cold War, western states supported human rights (at least as an ideology compatible with western notions of individualism). The contemporary 'War on Terror' has, since 9/11 and 7/7, turned the state against migration and hardened attitudes towards political refugees and stateless peoples, and globally states now emphasise their responsibility for securing the safety of their 'own' citizens. States place a priority on the provision of security, not the defence of civil liberties. While sociologists have talked much about globalisation and the erosion of the state, the modern security crisis has seen 'the return of the state'.[17] The attack on the Twin Towers produced the Patriot Act in the US and the

Terrorism Act in the UK. This legislation has, for civil liberty campaigners, dangerously infringed individual liberties and increased the power of the state to arrest and deport suspected terrorists and criminals. However, the bombings in London were not seen to be performed by outsiders, but by local citizens. The aftermath of 7/7 is in a sense more significant than 9/11, because the bombings and attempted bombings in London were undertaken by the children of migrants and asylum seekers, who were British citizens. In the new xenophobia, the 'friendly stranger' is now 'the hostile stranger', and every citizen has become a potential enemy within. The essential condition for new xenophobia is a political situation in which the majority feels that it is under attack, and that its way of life is threatened by social groups whom it does not understand, cannot identify, and consequently does not recognise. The old rituals of hospitality towards the stranger who warms himself by the fireside have collapsed in the rubble of the Twin Towers.

In summary, the new xenophobia involves a fear of strangers who are both in our midst but also connected to distant places in a global network of migratory channels and diasporic communities. It is fuelled by notions of incivility in global cities, and by the presence of minority groups who are connected with the informal economy, and hence with petty crime. The new xenophobia is associated with the erosion of social capital and by the decline of trust. Where there is low trust, there is a growing sense of the offensive nature of juvenile crime and vandalism, and this incivility is increasingly associated with migrant communities and their dislodged young men. As Abdelmalek Sayad observes, migration has produced a new 'state thought' in which the criminality of the migrant has become ontological, 'because, at the deepest level of our mode of thought (i.e. state thought) it is synonymous with the very existence of the immigrant and with the very fact of immigration'.[18] The stranger has become a free-floating, dangerous 'guest', who emerges periodically to commit irrational crimes, or monstrous and inhumane acts of terror. Whereas the old xenophobia was regulated by gift giving, co-operation and ritual, the new xenophobia confronts the violent stranger, whose behaviour (random violence against civilian targets) appears to have no logic. The modern stranger is has become *peregrinus*, that is somebody whose peregrination is global, without anchor, and hence without connections. The somewhat arcane noun 'peregrinity' means something which is foreign and outlandish.

State, Sovereignty and Strangers

With the ageing populations and low birth rates in the industrial world, there is an economic interest in and demand for porous borders between societies. Capitalism needs geographically flexible labour, and preferably cheap labour. Labour costs are problematic in the advanced economies because welfare benefits, accident legislation, and retirement benefits have dramatically increased unit costs by contrast with many labour markets in Asia. There is a pension crisis in North America and Europe, in which we have seen companies in the US reneging on pension entitlements, and in the UK there has been a move away from final-salary benefits by corporations.[19] Migrant labour, especially illegal migrant labour, tends to be cheap and is characteristically not protected by unions and state benefits. However, this economic interest in cheap migrant labour is contradicted by state's the need to preserve political sovereignty and the coherence of its cultural foundations. The state has an interest in creating a unified polity – that is in the language of Benedict Anderson an 'imagined community'.[20] More importantly, the state can be said to exist, from a sociological point of view, when a moral order is imposed on a community (however socially diverse).[21] This necessity is in part the related to German political and legal notions of *Ordnung* and *Ortung*, of sovereignty, rulership and territory. A state is that institution which can command moral authority over a territory in order to bring about *Ordnung* The distinction between religion and politics, between sacred and sovereign, is the question of the territorialisation of power. This question of space is nicely illustrated by the distinction between *Ordnung* and *Ortung*. The argument is beautifully presented by Giorgio Agamben when he states that 'What is at issue in the sovereign exception is not so much the control and neutralisation of an excess as the creation and definition of the very space in which the juridico-political order can have validity'.[22] In this sense, the sovereign exception is the fundamental localisation (*Ortung*) which does not limit itself to distinguishing what is inside from what is outside but instead traces a threshold (the state of exception) between the two, on the basis of which outside and inside, the normal situation and chaos, enter into those complex topological relations that make the validity of the juridical order possible.

One essential point is that the modern state has a contradictory relationship to multiculturalism and migration, on the one hand, and to order and sovereignty, on the other. In a capitalist society, the state wants to encourage labour migration, porous boundaries and minimal limitations on labour fluidity and flexibility. The state is under pressure from economic elites to reduce the resistance of labour to the logic of capital accumulation, and one solution to this problem is to import labour. But the state also has an interest in its own sovereignty, and hence wants to impose a cultural and moral unity on society. Its economic interests produce cultural diversity through labour migration, but its need to protect its sovereignty commits it to preserving a moral unity, to the reduction, of cultural complexity and to the assimilation of the migrant. As Michel Foucault has argued, the modern state is an administrative order that seeks to maximise the social potential of its population (and hence it has an interest in supporting migration), but it also has an interest in the enforcement of a particular type of governmentality.[23]

As a consequence of this contradiction, we can expect state policies towards citizenship and migration to vacillate between treating migration and multiculturalism as aspects of economic policy, and treating multiculturalism within a framework of asserting national sovereignty. Given the current climate of global conflict and uncertainty, modern states are giving priority to security over welfare, and to public order over civil liberties. In part this situation explains the new emphasis on civic integration over multicultural difference. The modern state is increasingly Schmittian in its cultural and political strategies.

Australian multiculturalism is often held up as a successful model by comparison with the social democratic societies of Scandinavia, the laissez-faire liberalism of the UK and the laicite policy of France. Nevertheless, Australian policies towards citizenship and migration appear to have this unstable characteristic in that they fluctuate between an emphasis on multiculturalism as economically beneficial, multiculturalism as part of national identity, and multiculturalism as a strategy of integrating ethnic minorities into a dominant culture that is Anglo-Saxon and white. The Galbally Report in 1978 argued that multiculturalism was beneficial to all Australians, and the nation-building function of multicultural policies was further re-inforced by the document of *Multiculturalism for all Australians* in 1982 defined the past as multicultural. These official documents equate national with multicultural, but as Christian Joppke has argued this equation has two problems.[24] It suppresses Australia's British heritage, and it became impossible to see what exactly was 'Australian' about multiculturalism. The notion that all Australians were 'ethnic' came under further modification in the Fitzgerald Report (1988) which recognised the economic importance of immigration, and tried to separate migration from the national identity of Australia. In a further document, the

National Agenda for a Multicultural Australia (1989) the importance of the British heritage in defining Australian identity was re-asserted and the limit of multiculturalism is that there is an obligation to an 'overriding and unifying commitment to Australia'.[25] The notion of multiculturalism as a national identity has been continuously down-played, while the utilitarian importance of immigration has been stressed, provided migrants have an 'overriding and unifying commitment' to the Australian state.

The government of John Howard has moved even further away from the policies of multiculturalism of the 1980s, and has asserted the idea of a unified Australia. This strategy has of course been intensified by Australia's involvement in the Iraq war and the Bali bombings. There is very strong evidence that western governments are moving away from the multicultural policies of the 1980s towards 'civic integration'. The criticism of multiculturalism from liberals has been that multiculturalism, far from preserving cultural difference in liberal democracies, has isolated and excluded ethnic minorities by institutionalising their difference and separation).[26] Multiculturalism is further criticised because, in concentrating on cultural identity, it has neglected the fundamental problem of the economic and political marginalisation and exploitation of migrants. Finally there is the criticism of so-called recognition ethics that recognition has to be mutual and reciprocal. In empirical terms, sociological research in the Netherlands and the UK has recently painted a picture of isolated, underprivileged, minority communities, who are totally disconnected from mainstream society. Recognition of differences and their positive celebration has not occurred. Judith Shklar developed the notion of 'the liberalism of fear' to describe the anxieties of American democracy which emerged in the context of slavery.[27] Modern critics of multiculturalism have borrowed her phrase to argue that there is a 'multiculturalism of fear'.[28]

These failures in multicultural policies are aggravated by the current 'War on Terror', and civilian panic about terrorist attacks. This crisis has meant that the benefits of multiculturalism are being denied and cosmopolitan virtues are under attack.[29] There has been a definite assertion of state sovereignty, which leads one to question the exaggerated claims made about the erosion of the state in the face of globalisation. Contrary to the claim that states are declining as a result of globalisation, nation state sovereignty is being forcefully and continuously asserted against globalisation.

The New Incivility: New Wars and Failed States

This instability in state strategies has been recently transformed by terrorism and the global problem of incivility. This global incivility can be related to the development of new wars. Because we live in a global world, new wars have a direct and immediate effect on stable societies and democratic governments. New wars are as much our problem as their problem.

In the recent sociology of the military, there has been an important debate about the distinction between old and new wars, providing a valuable insight into micro religious conflicts, ethnic-cleansing and genocide. In particular, the concept of new wars is helpful in thinking about the increased vulnerability of women and children in civil conflicts. This debate owes a great deal to the intellectual power of Mary Kaldor's *New & Old Wars*.[30] Old wars are said to be characteristic of the international system that was created by the Treaty of Westphalia, involving military conflict between armies that were recruited and trained by nation states. In the conventional inter-states wars of the past that involved large set battles and military manoeuvres, sexual violence against women on enemy territory was dysfunctional in terms of strategic, rational, military objectives, because it interfered with the primary objective of war, which was the decisive defeat of an opposing army by direct military engagement. Harassing civilian populations constrained military mobility on the battle field and delayed engagement with an opposing army. With these conventional inter-state wars, the development of international law to protect civilians was perfectly compatible with these military objectives.

The dominant theory of such wars was produced by Karl von Clausewitz.[31] Clausewitz's analysis of war as a contest between nation states involving a conflict between armies. This theory continues to shape modern assumptions about the nature of military violence. War in the twentieth century continued to be based on the notion of strategic military platforms – tanks, battleships and fighter planes – but there has been a so-called 'revolutionary in military affairs' (RMA) in which it is argued that the strategic advantage of the US must lie in information technology, surveillance and smart weapons.[32] Kaldor's argument is that both Clausewitz and RMA are irrelevant to modern warfare, and that military thinking has increased civilian casualties and has done nothing to contain civil conflict. The futility of western foreign intervention in Iraq and Afghanistan, or of Russia in Chechnya, or of Thai military intervention in its southern region has only contributed to growing international instability.[33] These crises have a 'knock-on' effect in societies as far a field as Denmark and Australia, and hence the analysis of new wars and failed states is directly relevant to Australian domestic policy, let alone it foreign policy.

In new wars, this military logic evaporates. Wars are now about destroying civil society and killing citizens. For example systematic rape of women (so-called 'camp rape'), and violence towards civilians generally, become functional activities in undermining civil authorities and undermining civil institutions. In wars between states, the majority of casualties are military personnel; in new wars, the casualties are almost entirely civilian. New wars involve the eroticisation of violence through the impact of Hollywood films depicting the 'glamour' of war and masculinity.[34] The other characteristic of such wars is the growing use of children as cheap combat troops. These wars are in part the product of failed states and the reduced cost of military equipment, such as the widespread use of personnel mines and the Kalashnikov rifle. The 'miniturisation' of modern weaponry has greatly contributed to their effectiveness and devastating power against civilians. New wars have occurred in Afghanistan, Bosnia, Chechnya, Kosovo, Darfur, Rwanda, Burma, East Timor and the Sudan. Recent conflicts in Bangladesh and the southern provinces of Thailand are troublesome, and it is evident that neither government has an effective strategy to contain these civil crises.

New wars produce growing social incivility and they are responsible for the increase in homeless and stateless peoples. Refugee camps and other intermediary zones of transition create conditions within which terrorism and criminality can flourish. They create a global network of drug trafficking, slavery and illegal arms sales. Given modern interconnectivity, new wars have the consequence of generally destabilising civil society. Insofar as new wars contribute to failed states, they have an important impact on human rights abuse. They fuel the spread of new xenophobia, and they make multicultural values and cosmopolitan virtue difficult to nurture and sustain. This leads Mary Kaldor to argue that we are faced by a stark choice between cosmopolitanism and nihilism, between defending humane values and an ethic of multiculturalism and fascism.[35]

Types of Multiculturalism

It is necessary to distinguish between multiculturalism as a social policy, as a moral argument about diversity and as the empirical description of a state of affairs in which a population is heterogeneous. The argument against multiculturalism as an empirical state of affairs is problematic, because as a matter of fact the majority of nation states are multicultural. To criticise this state of affairs can only lead to one rather extreme policy, which is repatriation.

Multiculturalism means the existence within the same society of a diversity of different cultures and communities, but the principal debate about multiculturalism is in reality about the cultural diversity that is produced by migrant communities. While liberal philosophers and western states appear to be withdrawing from multiculturalism as a policy, it does not follow from this withdrawal that diversity has ceased to be a value. It is simply that multicultural strategies may have failed to produce justice and equality, but the opposite of multiculturalism cannot be in practical terms involuntary repatriation. Such a regressive policy would, apart from anything else, confuse the legal migrant with the illegal migrant. But in order to have a discussion about multiculturalism, we need to consider its heterogeneity and complexity. Theories of multiculturalism in attempting to make a distinction between its social and the cultural dimensions have identified four types, namely cosmopolitanism, fragmented pluralism, interactive pluralism and assimilation.[36] This theory suggests that multiculturalism can involve a variety of combinations of association and cohesion, including a situation where social groups retain their internal solidarity, but the society as a whole is fragmented. In this model, social groups can be in a conflictual and competitive relationship with each other. Cosmopolitanism involves a normative vision of diversity in which individual civil liberties are preserved. Assimilation in this sense is not strictly multiculturalism since it is based on the assumption that difference is harmful and should be abandoned in the process of integration into the host society. Finally, interactive multiculturalism praises difference, recognises group rights, and accepts principles of recognition and reciprocity.

In historical terms, the modern concept of multiculturalism had its origins in North America in the 1970s and 1980s. In the Canadian political context, it was used by Pierre Trudeau to counter the political agenda of separation and cultural autonomy by the *Parti Quebecois*. In this respect, there are important similarities between Canada and Australia. They are both Commonwealth, federal, parliamentary systems, and they are both classical examples of white-settler societies. In Australia, multiculturalism replaced the white-Australia policy, and enabled Australian governments to welcome new migrants from Italy, Greece and Eastern Europe to provide labour for post-war expansion. Australian multiculturalism was nevertheless premised on the existing constitutional ties to the UK and the dominance of the English language as the medium of public communication. In the context of racial tensions in the US, the term came to mean anti-racism. It was developed as a policy to integrate white European post-war migrants into the American melting pot. The importance of multiculturalism is that it has been developed as a positive response to diversity, and hence to be against multiculturalism is to be against culture itself. Paradoxically as the cultures of advanced capitalism have become increasingly McDonaldised, there has been a policy emphasising the value of cultural diversity.

In European societies, multiculturalism was a late development in response to migration from Asia and North Africa. Whereas in the US, multiculturalism has been specifically and originally directed at the political integration of the black community, in Europe multiculturalism in effect means religious diversity. It is for this reason that many of the recent conflicts around multiculturalism have assumed a religious component, notoriously the head scarf debate in France, and more recently the debate over press freedom and responsibility to other cultures in the cartoon crisis. In this European illustration, multiculturalism is directed at outsiders – or at least to communities that are politically marginal.

One criticism of multiculturalism is that the emphasis on difference and identity politics has submerged the importance of economic equality. So-called 'critical multiculturalism' requires both mutual recognition and redistribution of national resources to create equality of objective conditions of existence between host and migration societies.[37] The economic conditions for multiculturalism include rapid and sustained economic growth, a safety-net welfare state and some redistribution of wealth through a progressive tax system. Perhaps the hall mark of citizenship is in fact a shared taxation system and low-levels of tax avoidance. These economic conditions will never in themselves be sufficient. The multicultural record of societies such as Denmark and Sweden is not particularly encouraging.[38]

Conditions for Multiculturalism

What are the conditions of successful multiculturalism? Any comparative examination of multiculturalism in North America, Europe and Asia suggests that Australia and Canada have been relatively successful multicultural societies – with one very serious proviso. These 'white settler societies' have failed miserably to come to terms with their indigenous native communities, but we cannot treat aboriginality as an aspect of the debate about multiculturalism. The history and status of Australian aboriginals is for example quite different from the status of Italian Australians.

The US is clearly diverse and culturally differentiated but its critics argue that multiculturalism 'is the price America is paying for its inability or unwillingness to incorporate into its society African Americans'.[39] British multiculturalism has failed badly, because there is relatively little interaction between the dominant and minority cultures. According to the Cantle Report,

> Separate educational arrangements, community and voluntary bodies, employment, places of worship, language, social and cultural networks, mean that many communities operate on the basis of a series of parallel lives. These lives often do not touch at any point, let alone overlap and promote any meaningful exchanges'.[40]

Britain is in this sense not a multicultural society but a 'plural society', because individuals or groups may interact in the market for the sake of an exchange of goods and services, but they have no social or cultural exchange.[41] The alienation of Muslim communities in contemporary Britain is an outcome in part of this social disconnectedness, on the one hand, and the negative consequences of 9/11, the Iraq war and 7/7.[42] The UK's policy of 'benign neglect' has produced conditions that promote youth alienation from the mainstream society.

The main plank of successful multiculturalism must be the creation of overlapping social and cultural ties to create social bonds and social capital between groups. One of the critical issues in cultural recognition is the question of gender, and this issue is reflected in and measured by rates of inter-faith marriage. Generally speaking, there is no solution to this problem since most religious groups encourage or prescribe intra-faith marriages. Issues surrounding gender equality, inter-communal marriage, female education, the veil, seclusion, cliterectomy and circumcision remain the most divisive aspects of the debate about multiculturalism. This conflict which is not just about Islam, but about all faith-based communities, is actually getting worse rather than better as religion becomes increasingly the basis of modern identity and the mechanism for political mobilisation. The notion that individuals can opt out of their own communities is perhaps the most problematic. In the case of minorities, the survival of their cultures and traditions requires continuity of socialisation and transmission – a process that has historically depended on women. Hence, women are typically subject to excessive (and at times brutal) subordination to group norms. But this fact offers no normative reason for supporting gender inequalities.

To some extent state educational systems that in principle provide children with intercultural experiences, a positive view of multiculturalism and encourage cosmopolitanism can only be partially successful when the home experience is monocultural and outside the mainstream of multiculturalism. In any case, private schools that are funded outside the state system would appear to enforce not undermine multiculturalism. In the UK, the state has diverted public funds to support Muslim schools, and we can argue that this is an example of institutionalised separatism. One cannot blame these private schools, since the publicly funded schools have hardly done better. In the case of Tower Hamlets in London, seventeen primary state schools had more than ninety percent Bangladeshi pupils, while another nine schools had only ten percent. Among the fifteen secondary schools, two schools had over ninety-five percent of the students from the Bangladeshi community.

In the UK, racial conflict is not simply between host and migrant community, but in the depressed inner city areas there is also considerable urban conflict. In October 2005, there was a rumour in Lozells district of the city of Birmingham that, following a shop-lifting incident, young black girl was allegedly raped by a gang of fifteen Pakistani men. There was no evidence to support this rumour but in the following riots, two people were killed, a policeman was shot, and thirty-five people were hospitalised. These riots were taken to be evidence of the failure of the community-cohesion strategies that had been promoted by the Cantle Report of 2001 in response to the Oldham, Bradford and Burnley riots.

The cultural argument for multiculturalism is that the national community can only be bound together by shared values. We might call these shared values an ideology, but clearly nationalism has been powerful in the US and, I would argue in Australia, as a means of binding diverse groups together.

In the absence of a compensating nationalist ideology, shared schooling and a common language, societies have to rely increasingly on political and juridical solutions. There must be governmental policies that promote tolerance and understanding, namely a set of government measures that are seen to support 'cosmopolitan virtue'. There should also be provision of relatively modest criteria of naturalisation and access to full citizenship. In this respect, Australia has been far more generous and open than either the UK or Germany. The rate of naturalisation therefore can be used as an objective measure of multicultural openness.[43] The critical bedrock of multiculturalism must however be the rule of law, and procedural guarantees of judicial fairness. It is unlikely that multicultural societies can achieve agreement about substantive issues of law and justice, but at least they may agree about juridical transparency and procedural norms.

In short, successful multiculturalism is based on the notion that migrants can achieve social mobility (at least in the second generation), that their culture receives some public endorsement from government, that there is a national ideology of inclusion, and that the rule of law guarantees some degree of legal security.

The conditions that undermine multiculturalism are numerous, but they include as a minimum situations where a government is seen to take sides in ethnic conflict, and appears to promote the interests of one group over another. Communal hostilities are then fuelled because the rule of law is overtly flaunted. Ethnic conflict creates conditions for the development of civil strife and civil strife can lead ultimately to 'news wars'.[44] Civil distrust is sustained by the lack of intermarriage, and the prohibition on intermarriage is typically sustained by fundamentalist religions. Finally there are important economic circumstances that contribute to conflict especially high levels of unemployment, low wages and exploitative working conditions. These circumstances make it difficult for young people to benefit from secular citizenship, and these circumstances in turn make militant or militaristic alternatives look attractive. These forms of social and cultural alienation are the breeding ground for social conflict, civil disorder and terrorism.

Rule of Law and Legal Pluralism

There are important connections between citizenship and social capital. Much of the discussion of social capital has assumed that trust will emerge informally from the everyday network of social relationships that are associated with church attendance, club membership or participation in neighbourhood groups. Under privileged neighbourhoods are urban areas in which the informal wellsprings of trust have run dry. This analysis of trust is parallel to conventional views about how money functions. Money can only function where there is confidence (or informal trust) in money. However, any growth of monetary relations across time and space requires some degree of public legitimacy and impersonal trust, and these conditions have historically been provided by nation states. In a large and complex social environment, informal trust requires the backing of the rule of law and state institutions. The disorderly character of societies with globalisation and the rise of transnational, diasporic communities whose relationship to the host state will remain problematic and uncertain, requires a legal framework that is fair and transparent. In summary the legal conditions for a critical theory of recognition that goes beyond poly-ethnic rights would involve:

1. recognition of the validity of different legal systems;
2. acceptance of claims of minorities to exercise their own jurisdictions;
3. mutual recognition that laws are socially produced and subject to dispute and hence to evolution;
4. acceptance of legal norms that function across communities – essentially the acceptance of the rule of law which I have interpreted as meaning acceptance of rules of debate and evaluation;
5. recognition of rights of appeal against sentences;
6. acceptance of some process whereby members can leave their own communities.

What are the implications of these norms? We might distinguish between weak multiculturalism and the strong programme of multicultural diversity. Kymlicka suggests that legal pluralism is an inevitable consequence of the strong doctrine of multiculturalism and it suggests further that Kymlicka's group-differentiated rights are at present underdeveloped by not recognising the importance of legal self-determination or 'poly-juridicality'.[45] Legal pluralism would thus stretch the assumptions of liberalism to its limits. These juridical limits are probably defined by the issue of gender equality. Can liberals recognise cultural difference, if it entails gender inequality? The fight of Muslim women to reform customs relating to gender equality is the obvious illustration. This question in fact brings out the difference between a universalistic politics that recognises the equal dignity of all individuals, and a politics of difference that insists that everyone is to be recognised for his or her unique dignity.[46]

The problem of legal pluralism may not be a particularly new problem. Before the development of the so-called 'law of nations' by Suarez and Grotius in the seventeenth century, Natural Law had been recognised as a universal juridical and ethical system that applied equally to international and intra-national relations. The growth of nationalism and nation states after the Treaty of Westphalia meant that Natural Law was applied indirectly through the various civil laws, conventions, customs, and contingent circumstances of the diverse nations that made up the international system. Weber's sociology of law is built on the assumption that Natural Law is dead, because we live in a world of what he called polytheistic values that is a moral world of competitive value systems that are incommensurable. Leo Strauss complained that, if Weber's fact-value distinction went unchallenged, it would be impossible to distinguish between just regimes and unjust regimes, or between authentic religious charisma and false prophets.[47] Weber's notion of power politics was closely related to Carl Schmitt's development of a theory of the politic.[48] In this Weberian model, law is command, the political is the struggle between friend and foe, and sovereignty is the capacity to decide that a state of emergency exists. The legality of law is dependent on the authority of a state to issue a command and to ensure compliance. We might say that the rise of human rights as a moral statement about human vulnerability recognises that there are crimes against humanity that are not context dependent, that human rights are based on international conventions, and that they are typically enforced to protect individuals against failed states. Human rights are in part a restoration of Natural Law – they are enforced and mediated through nation states, civil laws and local customs. The growth of extra-territorial human rights indicates the limitations of territorial citizenship, and the inevitable pluralism of modern legal systems.

This discussion of the legal framework of multiculturalism forces to a deeper level of analysis namely to a consideration of the nature of sovereignty in the modern world. State sovereignty has become an issue precisely because some political theorists argue that state sovereignty is in decline and national boundaries have become precarious. The globalisation of the law constrains state activity; economic corporations frequently have more power and wealth than small nations, and contemporary warfare especially so called new wars have often undermined states. Since 9/11 however, there is ample evidence that all such talk about the erosion of state sovereignty was premature.

Citizenship: The Limits of Globalisation

The problems of multiculturalism are connected to the erosion of citizen in modern democracies.[49] While national citizenship is often weak, there has been much discussion recently of the possibility of global citizenship and global governance. With the growth of the European Union, sociologists have considered the possibility of transnational citizenship. Anthropologists have examined the problem of identity in modern societies with the growth of transational communities and diasporic cultures. Aihwa Ong has examined 'the cultural logics of transnationality' and has described 'flexible citizenship' as 'a strategy that combines the security of citizenship in a new country with business opportunities in the homeland'.[50] While the sociological analysis of transnational identities is an important and interesting field of research, it is confusing rather than illuminating to use the concept of citizenship.

There are several possible arguments against my position. Firstly, the very existence of dual citizenship might suggest that the relationship between sovereignty and social rights is not as close as I have claimed. Secondly, there is a lack of fit between duties and rights, for example in the case of children's rights. Citizenship tends to assume a healthy and intelligent person who is capable of undertaking their civic duties, or at least capable of gainful employment. The physically disabled cannot always fulfil such expectations. Citizenship thus contrasts sharply with human rights since the latter do not presuppose any relationship between rights and duties. These hypothetical objections in fact strengthen my argument. Generally speaking, states are reluctant to admit dual citizenship, precisely because it creates divided loyalties and ambiguous identities, and it is seen as a clear challenge to sovereignty.[51] The lack of fit between rights and duties in the case of disabled persons accounts for the fact that they are discriminated against and often treated as second-class citizens. The elderly, while also discriminated against, are regarded as having retrospect claims on the state. The absence of a relationship between rights and duties in these cases only serves to reinforce the notion that citizenship is based on contributory rights. In the case of the US, where there has been a relatively weak development of welfare institutions, the underlying assumption of citizenship entitlements is that citizens will serve in the military, pay their taxes, raise children and generally contribute to the common good.

It is possible to take a cynical view of the growth of welfare rights in the post-war period, by arguing that these welfare states and the growth of civil liberties were an aspect of the Cold War in which western states wanted to demonstrate their liberal values against atheism and communism. The rights of free speech were particularly important in the case of internal struggles within Czechoslovakia and Poland for the rights of artists to publish creative works. In the aftermath of the Cold War, there is less pressure to uphold those rights and after 9/11 there have been increasing restrictions on personal liberties with the Patriot Act in the US and increasing restrictions of mobility in Europe where the UK, Spain and Italy have sought greater control over and surveillance of asylum seekers, refugees, and migrants. The attempt to impose greater security measures internally is clearly a response to the specific threat of terrorism when governments have to balance the preservation of civil rights against effective security measures.

Although these political and legal developments can be connected directly with the perceived threat of terrorism, there is a more general political movement to limit the growth of multiculturalism. In the US, conservative critics claim that multicultural education programmes distort the historical truth of the US's cultural origins and undermines national unity by the effective Balkanisation of the American republic.[52] Liberal intellectuals had historically assumed that Americanisation was unproblematic, because ethnic minorities would eventually be culturally assimilated and benefit eventually from growing economic prosperity. However, this optimism has been shaken by the fact that black progress appears to have stalled in the 1970s. The neo-conservative response to alienated black youth is not encouraging. It implies that alienated youth can either continue to experience social estrangement, unemployment, and low wages, resorting to criminal careers to satisfy their needs, or they can passively accept limited social inclusion into American society on terms that are dictated by the dominant white establishment. These developments in Europe and the US suggest that citizenship is not a flexible institution, and that it is tied inextricably to the sovereignty of the nation state. The political exhortation of the French Revolution – citizens of the world unite – appears to have definite institutional limits and shows that not all institutions can be analysed from the perspective of 'sociology beyond society', because the social world is not simply an ensemble of flows.

Conclusion: The End of Multiculturalism?

In the framework of Thomas Hobbes's theory of the state, we can only achieve some degree of personal security if we surrender a modicum of our own freedom in order to establish the sovereignty of the state. Herein is the great intellectual puzzle of political science, because politics can never be wholly universal; it is essentially about the struggle for resources between conflicting groups, whose motivation is to achieve power. Politics involves the contradiction between the state, which needs to achieve some level of legitimacy in order to function, and the struggle for power that appears to take place outside the framework of law, which is necessary for the continuity of the state. The legitimacy of the modern state is tied to the provision of security for its citizens. There appears to be an irreconcilable tension between any human rights regime which is universal, and the legitimacy of the state, which is particular and exclusive. Yet this tension between the state and citizenship, on the one hand, and global governance and human rights, on the other may turn out to be more apparent than real.

In the US and the UK, governments have been anxious to change the law, which is often seen to be unduly generous in protecting the civil liberties of individuals and groups, whose beliefs are seen to be hostile to western liberal culture. In these circumstances, there is little room for optimism, and the idea of cosmopolitanism appears to be increasingly out of step with contemporary political sentiment. What is the difference between terrorist violence and counter-terror measures, when the US detains suspects without trial in locations that are secret and outside international scrutiny? The coercive force which is available to the state is legitimate, if it is subordinate to legal norms, namely to the rule of law. Michael Ignatieff argues that state violence is legitimate only as a 'lesser evil' – only if it is ultimately restrained and made accountable as a consequence of due process of law.[53] In the twentieth century, therefore, the legitimacy of the state came to depend increasingly on the extent to which both domestic and foreign policy of powerful states were compatible with international human rights standards. The legal difficulty for the coalition forces in Iraq has been that the original invasion and subsequent treatment of prisoners do not appear to be consistent with UN requirements or human rights objectives. The notion that terrorism creates exceptional circumstances which permit states to act outside human rights norms is likely to be counter-productive. Such actions merely give further credibility to terrorist ideologies, and continue the erosion of the credibility of both the UN and US foreign policy. The political world has become increasingly precarious, and the contemporary international crisis is not well served by academic arguments supporting moral relativism. Recognition of our common vulnerability is the only starting point for the construction of a commonwealth in which security might be restored.

I have argued that the social and economic conditions for multiculturalism will include (1) sustained economic growth and opportunities for social mobility, especially for minority groups; (2) a national, secular education system that promotes social mobility, and integrates children of different ethnic and religious traditions; (3) freedom to choose marriage partners, intermarriage and liberal divorce laws; and (4) rule of law, and a government that is overtly committed to policies supporting multiculturalism.

In summary the social causes for failed multicultural diversity are the obverse, namely (1) declining economic growth and social inequality where stigmatised minority communities find their opportunities for social mobility are declining; (2) low level of cross-cultural marriage, and segregated educational systems; and (3) governments that actively intervene in society to the disadvantage of minority communities. Multiculturalism fails because social conditions undermine trust and social cohesion. Multiculturalism is likely to fail in the modern world, because the conditions that produce trust are being eroded.

I started this chapter with a quotation from a black British sociologist Paul Gilroy from a conference at Goldsmiths College in 1999. I conclude with a quotation from the US black intellectual Cornel West. In 1993, Cornel West pondering the condition of black Americans in his *Race Matters* (1993:8) commented that

> to establish a new framework, we need to begin with a frank acknowledgement of the basic humanness and Americanness of each of us. And we must acknowledge that as a people – *E pluribus Unum* – we are on a slippery slope toward economic strife, social turmoil, and cultural chaos. If we go down together.

The same could be said for our contemporary global condition. While current policies of multiculturalism may be under strain, and while some may have failed miserably, we cannot avoid a multicultural future in which citizenship and human rights will be our best defence against civil unrest and the erosion of civil liberties in the name of our security. The new xenophobia is a cultural product of these complex social and political circumstances in which there is currently a tragic corrosion of civic culture and the public sphere.

6

RISK SOCIETY AND
THE ISLAMIC OTHER

Sue Kenny

This chapter explores the context of the concerns of Islamic non-government organisations (NGOs) regarding their experiences of hostility towards them from non-Muslims. The chapter begins with a note on the promises of ethno-specific NGOs, including Islamic organisations, prior to September 2001. Since 2001, Islamic NGOs have been the target of government and popular media attacks, in Australia, as elsewhere in the Western world. Islamic NGOs in the West are searching for explanations of these attacks and the potency of the discourse of 'Islamic terrorism'. Similarly, Islamic NGO recipients in developing countries are sensitive to the need to satisfy Western aid agencies that they are not agents of Islamic terrorism, and they too are seeking clarification of their standing in the West. The aim of this chapter is to open up discussion of the perceptions of the Islamic NGOs. It is argued that it is important to understand how the backdrop of 'risk society' sets the scene for the provocative encounter between the contemporary discourse of terrorism, the concept of the Islamic Other and the development of xenophobia.

The Promises of NGOs

In the last ten to fifteen years we have witnessed renewed interest in the promises of civil society This interest has accompanied the erosion of trust in both the market and the state. Third sector or non-government organisations (NGOs), in particular, have promised a way to reinvigorate and reorient community life at the local level and to offer alternative global networks committed to pluralism and human rights.[1] Indeed, at the very turn of the century, in the years 2000–2001, the vast array of ethno-specific groups and NGOs around the world offered a force that could demonstrate the rich diversity of cultures and social organisation, respond to immediate needs at the grass-roots level and provide an independent voice for the powerless. It was in the context of this favourable imagery of the role of NGOs that governments in Australia provided resources and support for ethno-specific organisations, including Islamic organisations within a policy framework of multiculturalism and provided aid to NGOs in developing countries.[2]

The promises of NGOs as new and important agents of change and the interactions between NGOs and governments have provided the focus of much of the research that I, together with my colleagues, have been involved in over the last fifteen years.[3] One of the key ethno-specific dimensions in this research has been a focus on Muslim groups. Through studies of NGOs, social capital, capacity building and active citizenship, I have been involved in an exploration of the experiences and perceptions of Muslims in both Australia and Indonesia. The Australian research has involved working with local NGOs to study of the types and dimensions of social capital amongst Arab Australian groups, perceptions of the success and effects of multiculturalism in a local council area and the experiences of Muslim women in Victoria.[4] The Indonesian research has involved a study of the meanings and experiences of capacity building in a range of Islamic NGOs in Indonesia.[5]

The Experiences of Islamic NGOs

All Islamic groups in these studies report experiences of increasing hostility from non-Muslims. Islamic NGOs,[6] rather than contributing to civil society activities, are now often seen as sites for generating social unrest and political agitation, and more threateningly, as sites for training 'terrorists' or syphoning off funds for 'terrorist' activities. Such accusations have profound effects on the wide range of Muslim communities in Australia. For example, the research into the dimensions of social capital in Arab Australian communities reveals that Arab Australians feel less safe within their neighbourhoods than they did prior to September 2001. Bridging social capital (a term describing networks based on contacts between people of different backgrounds) *between* Muslim and other communities has diminished, whilst connectedness *within* Muslim communities (bonding social capital, comprising networks with homogeneous groups) has intensified. Muslim women report on escalation of verbal and even physical abuse by non-Muslims in public spaces. Whilst there have been attempts to keep racism and discrimination against Muslims at bay, raids on Muslim homes and subsequent arrests, media portrayal of a unitary Muslim community in

Australia, and the continual linking of Islam and terrorism, have helped to keep the idea of a generalised 'Muslim threat' alive.

In December 2004, the province of Aceh in northern Sumatra was struck by a devastating earthquake and tsunami. Working with Islamic NGOs in Aceh, the Indonesian study has been able to trace the reconstruction effort, and the perceptions of this effort, mainly from the perspective of Acehnese NGOs, but also taking into account the views and practices of Western aid agencies. This research has revealed suspicion and mistrust of Islamic NGOs in the attitudes and practices of Western aid agencies.

The Islamic groups in these studies have been trying to come to terms with the mistrust and suspicion with which they are treated by many non-Muslims. They understand the role of the events of 11 September 2001 in the US and subsequent 'terrorist' threats and attacks in the name of Islam. However, they emphasise that they have been equally, if not more offended and affected by these events. They argue that the current forms of Islamism and claims for a pure Islam undermine their views and presentation of the richness and diversity of Islam. They point to the great variety of agents and sites of terrorism over the last twenty years, including military adventures in Africa, Palestine and the Middle East, Asia and South America. They argue that the agendas of the Islamist terrorists are generated politically and socially. These agendas are largely the result of Western foreign policy actions. Moreover, the tactics of Islamic political activism have been adopted from the West.[7]

Islamic NGOs also want to understand the processes that are involved in the construction of the 'Muslim as threat', how they can respond to this construction, and how to counter xenophobia. This chapter begins to engage these questions. It explores some sociological analyses of the factors contributing to the environment of fear of terrorism and the construction of the 'Islamic Other'. In particular, it considers how ideas of risk society and the Oriental Other are shaping the discussion of human security and the policies of the Australian government and aid agencies in disaster management.

The Shifting Foci of Human Security

Human security involves protection from threats to people's lives, their livelihoods and rights. In the context of social policy, human security can be guaranteed by state institutions and processes, such as those developed by welfare states. NGOs have been implicated in the activities of welfare states as partners in the delivery of welfare and as advocates for the poor and powerless. Human security is also protected by military and policing activities. Historically we can trace the ways in which societies construct concerns about human security that is based on social initiatives 'to protect livelihoods' and human security that is based to military and policing activities 'to protect lives'. Many Western societies are currently shifting focus and funding away from human security through social policy, and particularly through the welfare state, to human security through increasing the powers and numbers of the military and police forces. This growth in the military and police has also involved a shift to the privatisation of military and policing roles. So far, NGOs have been largely excluded from these roles. However we are beginning to see NGOs brought in to 'trouble spots' as 'humane protectors', who can complement and 'soften' the impact of military and policing programs. One explanation of the recent remilitarisation of human security is a renewed focus on political insecurity, particularly the political insecurity generated by the resurgence of terrorism. While there have always been terrorist acts, it is a particular form of terrorism that has focussed the minds of Western governments since September 2001. This is Islamist terrorism.

There are a number of ways to consider the factors contributing to the environment of a fear of 'Islamic terrorism'. We could begin with the broad definition of terrorism as an activity directed against civilians or targets affecting civilians, using violence or threat of violence, for political ends. Within the context of this broad definition, the agents of terrorism can be civilians themselves (civilian or group terrorism), or military or police personnel (state terrorism). These agents can act alone or under supervision and guidance by other civilians or the state.

What does the research show? The data available is often difficult to read. However we can make a few preliminary comments. Most obviously, today, as in the past, the probability of a premature death as a result of a terrorist act, of whatever kind, remains universally very low in comparison with death through disease or a car accident.[8] If this is the case, how can we explain the focus on civilian terrorism today? First, whilst the data on the trends in terrorism is mixed[9] and the overall the number of terrorist acts has declined between 1982 and 2003, the number of 'significant' incidents, (namely, high-casualty attacks) of international terrorism had been increasing.

Importantly, there are four new features of current forms of group terrorism. First is the focus on the global scale of group terrorist acts and the apparent global networks, which indicate that no one and no country is immune from attacks. The radical Left terrorist acts of the 1970s and 1980s involved a loose network of revolutionaries but these networks did not have the same power or reach as the networks of today. Second, the political and media interpretations of new terrorism identify 'the West' and the so-called 'Western way of life' as the major target of these new activities. Most particularly, the object of the most publicised current attacks is the US, its allies and its interests. Whilst other Western countries, such as the UK and France, many South American countries, Sri Lanka, India and Pakistan and Russia have many years experience of 'terrorism' the US mainland has not. Being the only super-power, the US is able to frame much of the terms of the discussion of terrorism and present an attack on its shores as an attack on all humanity. Third, the expected response to the contemporary fear of terrorism is not resigned fatalism but deliberate action on the part of the citizens. That is, people are expected to take control of their own destinies, including responding strategically to any threats to them. Finally, the perpetrators of much of the strand of global terrorism that is receiving international attention is identified with Islamism.[10]

These new features of group terrorism provide one line of argument in the explanation of the current discourse of terrorism. But they do not account for why the current discourse regarding the apparent 'global threat of Islamic terrorism' has found such a receptive audience in Western societies. This explanation requires a deeper understanding of some of the characteristics of late modernity and the reconstructions of the Islamic Other. In the following sections, we explore how these characteristics and attitudes towards Islam have worked to provide fertile ground upon which to plant ideas of threat and intensify fear of the Islamic Other. We begin with the way in which risk has come to be conceptualised, and the idea of 'risk society' that has been developed by Ulrich Beck.[11]

Risk Society

Much of the populist discussion of risk locates the idea of a heightened awareness of 'riskiness' of life to the period following the events in the US on 11 September 2001. Yet these attacks took place in a context in which the discourse of risk was already well established. The idea of 'risk society' as a theme in late modernity can be traced back to the 1980s, with the seminal work of Ulrich Beck. Beck set out the idea of risk society in his book *Risk Society : Towards a New Modernity*, published in German in 1986 and English in 1992. The core thesis of risk society is that more and more aspects of our lives are framed by an awareness of the dangers confronting humankind at the individual, local and global level, and that humans are now concerned to develop strategies to confront these dangers. Indeed, the notion of risk offered a major new frame of reference in which to understand late modernity, and by the beginning of the twenty-first century ideas of a risk based society had begun to gain support amongst both academics and policy-makers. In his 1999 publication *World Risk Society*, Beck discusses further the cultural shift that has led to a preoccupation with conceptualising possible futures in order to avoid undesirable futures.[12] It is because we live in a society based on knowledge, information and ever developing new technologies that we can envisage what Beck calls the 'threatening sphere of possibilities'.[13] He argues that the concept of risk characterises a situation existing between security and destruction, where the perception of threatening risks determines thought and action.[14] For example:

> Believed risks are the whip to keep the present day moving along at a gallop. The more threatening the shadows that fall on the present day from a terrible future looming in the distance, the more compelling the shock that can be provoked by dramatising risk today … Established risk definitions are thus a magic wand with which a stagnant society can terrify itself … [15]

Of course, humans have always faced hazards and dangers, and all societies have developed ways of identifying and responding to risk, but our contemporary understandings of risk, and the ways in which risk assessments permeate both the choices we make in our everyday lives and public policy, are new. Mythen argues that this systematic identification, assessment and negotiation of risk has become routine.[16] It is this new pervasive construction of risk, and the responses to risk, that set the backdrop to the new forms of xenophobia constructed around the idea of the Islamic Other.

The key to grasping the importance of contemporary ideas of risk is to understand the way in which we conceptualise our lives within a future-oriented framework, as territory to be conquered, and within the control of human agency.[17] While all human choices are circumscribed by cultural context and physical limitations, late modernity is characterised by a belief in the largely unencumbered power of individuals to be the agents of their own destiny, with assistance from science and reason. Indeed, if there is a denial of human agency then there is little reason to identify risks, undertake risk assessments and develop risk avoidance and risk management strategies. It is this very focus on the responsibility of human agents to take action to avoid danger that leads to develop a radar for picking up evidence of an impending threat. Indeed, governments and the media have been quite effective in alerting us to the need to be watchful for signs of threat from Muslim populations and groups.

We now seek out knowledge of the factors that affect us personally with a vigour unknown in human history. One view is that our greater knowledge of risk derives not so much from the quest for knowledge, but from the way in which we are blitzed with the dangers of the world through the global mass media. Indeed, the media have played a key role in promulgating the threats to human security through terrorism. From this perspective, risk society is only possible when we have global media, and risk is made all the more real through the instantaneous communication possible today, where we are confronted with stories about the riskiness of life.

However, the more we attempt to 'colonize the future with the aid of the category of risk, the more it slips out of our control'.[18] This is because while risk society opens up new opportunities, it also carries with it the possibility of a never-ending spiral of unintended new risks, as part of what has been identified by sociologists as reflexive modernisation. That is to say, as we respond to the risks we see, we open up new unintended risks. The reflexive element of risk response is illustrated in the ways in which human security is managed. For example, the spiral of unintended new risks is evident in the ill-conceived invasion of Iraq by the 'coalition of the willing'. The reflexivity of the draconian so-called 'anti-terror' laws in Australia is yet to be played out, but given the way in which these laws will be used alongside 'profiling', which singles out Muslim Australians, the proposed laws are already having the effect of deepening the cleavages between Muslims and non-Muslims. In addition, the 'anti-terror' laws premised on the defence of human rights and security, actually put the principles of human rights and security on hold, in the name of responsible risk management.

As indicated above, the issues of how far risk is real or a construction and whether in fact life is more risky today than it has been in the past, or it just takes place within new constructions of risk, are the subjects of some deliberation.[19] People continue to be subjected to war, natural disaster, starvation and political repression, as they have been in the past. From this perspective comes the argument that there are always real risks in human life and it is the cultural perceptions of risk that change.[20] In fact risk objects do vary over time and space and several forms of risk have been identified. Several writers have distinguished between traditional type risks and the risks of early and late modernity.[21] Traditional risks, or what Beck calls natural hazards, include famine, flood, plague, and earthquakes. They were attributed to external forces, whether supernatural powers or nature. As science developed scientific understanding of these events rose, and technological interventions have been used to mitigate their worst effects. As we moved into through the 20th century these traditional risks were complemented by human made risks, or what is identified as 'manufactured uncertainty'.[22] Such new risks are caused by humans polluting the environment, manufacturing nuclear weapons and industries and manufacturing and marketing cigarettes, for example. These manufactured risks are produced socially rather than 'naturally.'

For most people however, the current culture of fear is significantly disproportionate to the actual probabilities of new threats to their lives.[23] Slovic et al have argued that individuals generally overestimate the threat to them of rare, but large and memorable risk events (such as a plane crash) and underestimate the risk to them of mundane risks (such as a car accident).[24] This is also the case in regard to terrorist acts. We have indicated the complexities in regard to the low probability of death by a terrorist act. Yet, particularly in Western countries, politicians and the popular media continue to highlight the threat of terrorism and to remind people of a continuing threat from Islam.

If the identification of threat is a key element of risk society, so too is development of strategies to confront the risks. Risk confrontation occurs on the level of individuals, the level of the state and the level of NGOs.

Individual Responsibility

As indicated above, in order to grasp how risk affects us in our everyday lives it is important to understand how assessing and negotiating risk has become an individual responsibility. A concept that helps us analyse the importance of individual responsibility is individualisation. Individualisation is based on a particular way of looking at and responding to knowledge. It is a process that involves individuals taking responsibility for collecting information and acting appropriately, that is, people becoming the agents of their own destiny. According to Beck,

> Individualisation means that each person's biography is removed from given determinations and placed in his or her hands, open and dependent upon decisions.[25]

Individualisation sheets home responsibility for human activities and life chances to individual decision-making. As Mythen points out 'everyday life becomes contingent upon an infinite process of decision-making'.[26]

We are continually caught up in a reflexive process of accessing information, decision-making, engagement and response and more decision-making.

In regard to human security, individualisation means that we are urged or required to equip ourselves with a veritable arsenal of threat detectors. It is the responsibility of individuals to make sure that they have relevant information about threats from terrorists. They need to monitor and respond to any personal risks. They learn how to recognise risk because they are continually reminded of risk threats by the media and politicians. Journalists monitor and report risk news stories. The individualisation of risk is clearly illustrated when people are condemned for being caught in risk situations that they could have avoided, such as when journalists or aid workers enter dangerous foreign locations in full knowledge of the risks that they are taking.

The Australian government regularly up-dates travel warnings and press releases. Individuals are also asked to identify risk agents, such as potential 'terrorists'; and monitor risk places, such as public transport and other public places, for example, in Australia we need to know who might be a terrorist, how to recognise terrorists and what to do when we spot 'them' (for example, report suspicious behaviour to security agencies).

The State and Risk

Whilst risk is identified and managed at the level of individuals, this does not mean that the state is released from its responsibility for the management of risk. To be sure, in late modernity the state needs and uses the concept of risk society as part of an effective armoury for the governance the populace. The state still has an important role in framing our understandings of risk and developing risk management strategies. Risk society is intimately connected with the administrative and technical decision-making processes of late modernity at both the national and international levels.[27] Beck points out that global risk society has led to a new politics of risk. For example, risks have become a major force in political mobilisation involving a new power-game with its own meta-norms about who defines and evaluates risk. In terms of international relations, this power-game is dominated by the US, supported by its English-speaking allies. Transnational alliances are constructed around perceived threats, such as the threat nuclear war and global terrorism). Responses include global and regional summits (summits on terrorism, for example) and the employment of selected 'experts' who can vindicate the ways in which governments have transformed uncertainty into decisions.[28] There is now a flourishing industry of human security and terrorism experts, whose services not only governments, but aid and development agencies in the new markets of risk assessment, risk management and disaster capitalism.[29]

The state also deals with risk at arm's length, under the imperative of the purchaser /provider split in which governments purchase the services of private providers who provide the risk management at the ground level.[30] The shifting of responsibility of risk management, of course takes place under the tent of privatisation. In Australia much of the privatisation of risk management is driven by the neo-liberal agenda of shifting activity away from governments to the private sector (this involves both for-profit and not-for-profit, or NGO, endeavours). Private operation of goals and detention centres are examples of this form of privatisation. There is a growing role of for-profit and not-for-profit organisations in the surveillance and incarceration of so-called illegal residents, such as visa over-stayers and asylum seekers. There is increasing use of private security forms in aid and development arenas and in war zones. In tsunami devastated Aceh, for example, a large proportion of the aid effort has been the responsibility of private contractors and independent aid agencies.

NGOs and Risk

Risk assessment and risk management also take place at the level of NGOs. In the West, particularly where a strong version of neo-liberalism and new forms of managerialism have taken hold, NGOs are required to undertake risk assessments and to establish risk management strategies. They are also subjected to checking and inspection regimes through audits, monitoring and the evaluation of their programs. These processes allow the state to manage and watch them at arms length'. NGOs can have other roles too. As stated at the beginning of the chapter, NGOs have been identified as sites for the development of civil society. In so far as they can harness labour (or volunteers) on the basis of their presumed altruistic goals, their flexibility and their responsiveness to their communities, they can provide cheap and effective services. As noted above, they are also convenient shunting yards for risks that are too threatening to the state or to market players: that is, unless they are Islamic NGOs. In an ironic twist, the very positive attributes that made ethno-specific NGOs so attractive to governments prior to September 2001, such as their ability to work at the grass-roots, their responsiveness and their flexibility, has made them the targets of suspicion and distrust and the objects of surveillance. That is, the new discourses of risk and terrorism now provide the lenses through which funding bodies, and especially government funding bodies, are perceiving Islamic NGOs. Of course, this is not to say that all Islamic NGOs are distrusted, but to underscore the line of thinking that has suspicion as the default, and requires sorting out those Islamic NGOs that are or could be useful agents of the state from and those Islamic NGOs that are a threat. Such sorting is taking place both in Australia and in the major international disaster arenas where Islamic organisations operate.

Surveillance and Risk

As indicated above, the discourse of risk goes hand in hand with suspicion and mistrust. Key policy responses to suspicion and mistrust are increases in regulation and surveillance. In late modernity a good deal of regulatory power is embedded in the repertoire of checking and inspection, through the processes of monitoring, auditing and evaluating. In the era of the proclaimed 'War on Terror' the most obvious form of surveillance response to risk involves a host of new measures invoked to find, watch and capture those responsible for terrorism. The rationale for the introduction of the new checking and surveillance regimes is that they provide a way of identifying, assessing and pre-empting or managing risks. Of course, the practice of watching others is not new. The French sociologist Michel Foucault (1979) traced the self-regulatory effect of the Panoptican system of observation (where people self-regulate because of the possibility that they are being observed) in the nineteenth century. Classificatory methods have long been the tools of the guardians of 'normalcy' to profile and identify 'the mad and the bad'. They continue to be used today, not only to classify Islamic NGOs, but also to ensure that potential terrorists are identified and the 'risk' of terrorist attacks is brought under control. The new forms of post 9/11 surveillance promise to control risk through increasingly sophisticated procedures for assembling data, and classifying and cross-referencing, such as through bio-metric data, in ways that none of us are immune to. It is these new forms of surveillance that Lyon alerts us to.[31] Like the many critics of the Australian government's 'anti-terror' laws, Lyon comments that neglecting the need for ethical care for the objects of surveillance is a serious mistake, with ramifications that we may all live to regret.

Risk in Need of an Agent

The power of risk discourse in regard to issues of human security is that it provides a 'forensic resource for providing an explanation for things that have gone wrong'.[32] One of the major challenges of much of the discourse of risk is to find the agent of risk, a person or phenomenon that can be blamed, or controlled and disciplined. The search for, and discovery of the agent of risk valorises government concerns over risk, and in turn, becomes a forceful tool in the hands of those in power.[33] Governments have always been able to find legitimacy through their naming of the risk agent. In Australia, the Howard Government has successfully played the 'risk card' in two elections, through its identification of agents of risk who were putatively threatening the 'Australian way of life'. In 2001, both the 'Tampa affair', in which a Norwegian tanker was refused permission to land 460 asylum seekers on Australian soil, and the manipulated portrayal of asylum seekers throwing their children overboard, contributed to a risk narrative that served the government well. The fear of asylum seekers has been clearly underscored by fear of agents of group terrorism penetrating Australian shores. The argument of this chapter is that this discourse of terrorism has effectively located the risk agent within the Muslim communities, whose backgrounds are Middle Eastern, North African or South–East Asian. This discourse seems to sit comfortably with the view that the agents of terrorism are those who experience political, social and cultural marginality. They are people who are not content in their homelands and who are the 'type' who will 'throw their children overboard'. This narrative of asylum seekers fails to mention that they are seeking to escape from oppression in their homeland.

The Metaphor of War ·

The contemporary discourse of terrorism has also been presented through the metaphor of war, in which nation states are rallied to support the 'War on Terror'. The metaphor of war conjures up the imagery of a zero sum battle between two coherent sides, of 'them and us' ('if you are not with us you are against us'), of good and evil. While the application of the metaphor of war is inaccurate, it serves the purpose of identification of the Other as a clearly definable, homogenous and dangerous entity. Much of the this discourse draws (oversimplistically) on the work of Samuel Huntington who argues that the new schisms that have replaced the Cold War are based on what he identifies as cultures and civilisations.[34] The metaphor of war serves the idea of risk society well. It reminds us of a palpable threat and allows governments to argue for the efficacy of pre-emptive attacks to prevent foreseen dangers, whether these dangers are 'terrorists' in our own backyards or overseas. This pre-emptive logic also opens the way for the burden of empirical proof to be discarded.

The Muslim as the Other

For many in the West, then, who hold an undifferentiated notion of 'a Muslim', all Muslims, as the Other, and the possible agent of threat, have come to be seen as being potential terrorists. The undifferentiated concept of 'the Muslim' is located in the global revival of Islam, and as Sayyid points out, marks the return of the repressed.[35] As such it is the source of considerable cultural anxiety in the West. Of course, the construction of the terrorist as the Other is a convenient artifice that has a long history. As Lupton argues (in contrast to Beck's position), notions of 'Otherness' are central to ways of thinking and acting in regard to risk.[36] The Other is someone who is different from 'the self', that is, someone who is strange. Because of difference, the Other can be a source of anxiety and even threat. 'Risky Others' can be the object of blame.

But the construction of the Other offers more than this. It offers a way of ordering our world for us. The dichotomy between self and the Other offers a framework for setting boundaries between categories of people. Yet as with all ordering through binary divides, the comfort afforded by the dichotomy between self and the others is not guaranteed, for this dichotomy also generates its own anxieties and fears.[37] First, there are the anxieties resulting from the transgression of boundaries of 'the self' and 'my world', by the Other or 'the stranger'. The threat to 'my territory' becomes more acute when there is an emphasis on the privatisation of responsibility, that we discussed above, and where public spaces become privatised. The fear of a stranger transgressing the norms and security of 'my world' is clearly evident in the discourse of the 'foreignness' of other cultures within our midst (in Australia this has presented as the growing unease with and criticism of multiculturalism) and the profound anxiety regarding the possibility of terrorist acts within our own territory. The possibility of the stranger penetrating 'my territory' is brought home graphically in the attacks on the New York Twin Towers in the case of the US and in the presence of the US military in Saudi Arabia in the case of the viewpoint of political Islamists.

Second, there are the anxieties resulting from the existence of anomalous and ambivalent categories that do not fit neatly into a relevant binary divide. For example, the fear resulting from the London bombings in July 2005 is a particularly uncomfortable fear, because it is underpinned by an understanding that the alleged bombers were both 'of us', clearly members of British society, and 'not of us', that is, strangers transgressing British norms and way of life. They are anomalous agents. Similarly, in Australia the popular support for increased powers of the state to 'fight terrorism' is underpinned by an anti-terror discourse that draws on the threat of the stranger transgressing the norms and security of 'my world', and being both 'of us' and 'not of us'. Contemporary fears of transgression of the boundaries of 'my world', by the Other and fear of the 'stranger within' give succour to xenophobia[38] in the popular media. But they are also given academic legitimacy in the idea of 'the clash of civilizations', mentioned above.[39] The anxiety generated by fear of the Other, of course, also generates its own solidarity, that is, the solidarity of anxiety. This solidarity of anxiety can be the driver of political movements, including nationalistic and racist ones.

In Australia, the anti-terror discourse has led to four policy developments. First, measures involving surveillance and interrogation of 'suspects' are to be extended through the recent anti-terror legislation. For example, the legislation will allow the detention of terrorist suspects without charge for a period of up to 14 days. Second, suspects can be controlled through incarceration or house arrest. For example, the new anti-terror legislation means that being a member of an organisation deemed to be a terrorist one can lead to a prison term or house arrest.

Third, suspected terrorists can be banished through deportation. Australia, like the US and the UK has all put in place more efficient methods of screening foreigners and expelling those whom it deems a threat to internal security. Finally, if the problem lies in acceptance of diversity and difference, then one way of resolving the problem of 'strangers' in our midst is to jettison multicultural agendas in favour of assimilationist ones. The move from multiculturalism to assimilation is just beginning.

Orientalism

The argument of this chapter is that risk society, the discourse of terrorism and the concept of the Other provide fertile ground for the development of xenophobia. However, there is another factor that provides an additional potent ingredient in the nexus between risk, terror and 'Otherness'. This is Orientalism. It is Edward Said's reflections upon Orientalism that have provided the most influential analysis of the idea and its power. Orientalism refers to an academic study of the Orient; a style of thought which is based on upon an ontological and epistemological distinction between 'the Orient' and 'the Occident'; and a corporate institution for dealing with the Orient, for describing it, authorising views about it and dominating it.[40] For Said,

> The Orient that appears in Orientalism, then, is a system of representations framed by a whole set of forces that brought the Orient into Western learning, Western Consciousness, and later, Western Empire.[41]

Orientalism draws on, and provides another layer to the Other. What is of interest for this chapter is the way in which Orientalism constructs the essentialist concept of the 'Islamic Other' as simultaneously vulnerable, exotic and a threat. Whilst the idea of the 'Islamic Other' exudes gender blindness, denying the personage of an individual and as a man or a woman, or even a young person or an old person, it is maleness and youth that dominate the imagery of the Islamic Other as dangerous and femaleness that dominates the imagery of the Islamic Other as vulnerable. As indicated above, these characterisations of the Islamic Other undermine the great complexity and richness of Islamic cultures, oversimplifying and profoundly limiting the possibilities for policy responses. In addition, the three policy directions indicated by the conceptions of the Islamic Other as vulnerable, exotic or threat are contradictory. Policy makers are confronted with the question: Is it better to protect vulnerable Islamic Others from harm, both from without and within, to keep them separate, or banish them to 'their own territories', wherever these territories might be, or is it better to embrace and even co-opt their exoticness?

Risk and Orientalism in the Reconstruction of Aceh

To illustrate the arguments made in this chapter it would be useful to elaborate how the foregoing analysis might help explain the way in which the response to the tsunami in Aceh has unfolded. The reconstruction of Aceh has been inexorably slow. People involved in local NGOs have queried where the promised millions of dollars in aid have been used. The major response to their queries has been to point to the need for both careful planning and to focus upon capacity building. Indeed capacity building has been the main rationale behind much of the reconstruction effort.

What has been interesting for the purposes of this chapter are the dominant forms of capacity building and the principles upon which capacity-building has been developed. There are three forms of capacity building.[42] First, capacity building has involved external contractors who provide the expertise to rebuild the physical and organisational infrastructure. Second capacity building has involved skills and attitudes development through training, largely undertaken by Western experts. Finally, there is some evidence for reconstruction programs based on community development methods, whereby local communities and NGOs control the direction and use of aid. The dominant reconstruction programs fall into the first two categories of capacity-building. These are based on a deficit approach to local development and the need for external expertise. They ignore the possibility that local people in Aceh could organise themselves independently, mobilise what resources they have, and take the initiative in planning and reconstruction. To understand this view of the Western aid agencies it is helpful to probe the constructions of the Acehnese as the Other.

The imagery of the Acehnese provides a clear example of the problematic contradictory characterisations of the Other discussed above. The first approach is to characterise the Acehnese are dangerous. They have a long history of fighting for independence. The Netherlands formally declared war on the Acehnese in 1873 and since Indonesian independence in 1949 there has been continuing conflict with the Indonesian government (conflict ceased in August this year when a new peace deal was struck in Helsinki). They are also strongly Muslim, living in a country that has experienced a number of Islamist terrorist acts. During the reconstruction period, there have been several warnings of threats by Islamists which have put out by Western governments. Second, the Acehenese are Indonesians. Given the imagery of the rampant corruption in Indonesian politics and business, it is logical to construct Acehnese life as vulnerable and corrupt. Finally, the Acehnese, as Indonesians, are part of the 'undeveloped' South. In economic terms, in particular, they lack competence and hence require Western intervention and assistance. The imagery of the post tsunami Acehnese is of a people who are weak and vulnerable. They need protection and support.

These three characterisations of the Acehnese have helped to develop a new politics of Orientalism, which, with the growing strength of the discourses of terrorism and the need for risk management, provide a sound launching place for renewed forms of imperialism. Most importantly, the new politics of Orientalism and the need for risk management have also set the scene for strengthening the marketisation of aid. This new configuration of aid draws in particular on the Orientalist idea of the underdeveloped Other as both threatening and vulnerable. The threatening Other promises lucrative contracts for private security firms. The vulnerable Other promises lucrative contracts for capacity building. The devastating material effects of the earthquake and tsunami have promised unprecedented access to contracts for physical reconstruction. The characteristics of the reconstruction of Aceh are part of the rise of disaster capitalism.[43] Klein argues that now that the traditional territories for capitalist adventure have largely disappeared new territory has to be found, and this new territory exists in countries that have been 'smashed to rubble, whether by so-called Acts of God or by Acts of Bush'. Klein refers to the rebuilding process in general. When the rebuilding is threatened by 'acts of terrorism', then it needs to be protected by security agencies, who can collect information, monitor and control the activities of the dangerous/vulnerable Other (threat capitalism). In this form, disaster capital provides a 21st century rendition of Orientalism and an indication of power and potential of the new discourse of terrorism.

The Coming Political Crisis of Risk?

Beck explains how large scale risks have the power to set off a dynamic of cultural and political change that can undermine state bureaucracies, challenge the legitimacy of experts and redraw the battle lines of contemporary politics, in what he calls the 'social explosiveness of hazard'.[44] This view of the power of risk is well illustrated in the case of the apparent global and national crises of human security. In particular, issues of human security have the power to delegitimise and destabilise state institutions with responsibilities to protect public safety.[45] In regard to issues of human security, neither the state nor individuals seem to be prepared for the task of dealing effectively with the 'social explosiveness of hazard'. As indicated above, the state is focussed on what Beck calls 'organised irresponsibility' the simultaneous acknowledgement of the reality of risk, the covering of its origins and the rejection of responsibility and accountability from within the state. Through the privatisation of responsibility, individuals and contractors face the daily tasks of ensuring the safety of themselves or their charges. Blame and responsibility are sheeted home through the focus on the agent of risk and threat. Of course, blame and scapegoating of the supposed or actual agent of risk and threat has always been a risk management strategy.[46] Yet such strategies are insufficient for the tasks of explaining and responding to the risks facing human security and in particular, the risk of terrorism.

Conclusion

In the light of the foregoing discussion, how can we respond to the questions posed by Muslim communities that were presented at the beginning of this chapter? We have some stark choices. First, one set of options revolves around seeking refuge in past beliefs and practices. We can try to return to a time of relative certainty and providentialism. We can try to withdraw into the certainties of 'our space' and 'our side' in the apparent the clash of civilisations, where the Muslim is always a unitary Other. Through this option, we can soothe our anxieties by investing confidence in the power of the state to 'protect us'. We can throw back on the state the responsibilities that have been given to us in the processes of individualisation. Indeed, the state itself can reclaim an authoritarian presence, as the governments in the UK, the US and Australia are doing. Second, we can deepen commitment to market logic by pursing further the option of privatisation of responsibility for human security. Private policing and other security forces can be brought in as the military front line in the so-called 'War on Terror'. Internationally this option can attend to the problem of human security by further developing the complementary institutions of military capitalism and disaster capitalism. Third, we can forget about attempting to control for risk through risk assessments and management. We can just learn to live with uncertainty.

Alternatively, we can take a fourth direction, one that begins with the view that risk is an opportunity. We can explore new possibilities for new relationships based on intercultural competence. Intercultural competence requires tolerance, irony, revisability and an ability to learn.[47] Fifth, we can take the democratic path, where, as Cooke suggests, there is a new deal between the public, the politicians and the experts. Through this option, we can use risk to develop mutual respect, active trust and skills in negotiation through democratic dialogue and informed deliberation.[48] The democratic path means that politicians will let the public know the limits of their own knowledge and identify the interests lying behind decisions and the presentation of events. The democratic path also requires governments to facilitate the development of institutions and policies that are committed to sharing information and dialogue These later tasks, of course, are very difficult in an environment where competition, distrust, suspicion and fear dominate

Sixth, we can unpack the imagery of the Islamic Other. In this regard, we can validate our common humanity, by initiating discussion of our common values and human rights. We can provide knowledge that challenges the unitary conception of Islam. Working at the local level, councils and local authorities can establish genuine partnerships between Muslim and non-Islamic NGOs in local community development initiatives. The populace can be informed about the culture of fear that accompanies risk society. The media can play a major role in disseminating all this information.

Finally, we can expose the links between risk society and xenophobia. If we take the position that it is not Islam as a religion that is the threat, but the political use of any religion in an essentialist or totalitarian way (including the political use of Christianity, Hinduism and Islam), then one strategy that can combat the xenophobia based on the fear that arises out of foreignness, is to underline the hybridity that has always been part of religious thought, including Islam. For example, there are many who point to the ways in which Arab Australian identities and Muslim Australian identities are being developed. The idea of an Australian Islam can challenge the concept of the 'enemy within'.

This brings us back to the discussion of the promises of NGOs that was commented on earlier in this chapter. NGOs have been identified as 'fronts' for Islamist groups. Research that I have been involved in reveals the increasing difficulties faced by people in Islamic NGOs. Is this enough to give up on the promises of NGOs as sites for social change, places to reorient community life and part of the global networks committed to pluralism and human rights? The answer is no. In regard to the Islamist NGOs, these organisations are more properly described as secret sects than NGOs, for NGOs are open and transparent in their activities.[49] It is exactly these open and transparent third sector sites that offer the best chance of facilitating dialogue between different ethno-specific groups. What will become important in the coming years is keeping the dialogue open, setting up processes for bridging and linking social capital and generating relations of trust. If there is a crises of the state generated by risk, this crisis will not be solved by the market or by individuals, and it will certainly not be resolved by further privatisation of responsibility. It will be the task of those NGOs committed to human rights, capacity-building and interfaith dialogue, for example, that will provide the best opportunity to deal with the challenges facing us. We already have some burgeoning NGOs of this type. One example is the Wahid Institute in Indonesia. The mission of the Wahid Institute is to promote democratic reform, religious pluralism, multiculturalism and tolerance amongst Muslims, both in Indonesia and internationally. The Wahid Institute is at once both cosmopolitan and local. It is a large and influential Muslim based organisation, that works at the grassroots level, as part of a broad network of Islamic NGOs. It is democratic, open and accountable. For a future that will be facing unprecedented uncertainty, we will need thousands of such NGOs. Many already exist. The task is to ensure that they are prepared for the new challenges of risk.

7

FROM DIASPORA ISLAM TO GLOBALISED ISLAM

Michael Humphrey

The recent suicide bombings on London transport in July 2005, carried out by home-grown (second generation British Pakistani) Muslims, has only served to increase suspicions about Muslim minorities in Australia and made them the focus of intensified counter-terrorism measures. In response, 'homeland security' has enhanced the surveillance and pre-emptive powers of the Australian state to manage potential invisible threats made visible by the London bombings and by the recent detention of seventeen Muslims accused of the crimes of belonging to a proscribed organisation and plotting a terrorist attack. Key to these counter-terrorism measures has been new anti-terrorist legislation directed at subversive threats of potential terrorists but which are publicly implicitly understood as code for 'dangerous Muslims'. In Australia, as elsewhere, Muslims have become securitised and classified as either 'extremists' or 'moderates.' When the Australian government states that the anti-terrorist laws are not against Muslims, it in fact means 'moderate' Muslims. Because of the invisibility of dangerous 'intention', profiling necessarily targets sub-populations. The Australian government's creation of the Muslim Community Reference Group made up of 'moderate' leaders is a public expression of the intensification of classification with the purpose of producing order. The consequence is that Islam is becoming further globalised by being securitised.

The London bombings changed the relationship of Muslim minorities to the state in the UK and the West generally. It is a measure of the globalisation of international jihadist terrorism, as a perceived ubiquitous 'threat', that events in one Western country now produce high level inter-government cooperation as well as harmonisation of counter-terrorism policy. After September 11, and President George Bush's declaration of the 'War on Terror', Western governments largely upheld the view that (immigrant) Muslim minorities should be geographically (if not politically) differentiated from the radical and extremist currents in parts of the Muslim world. Western governments widely defended 'their Muslims' as 'having nothing to do with' the politics, aspirations, networks and violent methods of extremist jihadists – while at the same time intensifying surveillance and scrutiny of their activities. But after the London bombings counter-terrorism and the war against terror merged as part of the same struggle. With borders becoming more porous and a growing perception of risk arising from the global circulation of invisible threats – dangerous goods, people, ideas, and laundered money – national security has become de-territorialised. The national space (in the West) has been turned into a paranoid space where all forms of disorder (things and people out of space) are now put under surveillance and investigated. The securitisation of everyday life is evident in the invitation to phone the terrorist hotline if you see something/someone suspicious (i.e. out of place). When terrorist incidents occur, news broadcasters (e.g. BBC news) now post requests on their websites asking the public to send in copies of any digitised images of the events knowing the ubiquitous use of the digital technology now in phones and cameras. But rather than trying to bring about order the new security measures seek to manage disorder.[1]

This chapter explores the emergence of a 'globalised Islam', a term coined by Olivier Roy, to contextualise contemporary expressions of Islamic belief and practice in amongst Muslims minorities in Western societies.[2] He defines 'globalised Islam' as 'the way in which the relationship of Muslims to Islam is reshaped by globalisation, westernisation and the impact of living as a minority. The issue is not the theological content of the Islamic religion, but the way believers refer to this corpus to adapt and explain their behaviours in a context where religion has lost its social authority'.[3] In this chapter I will extend Roy's analysis of 'globalised Islam' – neo-fundamentalism as religious innovation – by exploring its relationship to 'securitised Islam', the product of the state's attempt to regulate dangerous global circulation of illicit commodities, illegal migrants, drug smugglers, laundered money, terrorists and new exotic diseases. The relationship of Muslims in the West to Islam has also been changed by the impact of Islamic international terrorism (international jihadism) and the West's counter-terrorism responses. Muslims in the West are confronted with the consequences of radical jihadist violence, which has even led to the political questioning of their right continued membership and citizenship (e.g. public speculation that anyone convicted under the anti-terrorism laws could lose their Australian citizenship).

The state has now been forced to manage global circulation as a threat to disorder. Feldman describes the new security paradigm as the defence of sovereignty globally through de-territorialised 'public safety wars'.[4] These wars are not focused on territorial conquest, or an easily identified enemy, but rather are aimed at countering territorial contamination or transgression. That is, the 'securocratic ideology fixes upon an iconography of demonised border-crossing figures and forces, including drug dealers, terrorists, asylum seekers, undocumented immigrants and microbes'.[5] Public safety wars have no clear political end because their objective, Feldman argues, is to regulate threats in a world in which borders have become porous. Sovereignty and national security are no longer based on the defence and control of territorial boundaries but on a multi-tiered surveillance and intervention (reach) against threatening forms of global circulation that can never be completely extinguished. Thus, these wars 'require the continued symbiotic presence of the policed object in order to justify the continuation and new elaborations of state sovereignty'.[6] State legitimacy is being closely tied to its capacity to police the object of disorder, the terrorist.

In the same way that Islam has become de-territorialised through globalisation (migration to the West), so too has national security become de-territorialised through 'the war against terror' and 'counter-terrorism'. The new character of national security as the management of disorder offers no resolution to political conflict, only 'eternal' surveillance, pre-emption and intervention. I will argue that 'globalised Islam' is now being shaped by, and locked into a symbiotic relationship with a security paradigm in which national sovereignty is defended globally by strategically focusing on Muslim sub-populations for carrot and stick treatment – intervention, war or therapeutic persuasion. Hence the relationship of Muslims to Islam in the West has not only been shaped by the existential experience of social marginalisation, de-industrialisation, racism, and Muslim terrorist violence but also by the state's securitising of Islam/Muslims as a response to the invisible threat of terrorism arising from global circulation. 'Islam' is being transformed by the consequences of globalisation; through the dispersal of Muslims, the mediatisation of culture, the securitisation of dangerous global circulation, and neo-fundmentalism's reconstitution of a self-conscious transnational umma galvanised by terrorist violence.

This chapter will explore the changed relationship between Muslims to Islam and Muslim immigrants/minorities to the state in the shift from diaspora to globalised Islam and the impact of securitising Islam/Muslims as a strategy of risk minimisation.

From Diaspora to Globalised Islam

'The attempt to abolish uncertainty has failed' comments Michael Herzfeld about the era of globalisation.[7] The forms of bureaucratic organisation and organised community – the institutions of modernity – designed to reduce risk and danger have proliferated but have only made understanding human life more opaque. One of the most obvious victims of this process is the bounded human group – 'society' or 'culture'. Islam, the nation-state and minorities are all being transformed as bounded entities in the context of globalisation. This is not merely a question of porous borders or global communication but the very scale of what society and culture have become in a de-territorialised and mediatised world. The anthropological comfort zone of locality and community can no longer contain the source of social and cultural reproduction.

Muslim communities formed in the West as a result of state immigration policies.[8] In Australia, unlike the pattern of recruitment of Muslim migrant labour by the UK, France and Spain from former colonies, Muslim immigrants arrived as a result of the expansion of a post-war mass immigration policy designed to sustain planned population growth and meet labour needs for national economic development. Immigration policy is also an expression of the state's capacity for social reproduction on its own terms. It defines the borders and determines who can enter on the basis of bureaucratic classification of who are the most 'desirable' migrants – who will fit in, course no trouble and not present a security risk domestically of internationally.

While immigration policy as an instance of bureaucratic planning might approach migrants as workers, it also constructs them socially as culturally the same or different. In Australia, the relationship between immigrant communities (minorities) and the state has been shaped by a dominant narrative of cultural assimilation and naturalisation (citizenship rights). Social order was conceived as a process of social incorporation of migrants into the national culture, as in all modern Western states. The classification of difference signified distance from assimilation. As Rosaldo observed in his study of the borderzone (US – Mexico) cultural difference and visibility (ethnicity) is about distance from full citizenship and agency while cultural invisibility is a sign of full citizenship and agency.[9] In the 'assimilation' or 'integration' model of immigration, the dominant assimilating space was the nation-state. The history of immigration policy in fact neatly summarises the way the transnational movement population was to be managed and ordered.

Although Australia's mass immigration policy (White Australia) assumed recruitment from Western European (especially the British Isles), the programme became increasingly culturally diverse as the immigration net was widened in order to maintain population targets. The modernist assumption was that migrants would assimilate. Cultural difference under this nation-building project was seen as a temporary attribute of migrants that would be transformed through the culture-stripping experience of settlement, social mobility, second-generational distancing from origins and culture, and naturalisation. Characteristically the Australian mass immigration programme involved family chain migration, especially from the Mediterranean, which shaped the process of settlement, community formation and identity. In Australia, the word 'migrant' became synonymous with Mediterranean migration and came to mean a non-English speaking unskilled worker embedded in family and village community relations. Community meant 'village community', which became the basis for social and religious organisation.

In addition to opportunities created by widening the immigration catchment area, Muslim immigration to Australia has been specifically shaped by war and population displacement in the Middle East on one hand, and the introduction of multiculturalism as an ideology of national pluralism in the mid-1970s. Muslim migration rapidly increased as a direct result of the state's management of sectarian demands for equal treatment in administering a special humanitarian migration from Lebanon under multiculturalism.

I use 'diaspora Islam' to refer to first generation Muslim communities whose identities and social worlds have been largely constructed and imagined as socially bounded worlds constituted through kinship and reinforced by reconstructing family and community life in settlement. The village is a space of social intimacy, which has provided the focus for maintaining the continuity of social life. Immigrant experience was largely shaped by ethnic differentiation in the context of multicultural politics and the challenge of establishing Islam as new a minority religion. In this period Islam established itself as a multiplicity of organically developed ethnic community religions that had to work out their relationships to other Muslims as much as other ethnic communities and the dominant society. Muslims represented just another religious/ethnic migrant constituency competing for support and recognition from the state and political parties. Muslim immigrant experience of settlement involved negotiating permission to be culturally different in distinct ways. Much of the literature on Muslim presence in Australia is about different forms of discrimination Muslims faced in relation religious practice: prayer in public places (e.g. at work), dress codes, burial practices, mosque-building, and community rituals.

The immigrant relationship to the state continues to be influenced by the bureaucratic demands of the national immigration policy to be audited for 'outcomes' – i.e. immigrant 'contribution to' and 'fit with' the nation-building project. The Hansonite debate about Asian migration (the old national fear that we're going to be overrun by the 'Yellow Peril') captured the nostalgic fusion of state and nation as an ordered and homogenised sovereign space. In the same way that immigration policy determined exclusion so the auditing produced internal marginality and boundaries. Migrant categories (read 'races' or 'cultures' according to the period) have been always policed as a symbolic boundary of the state's active concern with contamination of the national body. Ironically, the social history and everyday life of minority communities, identified as suspicious, are often better known than the dominant society because of the detailed police records kept on their activities and lives – e.g. the history of Lebanese settlement in 19th and early 20th century Queensland (Anne Mansour gained invaluable insights for her PhD study on the early Lebanese migrants in Queensland in part because of these official sources).

In Australia, politicians, commentators and public opinion have made scrutinising and comparing the social 'performance' of migrants a national passtime. The use of ethnic (overseas born) or religious classifications have constantly been used to essentialise individual behaviour as cultural with the result that these categories quickly become socially stigmatised – e.g. ethnic/religious groups blamed for high levels of unemployment, anti-social behaviour of youth (gangs) and serious crime (drugs, gang rape). At an organisational level the state was more concerned managing Muslim communities and their mosque based leadership and focus through a national body such as the Australian Federation of Islamic Councils (AFIC) thereby regularising, if not centralising, the appointment/recruitment of imams and marriage celebrants. The absence of any church like or parent religious organisation in Sunni or Shi'a Islam created very democratic and organic religious organisation around specific ethnic and regional communities.

Immigration policy and national identity have always been in tension in Australia over the nature of difference that can be accommodated and the extent to which immigrants will blend in. There has always been a policing of culturally differences that are seen by the dominant society as culturally repugnant or unacceptable. In the case of Islam/Muslims there has been a consistent focus on public expressions of gender difference in Islam as symbolic of gender oppression in Islam. These include the question of the wearing of *hijab* at school and at work, legislation against female circumcision and recent laws against forced (arranged?) marriage. While these laws were not made culturally specific, they were widely understood as targeting Muslim communities.

The state's demands that minority communities take responsibility for policing themselves and addressing social problems, especially among their youth, fails to understand the nature of the crisis in Arab/Muslim diaspora organisation and authority. Hence the formation of an Arabic Council in Sydney to address the needs of second generation youth in response to public alarm about the role of Lebanese gangs and the conviction of Lebanese Muslim youth for gang-rape, and the recent formation of the Muslim Community Reference Group, are more symbolic acts of making others accountable than reflecting any actual authority or representation in these councils of elders. It is once again an expression of the state's effort to construct taxonomies of order rather than a statement about actual social organisation.

Globalised Islam

The study of Islam/Muslims in the West has largely been approached as community and immigration studies, as 'diaspora Islam'. My own study on Lebanese Muslim communities in Australia is an example.[10] Roy points out this approach was appropriate then but now there is a 'growing discrepancy between the forms taken by Islam in the West and in the cultures of origin'.[11] Islam in the West, in Australia, Europe and North America where there has been a shift from a socially embedded 'diaspora Islam' produced through immigration and settlement to an increasingly socially and culturally detached 'Islam', 'globalised Islam'.

Diaspora Islam has evolved into differentiated identities and social orientations. Roy lists five kinds Muslim socio-cultural identities amongst immigrant minorities: the kinship based community; the ethnic or national community based on language, culture and citizenship; neo-ethnic Muslim identity based on their shared origins from Muslim communities and shared culture and religious values; Muslim identity based on religion but without specific culture or language; and secularised and westernised Muslims who retain a Muslim sub-cultural ethnic identity defined more by a multicultural urban environment than by their parents ethnicity.[12] Hence, Islam/Muslim refers to a diversity of identities and social entities amongst Muslim minorities in the West.

Roy emphasises the experience of becoming a socially marginalised Muslim minority in the West, as an important factor in what he describes as 'de-culturalisation' of Muslims in the West. By 'de-culturalism' Roy means the loss of Islam's social context and thereby its social authority in the West. Thus despite the best efforts of first generation Muslim immigrants to reconstruct and reproduce social and religious life the experience of unemployment, racism and secular culture has been socially and culturally corrosive for the second generation. The new expressions of Islam in the West, especially neo-fundamentalism calling for the recovery of pristine religion, are the product of the re-islamisation of the alienated and marginalised. Religious identity is no longer contextualised in ethnic communities but by a sense of victimhood shaped by their existential experience of disadvantage in the second generation in Western cities and by the mediated witnessing continuing Muslim suffering in conflict zones.

Religious expressions of de-culturalisation are the neo-fundamentalist and Islamist movements whose concern to determine what is Islam and what is not. As Roy comments, 'the need to formulate what it means to be Muslim, to define objectively what Islam is – in short, to 'objectify' Islam – is a logical consequence of the end of the social authority of religion, due to westernisation and globalisation'.[13] Re-islamisation is a response to de-culturalisation, the loss of context of social and cultural reproduction. De-culturalisation creates the context for the cultural imaginary of recovering 'pristine' ahistorical Islam uncontaminated by cultural/ethnic influences. Globalisation also reinforces fundamentalism by creating the opportunity to build 'a universal religious identity' and by presenting itself as defence against the cultural products of globalisation – ie. corrupt and decadent westernisation.[14]

'Globalised Islam' is also distinguished from 'diaspora Islam' in its individual, rather than collective, orientation. Today, Roy argues, Islam and culture have become de-territorialised. It is no longer based on social authority or conformity but on personal belief and choice. It is about the self and the realisation of the self through faith. The globalisation of Islam is leading to its secularisation. 'Islam is experiencing secularisation, but in the name of fundamentalism'.[15] From the neo-fundamentalist perspective, the reconstruction of a true Muslim community begins with the individual and is based on 'an individual reappropriation of Islamic symbols, arguments, rhetoric and norms'.[16]

Neo-fundamentalism's project is to reconstruct 'pure' religion outside culture. Because their community is not based in actual social relations, it has to be reconstructed and experienced as an act of faith. Their global community is a virtual *umma* (community of believers) whose existence relies on their behaviour and deeds. With the de-territorialsiation of Islam there is no longer a distinguishable religious geography of *dar al-harb* and *dar al-islam*. The obsession about blasphemy and apostasy goes hand in hand with the vanishing of the social authority of Islam. Boundaries become embodied and both sides – the neo-fundamentalists and the host state – become obsessed with assessing loyalty and transgression from very different perspectives. The boundaries of Islam have to recreated daily. 'They work in minds, attitudes, and eagerly endorsed and defended because they have to be invented, and because they remain fragile and transitory'.[17]

In the Netherlands, the murder of the filmmaker Theo van Gogh by Mohammed Bouyeri was about the transgression of the filmmaker against Islam and the Somali-born woman politician Ayaan Hirsi Ali who participated in making the film to convey Islam's oppression of women. 'By slaughtering a 'blasphemer', Mohammed B. literally inscribed the boundary on his victim's throat. Do not trespass'.[18] Netherlands is probably the most liberal and secular (in the sense of allowing difference) society in Europe and the filmmaker Theo van Gogh was described in one controversial article as a 'free-speech fundamentalist on a martyrdom operation.'[19] In a society which had actively promoted multiculturalism, developed social policies towards cross cultural communication and understanding with Islam and Muslims (eg. a school for new imams), and made extensive efforts to promote equity and understanding in Holland the conflict was embodied in transgressive individuals. Socially disembedded Islam has resulted in individuals being made the surrogate borders. The intensification of the work of boundary maintenance is needed precisely because it is so fluid and de-territorialised. Therefore, these borders 'work in minds, attitudes, and discourses. They are more vocal than territorial, but also so much more eagerly endorsed and defended because they have to be invented, and because they remain fragile and transitory'.[20]

Islamic religious identity has expanded from kinship/community groups to include de-culturalised and de-territorialised forms of identity. Acculturation to globalisation as experience in the West has included the growing consciousness of Islam as a political issue – eg. the political and religious significance of Iranian revolution in reasserting Islamic authority and relevance in world affairs, the role of Hizbullah in resistance to Israeli occupation of South Lebanon, the growth in popularity of Islamic over secular nationalist parties in Palestinian politics. As a consequence the most radicalised ideological jihadists living in Europe joined up with international Islamist causes rather than going back home. Hence French neo-fundamentalists of Algerian origin went to Afghanistan, Yemen, Kashmir or even LA but not their home.[21] Jihad then was something very symbolic, martyrdom for Islam and not a bid for national power.

Integral to the cultural imagining of 'globalised Islam' and the creation of a virtual *umma* are the new global communications media; television, internet and phone. The scale of the social and cultural has been de-territorialised as a result. The state no longer has a monopoly over the production of social reality as normative and experienced as managed image flows and meanings. The global media opens up the social and cultural imagination and becomes what Appadurai calls a 'global ethnoscape'.[22] The contemporary displacement of huge numbers of people has given the imagination – or, as we might perhaps more accurately say, the exercise and representation of imagination – 'a singular new power in social life', for which the mass media are a primary source, providing a 'rich, ever-changing store of possible lives'.[23]

A vital source of this experience of the *umma* has been the global media. Moreover, now a range of alternative global TV channels such as Al Jazeera and Al Arabiyya provide regional perspectives on politics and unfolding crises in the Middle East and the Muslim world. These networks provide a counter-point to the international dominance of global western media (CNN, SKY, BBC) and they interpret the event driven course of politics within a distinct narrative with the Arab/Muslim as the focus of attention and invariably as victim. *Umma* consciousness has been raised by media globalisation, which has allowed Muslims everywhere to witness the lives of other Muslims, especially those suffering as a result of war. Solidarity with suffering co-religionists is strongly felt, as in earlier times was solidarity on the basis of Arab nationalist identity. Muslims are made witnesses to a narrative of disasters, which reiterates the long-standing theme of Muslim decline since the 19th century.

Another major source of information and communication to large remote audiences is the internet. This new global medium has created opportunities for new religious interpretation and culture across the political spectrum.

On one side, the internet has created the opportunity to establish an authoritative source of religious interpretation that is readily accessible for dispersed Muslim populations such as in the West. Hence, in Europe the 'European Council on Fatwa and Research' provides a religious internet service to give opinion on how to live a good Muslim life in the secular West. It can be argued that this one-on-one form of question and answer in private through the internet further secularises Islam by emphasising individual religious consciousness, reflection and decision making. However, the internet also provides new opportunities for religious entrepreneurship promoting a diversity of views and messages. A recent Australian initiative has been the establishment of *Darulfatwa* High Council of Australia to provide religious advice, help and leadership. It was set up with the purpose of providing an alternate leadership to AFIC and the Mufti Sheikh Hilali.[24] It sees its role as innovative and providing religious advice in new ways such as via its website.[25]

On the other hand the internet has become a source of more radical Islamic interpretation and politics, for example international jihadist messages about oppression and liberation from the West and its corrosive and decadent globalising culture. The development of the ideology and culture of martyrdom – especially suicide bombing – has been significantly reinforced through the internet where streamed videos of the messages of martyrs and their 'operations' are presented as heroic and sacred acts of violence. As Roy comments: 'At a time when the territorial borders between the great civilisations are fading away, mental borders are being reinvented to give a second life to the ghost of lost civilisations: multiculturalism, minority groups, clash or dialogue of civilisations, communautarisation and so on'.[26]

As well as the experience of marginalisation and generational disembedding of Muslims in the West, the emergence there of neo-fundamentalist outlooks in the desire to recover the pure religion and the role of global media in facilitating a new *umma* consciousness and counter hegemonic interpretation of events and political turmoil in the Muslim, another important aspect of 'globalised Islam' is the way it has become securitised – ie. become the bureaucratic object of classification and surveillance as a strategy of national security to manage new forms of dangerous global circulation.

Securitised Islam

The securitising of Islam/Muslims is a case study in the new strategies for the global management of disorder, which targets social categories for repressive or therapeutic treatment at home and abroad. The security focus is human security, the safety of population, homeland population. Prior to September 11, human security had been primarily concerned with underdevelopment and vulnerability of populations in failed states. It combines the technological intensification of classificatory systems with the ability to control image flows of events and spectacles as an integral part of security management.

The advent of international jihadist terrorism in Western global cities has transformed the state's relationship to its Muslim minorities. 'Homeland security' now constructs Muslims as a source of 'risk events'. The state's response to this new increased risk has been 'public safety wars' based on the to intensification of surveillance, classification and pre-emptive intervention on the one hand and maintenance of the appearance of order through the management of image flows on the other.

Public safety wars seek to manage global circulation as a threat to disorder in the name of human security – ie. *biopolitics*, the security of population. Pre September 11 the concept of human security sought to widen 'security concerns beyond those of the state to include the needs and well-being of people'.[27] It addressed the shift from geo-politics, the security of states, to *biopolitics*, the security of people, with particular emphasis on failed states and humanitarian crises. Although originally human security defined populations according to their vulnerability and lack of development, post September 11 'the security of 'homeland' livelihood systems and essential infrastructures (has) moved centre stage'.[28] Borderland populations have changed from being targets for protection to targets for intervention. Also global populations are now conceived as 'interconnected flow of people, information, livelihood systems, cultural networks and political dispositions' linking homeland and borderland. 'Issues of poverty, conflict and development assistance … vector through displacement, migration and asylum into the domains of immigration and homeland security'.[29]

The November riots by marginalised North African French – the word immigrant is used even though they have been in France two or more generations – demanding to be included in French society (have jobs especially) were an example of the historical legacies of the connection of homeland and borderland. When the French government decided to declare a state of emergency to control the rioting and property destruction they invoke a law first used in 1955 to manage the situation produced by the Algerian War of Independence.[30]

What Feldman calls the 'public safety wars' and Duffield outlines as the shift in focus of human security to the priority of homeland security Agambem describes as the search for security through 'a worldwide civil war which destroys all civil coexistence'.[31] National security is no longer territorially contained but de-territorialised in a new imaginary of global order, which he calls 'the worst of all orders'.[32] Because of the limitiations of any state or coalition achieving planetary order, 'security finds its end in globalisation'.[33] Globalisation is expressed as the dangerous circulation of people, goods, and ideas from danger/war zones/failed states. And because of the invisibility of these dangers human security (of one's own citizens) leads to the constant need to identify a state of exception whose initiatives (anti-terror laws, detention without charge) only lead to the de-politicisation of society (trust us!). Having worked on Argentina and the truth commissions such statements resonate with ominous consequences. In Argentina, the National Security Doctrine of the military junta (1976–1983) against subversion led to the mass abduction and disappearance of 'suspects' whose fate the public acquiesced in – 'They must have done something, we're safe because we haven't!'

Agamben points out that the new paradigm of security is articulated with globalisation. Specifically, while 'the law wants to prevent and prescribe, security wants to intervene in ongoing processes to direct them. In a word, discipline wants to produce order, while security wants to guide disorder'.[34] At the same time security has become the overwhelming priority of the state and the principle source of legitimation. Biopolitics, the governance and protection of populations, has become the focus of security. The state has raised public consciousness of its role as protector in the official terror 'alerts' advertising the level of risk and threat. This emphasis on crisis has the dual effect of demonstrating state diligence and responsibility while at the same time displacing responsibility onto individuals should anything happen – 'well we warned you'. But heightened security consciousness and biopolitics can also engender a crisis of political legitimacy if governments are seen to fail that duty of care – e.g. President George Bush's lack of urgency in response the New Orleans hurricane disaster. Security is focused on risk to populations and the failure to control risk is a threat to state legitimacy. The Australian government's response to both Bali bombings of tourist sites getting injured Australians home quickly was an important and successful expression of its management of disorder – security as biopolitics.

Integral to the new security paradigm of risk reduction is the construction of virtual worlds through technologically intensified surveillance on the one hand and the production of security as 'normality' conveyed through event and non-event management of image flows in the media. This is the production of 'the police concept of history', which divides space into ideal and safe space and risk-laden space. Police history is more about function than repression: 'that of constituting the politically visible and invisible, which includes profiling systems, militarized and surveillance-centred sitting prisms and stratagems of erasure, such as detainees without charge, trial or legal representation, and the ideology of collateral damage'.[35]

Thus profiling seeks to identify, through visual techniques, threats to the 'visible spaces of order'.[36] This idea of normative space operates at the level of the street and transnationally as global orderly circulation. 'Improper or transgressive circulation, symbolised in icons of mobile biosocial pollution such as HIV/AIDS, mad cow disease, SARS migration, the drug trade, and illegal immigrants is feared and attacked' (Feldman 2004: 33). The shift to the focus on 'improper circulation' occurs in the context of globalisation, at the moment when physical national borders have become less and less enforceable. The state in response creates 'new boundary systems that are virtual, mediatized, such as electronic, biometric and digital surveillance nets'.[37]

This surveillance however does not just watch and wait but now 'diagnoses, pre-empts, and intervenes'. All behaviours, communications and consumption, as well as racial and ethnic characteristics become digitised, dissected and archived producing a digitised citizen. These archived images will be available for retrospective reading detached from context, subjectivity and intentionality long into the future.

The attempt to reduce risk through the intensification of surveillance may deepen globalisation but may expose the limits of making the invisible visible. Laws on terrorist financing checks introduced under the US Patriot Acts have forced compliance amongst banks globally. However, the costs of global screening by private banks are enormous. The costs for a mid-size bank to check names of transactions against a UN and US 'known terrorists' list is around UK£3–4 million each time.[38] For a large multinational bank to carry out 'remediation', a time-time checking of names and details against terrorist lists, costs between UK£20–30 million. Banks comply for fear of being cut off from business with the US. As one KPMG consultant commented, 'the cost to our global economy is so large, they've (the terrorists) already had the effect they wanted.'[39] What is technologically possible may be economically unsustainable, especially when the benefit is dubious.

The other side of the security paradigm of risk reduction is spectatorship and the production of spectacles. Herzfeld points out that spectacle has been integral to the production of modern bureaucratic order where 'Spectacles are mirrors that present and reflect impressive statist visions of social order. These visions mask the formative power of statist bureaucracies to shape, discipline, and control social order'.[40]

Bureaucratic spectacle is a means of national and political homogenisation and spectators are supposed to 'relate to surface as depth'.[41] The new public safety regime requires the labour of the 'spectator-citizen' to be attentive to the unfolding of event and non-event. This creates a perpetual tension in which the non-event, the normality of uninterrupted circulation, anticipates the risk event. The Prime Minister John Howard's constant warning after terrorist attacks in Europe that we too are targets has that structure – i.e. we are waiting for the confirmatory event/spectacle.

The circulation of images articulates the police concept of history as normative. Through the prosthetic of the screen, it creates an experience of order unavailable in everyday experience or perception.[42] This normative discourse and visual culture structures events and their meaning. These digitised images produce 'a massive expansion of objective guilt as a structure of governmentality'.[43] In the 'total information awareness' approach of homeland security there will be collateral damage because of the problem of invisibility, the way security services have to act on intelligence rather than proof, because intention is constructed as collective (conspiracy) rather than individual (criminal responsibility), and because the act of revealing terrorist threats is essential for objective security (discovery of real plots) as much as for affirming the reality of subversion through visual culture.

The recent arrests of seventeen young Muslim men in Sydney and Melbourne on charges ranging from belonging to a proscribed organisation to plotting a terrorist attack was an event which made visible the risk of terrorism in Australia. Solicitors for the accused complained that the level of coverage and unconstrained commentary by politicians and police chiefs was effectively trial by media. As an event in the public safety wars, its significance was the message that the state could manage dangerous global circulation by making visible the threats and justifying with results the intensified techniques of surveillance and profiling.

The London bombing made real the risk of a homegrown terrorist attack to the Australian government and public. Up until then warnings that a terrorist attack was possible but the images of death and destruction in London and the invisibility of the plot until it happened all the more real. The government actions included strengthening their policing power by introducing more anti-terrorist legislation and by demanding that 'moderate' Muslims police their own communities for extremists. Prime Minister John Howard told the Muslim Community Reference Group – the government selected Muslim leadership group –

'to make it their 'absolute responsibility' to rein in inflammatory clerics.'[44] The targets for policing were the radical Islamic preachers and their followers in the suburbs and the visiting clerics who were prone to making extreme statements: eg the visiting cleric Sheikh Khalid Yasin who declared that the penality of homosexuality is death under shari'a and that the university was a gateway for deviation.

Prime Minister John Howard's consultation with 'moderate Muslim leaders' followed hard on the heels of an almost identical meeting Prime Minister Tony Blair held with moderate Muslim leaders in the UK in response to the London bombings in July 2005. At the end of that meeting, Blair announced 'the creation of a task force to tackle the 'evil ideology' of militant Islam, to combat social exclusion and encourage political engagement.' Abdul-Rehman Malik questioned the effectiveness of addressing Muslim radicalisation by talking with government selected representative leaders who were neither representative nor trusted by those they were supposed to speak for, and certainly not the most marginalised, disadvantaged and prone to militancy.[45] He argued that it was under their moderate ethnic/religious leadership that a more puritanical and neo-fundamentalist Islam gained popularity amongst the marginalised in the UK. 'No one group should bear the burden of representing the unrepresentable. If the government wants to eradicate the causes of terror through a battle of hearts and minds, then it will not waste time with figureheads. It must get into the inner cities and join grassroots workers in their struggle to put Muslim Britain right.'[46]

By securitising Islam/Muslims as the focus of public safety wars Islam/Muslims have been locked into a project of managing disorder globally. The limits of states being able to police dangerous global circulation is a measure of the difficulty Muslims face in trying to redefine what their religion, societies, communities and hopes are about..

Conclusion

Sociologically we face a major challenge in understanding the very notion of the scale of society and culture in a globalised and mediatised world. The response of the state (in the West) to international jihadist terrorism has been to try to extend the organisational principles of modernity – bureaucratic classification as the basis for ordering – by intensifying the same bureaucratic techniques globally. However there are no clear boundaries and the threats remain largely invisible. The strategy is to project sovereignty globally in an effort to minimise risk to one's citizens – bipolitics.

Integral to the management of risk is the production of normality through a police concept of history to demonstrate everything/body is in its proper place. Normality is produced as a virtual experience through a visual culture managing the flow of images as non-event – the news that nothing happened today. The very structure of non-event is that it anticipates the event, the terrorist act/catastrophe that threatens to bring death and disorder. Such terrorist produced spectacles are a challenge to the state's legitimacy precisely because they expose the limits of the state's capacity to effectively produce security, now focused on biopolitics (safety of populations), rather than geo-politics, and concerned with managing disorder rather than establishing order.

Contemporary Muslim experience in the West has contributed to the emergence of a globalised Islam, a de-culturalised and de-territorialised neo-fundamentalist 'pure Islam'. Diaspora Islam has been transformed by the experience of marginalisation and the loss of social authority of their cultures and relgion. But the way public safety wars have targeted Islam/Muslims as a potential source of dangerous global circulation has had the consequence of locking them into an endless symbiotic relationship because the former can never guarantee security, it can never control the dangerous global circulation of risks.

8

CONCEPTIONS OF JIHAD AND CONFLICT RESOLUTION IN MUSLIM SOCIETIES

Riaz Hassan

'Jihad' is one of the foundational concepts in Islamic religious and socio-political thought. It appears in numerous verses of the Quran and with varying connotations (see Appendix A). There is no single 'reading' of the Quranic verses which can claim primacy. Consequently, in Islamic history competing meanings of jihad have vied for their authenticity and legitimacy. An important feature of the meanings ascribed to jihad and the doctrines that have evolved around it, is that they have been profoundly shaped by the prevailing political, social and economic conditions in Islamic societies. This chapter will examine the Quranic genesis of the jihad and the doctrines associated with it. It will offer a periodisation of jihad doctrines to show their evolutions through history of Muslim societies and conclude with a discussion of contemporary Muslim opinions of conflict resolution.

The Quranic Origin of Jihad

The concept of 'jihad' predates Islam and has its origin in pre-Islamic Arabia. Etymologically the word 'jihad' is derived from the Arabic word *jahada* or *juhd* meaning ability, exertion or power. In this sense it literally means the using or exerting of one's utmost power, efforts, endeavours or ability in contending with an object of disapprobation which may be a visible enemy, the devil or one's self (*nafs*).[1] In modern Arabic the word jihad has wide semantic spectrum. It has been used to mean class struggle and the struggle between the old and the new. Even when it is used in an Islamic context, it does not always denote armed struggle. It may mean spiritual struggle for the good of Islamic society or inner struggle against one's evil inclinations.[2]

This etymology of the word 'jihad' is reflected in its usage in the Quran. It can denote any effort towards a subjectively praiseworthy aim, which need not necessarily have anything to do with religion. The meaning ascribed to it in the Quran was influenced by the ideas and warfare practices prevalent in northern Arabian tribes. Among these tribes war was a normal state and a lawful act if it was fought as a defence against aggression by other tribes. The warfare protocols followed by combatants in the tribal wars forbade killing of non-combatants, children, women and old people. These rules were also incorporated in the jihad doctrines.[3]

There is a consensus among scholars that in the Quran, the word jihad is used to call upon believers to surrender their properties and themselves in the path of Allah to make it succeed. The principle purpose of this is to 'establish prayer, give *zakat*, command good and forbid evil'. It also enjoins believers to struggle against unbelievers to convert them to Islam. The first type, which entails peaceful means, has been described as 'jihad of the tongue' and 'jihad of the pen' and is regarded as 'the greater jihad'. The second type, involving struggle and aggression, is regarded as 'the smaller jihad'.[4]

The main verses of the Quran relating to jihad are identified in Appendix A. The earliest verse sanctioning the fighting of unbelievers was revealed soon after Hijrah. ('Leave is granted to those who fight because they were wronged – surely God is able to help them – who were expelled from their habitations without right, except that they say 'Our Lord is God'. 22.44). The early Quranic verses are primarily 'instructive' in the sense that they stipulate the broad nature of jihad. The Quran calls upon the believers to surrender their properties and themselves in the path of Allah in order to achieve its principal purpose: to command good and forbid evil – in short, to establish Islamic socio-moral order.[5]

As the social and political circumstances of Muslims changed after the establishment of a nascent Islamic state in Medina, the Quranic revelations expanded to include the promise of a 'reward' for those who are killed in the jihad and to threaten the non-participants with severe punishment in the Hereafter (9.81–82; 48.16). Unlike the 'instructive' orientation of the earlier verses, these verses are oriented to 'motivating' and 'mobilising' the believers to participate in jihad. There is disagreement among scholars whether the Quran allows fighting the unbelievers as a defence against aggression or under all circumstances. As the verses in Appendix A show, both options are supported in the Quran (2.190; 9.13; 9.5; 9.29). Islamic scholarship appears to have favoured interpretations of jihad under all circumstances. The verses invoked to support this position are known as the 'sword verses'.

Within a century of its rise, Islam had expanded across much of the Middle East and had become an empire. This was a period of great Muslim conquest and consequently engendered the need for a comprehensive treatise on the nature and law of jihad. Such a treatise was written by Abd-al-Rahman al-Awzai (d 774) and Muhammad al-Shaybani (d. 804) and was the result of the consolidation of discussions and debates that have taken place on the subject since the origin of Islam. They reflected the needs and exigencies of the prevailing social and political conditions. Over time as these conditions changed with the fragmentation of the Islamic empire into several autonomous empires, the meanings of jihad doctrines also changed and were transformed into a barely disguised ideology of power, resistance and business.

Periodisation of Jihad Doctrine
The Formative Stage

In Table 1 (below), I have attempted to offer a preliminary periodisation of the jihad doctrine. The underlying logic of this periodisation is that the material conditions, and by that I mean the prevailing political, social and economic conditions, have been instrumental in shaping the dominant meaning(s) of the jihad doctrine. My argument is that *ideas have consequences*; it is the exigencies of the *consequences* desired or sought by jihadis in different periods of Islamic history that have shaped the dominant nature and meaning of the doctrine of jihad.

In the early stages of the rise of Islam in the 7th century, the practical realities would have made the political and social well-being of the Muslim community, umma, a sacramental value for Muslims. If umma prospered it was an indication that Muslims were living according to Allah's will. The experience of living in a truly Islamic community was both a cause and a consequence of observing the sacred commands. A defining characteristic of this period is that the Quran calls upon believers to undertake jihad, which is to surrender 'your properties and yourselves in the path of Allah'; the purpose of which in turn is to 'establish prayers, give zakat, command good and forbid evil'.[6]

In this period, the dominant function of the ideology of jihad was 'instructive'- instructing the believers to strive and establish the Islamic social and moral order. As long as Muslims were a small, persecuted minority in Mecca, jihad as a positive organised thrust of the Islamic movement was unthinkable. Meccan suras of the Quran are circumspect on the subject of the use of violence and generally appear to counsel

Table 1. The Jihad Doctrine: A Historical Trajectory

Historical Period (CE)	Political and Social Conditions	Doctrinal Emphasis	Type of Jihad	Comments
Early Islam 7th Century	Beginning of Islam Hijrah Establishment of the nascent Islamic state in Medina Expansion of the Islamic State/Empire	Instructive Motivational Individual duty to achieve higher piety Collective Islamic duty	Defensive Jihad Offensive Jihad	Period of Islamic expansion through conquests Rules for coexistence with non-Muslims/*dhimmis* Rules re warfare
Empire Stage 8–16th Centuries	Multiple Islamic empires Internal dynastic conflict Mongol conquests in the Middle East End of Islamic expansion	Motivational Mobilisational State sponsorship/ Individual/Collective duty Establish Islamic hegemony	Offensive Jihad against non-Muslims and Muslims	Emphasis on martyrdom Divine rewards Enhancing legitimacy of a ruler Ibn Taymiyya '*Fatwa*'
Colonisation of Muslim countries 17–19th Centuries	Colonisation of Muslim world Capitalism and Muslim economic, political and social dispossession Rise of resistance movements against colonialism, Islamic political and radical movements (Jihadi movements)	Motivational/Mobilisational Muslim duty for Jihad emphasised Jihad as ideology of resistance Apologetic/ Modernist	Defensive but largely offensive against non-Muslim Colonial rulers	*Dar ul-Islam* and *Dar ul-Harb* Territorial Islamic identity Non-State actors mobilising Jihad Apologetic/Modernist orientations

Post-Colonial and Cold War period, mid–late 20th century	Failure of the 'national project' Economic underdevelopment and political instability; Alliance with the West Islamic radicalism2	Mobilisational. Jihad for an Islamic state Fighting Soviets in Afghanistan Muslim societies as 'jahiliyya'	Offensive Jihad targeting governing elite in Muslim countries and their Western allies	Rise of political Islam Operation Cyclone US funding of Jihadi Groups Privatisation of Jihad; Competing visions of Islamic state – Iran and Taliban State and non-State actors as sponsors. Revivalist Orientation
Post-modern/Post Cold War period 1990 -	Failure of 'national project' Repressive authoritarianism Globalisation and democratizing movements increasing access to global financial network Increasing literacy Sense of humiliation due to Muslim subordination to the West	Islamic fundamentalism Struggle for Islamic state Offensive Jihad against the West/US Jihad as defence of *Dar ul-Islam* Duty to Allah Martyrdom operations	Defensive Offensive	Jihad as a business Terrorism as the main tactic under asymmetrical distribution of military and economic power Reinforcing territorial and national project identity Declining state/public support of Jihadis Increasing privatisation of Jihad

its avoidance.[7] When Hijrah (emigration) was forced upon Mohammad and his followers by the Meccan opponents of Islam, resulting in their migration in 622 to Medina, all that changed. The Quranic revelation, 'Leave is given to those who fight because they are wronged ... who were expelled from their dwellings without right' (22:39), essentially granted permission to take up arms against the Meccan opponents.

After the establishment of the Islamic state in Medina, the situation changed and there is hardly anything, with the possible exception of prayers and *zakat*, which receive greater emphasis than jihad.[8] The mandate for force granted at Medina was eventually broadened (2:191,217) until, it would appear, war could be waged against non-Muslims at almost any time or any place. Quran 9:5 – 'Slay the idolaters wherever you find them' – is a broad permission for war against the unbelievers. In the traditional Muslim understanding of this revelation, it was thought to have abrogated all earlier limitations on the use of violence against unbelievers.[9] During this period jihad was viewed as a duty to achieve greater piety, in order to establish Islam's moral and social order. It was carried out under the aegis of *umma*. It was, in short, a means to construct and establish an Islamic identity.

The Empire Stage

The period from the 8th to the 16th century was remarkable for a number of reasons. First, this was a period of full tide for Muslim expansion and second, it saw the fragmentation of the Muslim empire into several autonomous empires ruled by local political and Islamic elites. Expansion of Islam during this period brought Muslims into contact with non-Muslims as subjects in the conquered territories. For Muslim religious and political elites it forced the question about the terms of co-existence with other religious ideologies and their followers who had come under Islamic rule.

The expansion of the Islamic empire, its subsequent fragmentation and its coming into contact with other ideological systems created the need for the development of a coherent doctrine of jihad. This led Muslim jurists al-Shaybani (d.804) and Shaffi'i (d. 820) to bring together the Quranic texts and hadith about jihad to formulate a doctrine of jihad. In this doctrine the world was divided into the Abode of Islam (*Dar ul-Islam*) and the Abode of War (*Dar ul-Harb*). In the first Islamic law and sovereignty prevailed and the second included lands that were not yet under the moral and political authority of Islam. According to this doctrine the Abode of Islam is in a permanent state of warfare with the Abode of War until the latter submits. Jihad is the instrument by which that subjection will be accomplished. Hostilities between the two spheres may be suspended by armistice or truce, but they will never be concluded by peace, only by submission. This doctrine also stipulated the duty towards jihad, people eligible to participate in it, the conditions of provocation of jihad and rules of warfare.[10]

Jihad doctrine from the early days of Islam stipulated that there was a religious obligation for Muslims to resist the enemies of Islam. The division of the world into *Dar ul-Islam* and *Dar ul-Harb*, besides delineating the boundaries between *umma* and enemies, also implied that the threat to the Islamic community came from external sources. During the period of rapid expansion of Islam and the subsequent fragmentation of its empire, it became apparent that Islam also had internal enemies who threatened the faith either as apostates or because they refused to meet their Islamic obligations such as payment of *zakat*. By the thirteenth century, the problem of internal enemies involved Muslim rulers such as the Mongols. The Mongols after having conquered and destroyed the heartlands of Islam had converted to Islam and became its rulers. Was it then permissible to fight the destructive Muslim warlords?

According to the noted Syrian jurist Ibn Taymiyah (d. 1328), the profession of Islam was not enough. Though by criterion of the *shahada* they were Muslims, the Mongols violated the broader requirements of Islam. They still lived according to their own pagan law, which rendered them unbelievers. According to Ibn Taymiyah a true Muslim must live according to Islamic law and must not attack the lives and wealth of Muslims. He argued that, 'any trespasser of the law should be fought… provided he had knowledge of the mission of the Prophet. It is this knowledge that makes him responsible for obeying the orders, the prohibitions, and the permits (of the shari'a). If he disobeys these, he should be fought'.[11] As Mongols lived according to their personal law which rendered them unbelievers, it was an Islamic duty to fight them. Jihad against them was not only licit but required. Ibn Tymiyah's fatwa still resonates today among fundamentalist Muslims.

Throughout Islamic history, governments and opposition movements have declared their Muslim opponents as heretics or unbelievers (*kafir*) in order to justify their struggle against them. The *fatwas* of Ibn Taymiyah influenced the views of the ideologues of modern Islamic radicalism like Abu A'la Al-Mawdudi and Sayyid Qutb and are often invoked by contemporary radical Islamic groups to give legitimacy to their use of arms against Muslim rulers they oppose. (This view was forcefully articulated in the pamphlet *Al-faridah al-ghaiba* (*The Absent Duty*) authored by Abd al-Salam Faraj, the leader of the jihad organisation which assassinated President Anwar Sadat of Egypt in 1981.[12] Al-Qaeda's leaders have used similar reasoning to incite Muslims in Pakistan, Saudi Arabia and other countries to take up jihad against the ruling elites in these countries. The financial support for jihad during this phase came from the state and from the war booty distributed among the fighters.

The Colonial Period

Between the 17th and 19th centuries, much of the Muslim world was conquered and colonised by European countries. The political aspects of colonialism had effectively resulted in the disenfranchisement of Muslim elites. The economic consequences, which flowed from the expansion of capitalism under colonialism, resulted in a massive economic dislocation of the Muslim bourgeoisie, artisans, peasants and a whole range of other groups. This economic and social dispossession was accompanied by cultural devaluation. Sociologically, it was not surprising that colonial rule and the political, economic and cultural domination that followed, led to the development of resistance movements across all Muslim countries.

Resistance among the local populations against the foreign rulers, at least in the initial stages, was organised by politico-religious movements under the banner of jihad. A partial list of these movements included the following: the Aceh war (1873–1904) in the Dutch East Indies; the Mahadist movement of Muhammad ibn Abdallah (1899–1920) in Somalia; the Tobacco revolt of 1891 in Iran; the Tariqa-i- Muhammadi Jihadi movement of Sayyid Ahmad Barelwi (1786–1831) and the Faraidi movement (1781–1840) in India; Algerian resistance against the French led by Abd Al-Qadir (1832–1852); the Mahadist movement of Mohammad Ahmad against the British and the Egyptians in Sudan in the late 19th and early 20th centuries; Egyptian resistance led by Ahmad Urabi against the British occupation; Sanusi resistance against Italian colonialism in Libya; the Ottoman Jihad –declaration of 1914; and Palestinian resistance against British colonialism and Zionism in the early and mid 20th century.

In the resistance against Western colonialism, the doctrine of jihad was of paramount importance. However, it was not the only religious doctrine that was invoked by the leaders of these movements. Just as the Prophet did during his lifetime, the call for jihad was often accompanied by the call for emigration (*hijrah*) from territory ruled by unbelievers. Another concept employed frequently in these movements belongs to the realm of Islamic eschatology. This is the belief in the coming of the

Mahdi, the rightly guided one, who will restore justice on earth and put an end to corruption and oppression.[13]

These movements were also Islamic revivalist movements, striving for reforms in order to ban all pernicious religious innovations (*bida*) and to achieve an amelioration of the present corrupt society with political and social organisations working for the liberation of the Muslim community from unbelievers. They all had popular mass support among the rank and file of local Muslims. Some of the contemporary jihadi movements trace their roots to these movements or were inspired by their example. They were very much motivational in mobilising movements for defensive and offensive jihad. It is this legacy that they passed on to the contemporary jihadi movements. The emphasis of the jihad doctrine was on expansion and was offensive. Financial support came from non-state organisations and from individual Muslims and Muslim religious institutions.

The Post Colonial and Cold War Period

By the middle of the 20th century, most Muslim countries had achieved independence from direct colonial rule. This was also the period characterised by the 'Cold War' between the two global super powers – the Soviet Union and the US. The independence of Muslim countries from colonial rule did not bring the promised economic, political and social rewards by way of better economic opportunities and political and social freedom and stability. Most Muslim countries were ruled by authoritarian, oppressive and corrupt regimes. In short, the 'national project' had failed dismally. These conditions shaped the nature and scope of jihadi movements in the Muslim world. The ideology of jihad, which these movements advocated, had some historical continuity with the preceding epochs but certain new features were added to the jihad doctrine.

The failure of the 'national project' had given rise to the ideology of the Islamic State. While there is no clear enunciation of this concept, it generally involved the introduction of Islamic economics and Islamic shari'a law. The origin of the idea of the Islamic State probably was laid down in the works of Pakistani social thinker Abul-Ala Mawdudi. In his voluminous writings, Mawdudi exhorted that Islam is much more than a set of rituals. It encompasses all domains of human existence including politics, law, art, medicine and economics.[14] The realisation of an Islamic utopia required the establishment of an Islamic State. Given the erudition and scope of Mawdudi's scholarship, this is puzzling since, of the 6666 verses of the Quran, less than 300 refer to institutional rules.

The other seminal contributions to the notion of the Islamic State came from Egyptian Sayyid Qutb (1906–1966) and Muhammad Baqir al-Sadr (1931–1980), an Iraqi.

The genesis of the notion of an Islamic State can be traced back to the classical formulations of *Dar ul-Islam* and *Dar ul-Harb*. *Dar ul-Islam* was the domain of Islam based on Islamic law, which was in continuous war with *Dar ul-Harb*, the domain of the infidels. The essential character of the *Dar ul-Islam*, therefore, was territory. It was the territory of Islam which had been taken over first by the infidel colonial rulers and then by the secular Muslim elites who were subordinated to the former rulers. The idea that Islamic identity could only be realised in an Islamic state was, in the final analysis, an expression of territorial identity politics.[15] This identity was aided by increasing literacy, urbanisation and industrialisation.

The territorial identity politics aimed at the establishment of an Islamic State was the inspiration for a number of Muslim organisations that advocated jihad for its realisation. These included Jammat-e- Islami, Muslim Brotherhood, Islamic Jihad, Hizbullah, Hammas, Jammah Islamia, Islamic Salvation Front, Islamic Republican Party, the Taliban and al-Qaeda. Many of these organisations now have several splinter groups and affiliates striving for jihad in most Muslim countries.

The Cold War aided the development and support of Islamic jihadi movements. During the period of the Cold War, the two super powers funded and supported various proxy wars at the periphery of their sphere of influence. This is best illustrated by Afghanistan. After the Soviet 'occupation' of Afghanistan, the US and its ally, Saudi Arabia, provided financial and military support to the Mujahadeen fighting the Soviet occupation. According to some estimates, the Central Intelligence Agency (CIA) of the US, under its operation code named 'Operation Cyclone', provided four billion dollars to the promotion of Islamic Mujahadeen activities.[16] Saudi Arabia and Pakistan gave substantial additional financial support. In the course of supporting the Afghan war, which culminated in the Taliban ruling the country (until they were overthrown by the US after the September 11, 2001 attacks by al-Qaeda in New York and Washington DC) the Pakistani military intelligence agency ISI was transformed into a major clandestine supporter of the jihadi groups in Afghanistan, Pakistan and Kashmir.

In short, the jihadi movements in this period were driven by Muslim territorial identity to explain the failure of the national project in the Muslim world in the postcolonial period. Individuals derive inner satisfaction from a secure and unambiguous identity. Such an identity was found to be wanting in most Muslim lands because of economic and social dispossession during colonialism and by their dismal economic and political performance. Just as a person whose house suffers damage will undertake repairs, people whose identity have lost focus or become depreciated will try to redefine themselves and establish a clearer sense of who they are. This was the sociological driver of the Muslim intellectuals' search for an Islamic state governed by Divine law.[17]

The establishment of an Islamic State in the lands of Islam, Darul-Islam, required ridding Muslim countries of secularist pro-western ruling regimes. Jihadi activities were spearheaded by generally well organised Islamic organisations which were funded through Islamic institutional philanthropy and private donations in cash and kind. Some of these organisations began to receive financial support from Iran after the Islamic Revolution of 1979. Ironically, some of the jihadi groups were supported by the US, Saudi and Pakistani governments during the Cold War period to fight the Soviet occupation of Afghanistan.

The Modern and Post Cold War Period

By the late 1980s and early 1990s the Cold War had ended and with it the aggressive super-power rivalry. After the disintegration of the Soviet Union in 1991, there was only one super power left. The failure of the national project in all Muslim countries had become their defining characteristic. The absence of any viable secular revolutionary alternative had led to the entrenchment of repressive authoritarian regimes of all ideological persuasions – Islamic, secular, fascist, nationalist, and socialist. Muslim societies had generally failed to incorporate the growing numbers of young people into productive economic activities. The key societal institutions such as the public education system, judiciary, public bureaucracy and municipalities, began to lose public support. The result was the large-scale alienation of a growing segment of the population, especially the young, from the national economy and polity.

This period coincided with the growth of globalisation, the communication revolution led by computers and the Internet and the growth of global capital and labour markets. In the 1980s with the Afghan 'jihad' funded mainly by the US and Saudi Arabia, a large number of 'madrassas' (religious schools), the main supplier of jihadi labour, had been established in Pakistan. Prior to 1980 there were only 700 religious schools in Pakistan and their growth rate was around 3 per cent per year. According to one estimate, by the late 1990s there were 7000 religious madrassas in that country with some even awarding postgraduate degrees.[18] Their students were the mainstay of the Jihadis.

There were also a growing number of Islamic minded students in the high schools, colleges and universities in most Muslim countries. After the Afghan war, which heralded the demise of the Soviet Union, the US funds for Jihadi activities had dried up and Saudi state support had waned. Official Saudi support was replaced by support from Saudi charities.

A striking feature of this period is the 'privatisation' of Jihadi activities. Jihadi activities and culture were being promoted under the aegis of well and not so well organised jihad organisations funded by Islamic charities (some of the jihadi organisations in Pakistan collect donations by force).[19] The Jihadis are also being funded by an international network of terrorist organisations. According to one estimate, the global terrorist economy can be as large as US$500 billion.[20] There are now hundreds of religious and sectarian jihad organisations in Pakistan alone and the same pattern may well prevail in other Muslim countries although there aren't reliable estimates of that as yet.

The movement towards privatisation has added a new dimension to jihadi activities in many Muslim countries. The ideology of jihad is driven by the need to repair Muslim identity, with the honour of Islam having been damaged by the ruling classes who are seen as secular and anti Islamic. A jihadi ideologue like Osama bin Laden has declared that the profanation of Islam's holy places justifies jihad against the ruling elites and the Western powers that support them. He has also declared that when an enemy enters the land of Islam, jihad becomes individually obligatory. This territorialised religious identity is a resistance identity. It offers no program of reform and only relatively vague notions of establishing an Islamic state. There are significant differences between different jihadi organisations as to what these notions might mean in practice and reality.

Privatisation has transformed jihad activities into a kind of 'business'. The *madrassas* are given money to recruit young men for jihad. The teaching imparted in these *madrassas* is limited to particular and often uncritical reading of the sacred texts. From Imam Masjids to *madrassa* teachers and *ulema*, it is just something they do as a 'job' and not out of a deep ideological commitment through an understanding of Islamic teachings and history.

During my fieldwork in Pakistan in early 2005, I came across examples that signified the business like orientation to jihad. According to a report in the English language newspaper *International News* (January 5, 2005), Islamic 'terrorists' arrested in Lahore for a series of rocket attacks against international and national targets were unemployed youths and small-time 'hoodlums'. They were reported to have admitted that they had close contacts with a senior al-Qaeda operator in Lahore.[21] According to another press report the Government of Pakistan paid huge amounts of money to four of the most wanted Islamic militants fighting the Pakistan armed forces in northern Waziristan who had surrendered and signed a peace deal with the authorities. The payment was made to enable them to repay al-Qaeda who had given them money to fight Pakistani forces.[22]

Jihad in the Contemporary Muslim World

It is important to note that not all Muslims are jihadis but all jihadis are Muslims. Recent studies show that the Muslim world is undergoing a religious renaissance. Islam plays an important role in the lives of an increasing number of Muslims around the world. For a very large majority of Muslims this entails increasing their commitment to the observance of Islamic tenets. Many Muslims are sympathetic to re-establishing the purity of their faith by following its practice during the Prophet's time. Many also believe in the establishment of an Islamic state based on Islamic law and in strengthening the concept of *umma*.[23] These Muslims, who constitute a large majority, may be described as Islamists. Jihadis on the other hand would include Muslims who combine these beliefs with reviving the anti-imperial warrior tradition, adding the duty of *qital*, combat against enemies. They add active aggression and *qital* to devotional religiosity.[24] This chapter deals with the latter who comprise a very small group of Muslims.

Jihadi religious movements now span the Muslim world. Most of them are loosely structured national movements. These include Jemaah Islamia, Laskar Jihad, Indonesia; Kumpulan Mujahideen, Malaysia; Pattani United Liberation front, MILF and Abu Sayyaf Group, Laskar-e Toiba, Hizbul Mujahideen, Taliban, Joishe Mohammad, Harkutul Jehad; Islamic Movement of Uzbekistan; Hamas; the Armed Islamic Group of Algeria (GIA); Egyptian Islamic Jihad (Tanzim al-Jihad); Al-Ansar Mujahdin of Chechnya; Ansar al-Islam and Abu Musab Al-Zarqawi Network in Iraq.[25]

A few, such as al-Qaeda and Hizb ut Tahrir, are loosely organised international networks. There is little unity in the meaning of the doctrine of jihad enunciated by these and similar groups. Their interpretations and practices depend on the political and strategic positions taken by their leadership. However, there are some common threads that bind them. They subscribe to the ideologies of Islamic ideologues like Sayyid Qutb and Abu A'la Al-Mawdudi, that the Lands of

Islam have been corrupted by un-Islamic and secularist regimes in Muslim countries and by their Western allies resulting in their profanation. To establish an authentic Islamic identity these regimes must be overthrown and replaced by an Islamic state.[26] The Declaration of Jihad by The Islamic Movement of Uzbekistan in Appendix B is typical of such declarations.

Modern jihadi movements are largely secretive, cellular organisations led by charismatic leaders. Their members are drawn from a cross section of society. Most of these organisations do not enjoy active mass support although many Muslims may be passively sympathetic to their cause for a variety of reasons. According to one study (based on 130 cases) 'international jihadis' are a heterogenous group. About 60 per cent came from core Arab countries, mostly Saudi Arabia and Egypt; 30 per cent from Maghreb Arab countries and 10 per cent from Indonesia. Two thirds came from established upper and middle class background. Most of the others came from alienated Maghreb immigrants and Western Christian converts. They came from in tact families and most but not all were devoutly religious. The average age for joining the jihadi movement for Arabs was 23 and for Indonesians it was 30 with 26 years being average for the group as a whole.[27]

They were well educated with over 60 per cent having some college education. Only the Indonesians were exclusively educated in religious schools. Most had good occupational training. Only a minority were unskilled with limited economic prospects. Three quarters were married and most had children. None suffered from mental illness or showed any common psychological predisposition to terror. Over 80 per cent had joined the jihad movement while they were living in a country away from family and friends where they felt cut off from their cultural and social origins. The most striking feature revealed by the study was that these jihadis felt isolated, lonely and emotionally alienated.[28]

The funding of jihadi activities is primarily through private sources and Islamic charitable donations. The organisations sponsoring them tend to be male dominated and often characterised by misogynist attitudes and male chauvinism.[29] The ideologies of Islamist movements in general and jihad movements in particular have been criticised for their lack of viable economic and political programmes that are seriously flawed. In addition, their highly skewed interpretations of Islamic texts and Islamic history, and the sanctioning of the killing of innocent Muslims and non-Muslims have been criticised.[30]

Attitudes toward Conflict Resolution

Given that jihadi organisations span the Muslim world and are actively pursuing their agendas, does this mean that they have popular support among the Muslim masses? There is no empirical evidence to answer this question reliably. There is evidence, however, which has an indirect bearing on this question. An increasingly popular tactic used by some of the main jihadi organisations against their perceived enemies is suicide bombing. The attitudes of the Muslim masses towards this phenomenon can provide some indication of their support of, at least, this tactic of the jihadi movements.

In 2003, the Pew Research Centre in Washington D.C. surveyed attitudes of Muslim respondents in Turkey, Pakistan, Morocco and Jordan towards suicide bombings by Palestinians against Israelis and by Iraqi jihadis against Americans and Westerners in Iraq. The findings (see Table 2), show that a significant majority in Morocco and Jordan supported suicide bombings against Israelis, Americans and Westerners in Iraq, and about half of the Pakistanis expressed the same attitude. Only in Turkey a majority of the respondents did not support suicide bombings. If we were to use the level of support for suicide bombings as a proxy for the support of the jihadis, it would indicate that these tactics command moderate to significant levels of support in the surveyed countries. The reasons for the support probably would vary from one Muslim country to another. From this evidence one can infer that jihad may have popular support in some if not in all Muslim countries.

Table 2: Attitudes of Muslims towards suicide bombings

Suicide bombing is justifiable by Palestinians against Israelis		YES	NO
	Turkey	67	24
	Pakistan	36	47
	Morocco	22	74
	Jordan	12	86
Suicide bombing is justifiable against Westerners and Americans in Iraq	Turkey	59	31
	Pakistan	36	46
	Morocco	27	66
	Jordan	24	70

Source: The Pew Research Center for the People & the Press, 2004, *A Year after Iraq War; Mistrust of America in Europe Ever Higher*

Table 3: War is justified when other ways of settling international disputes fail %

Countries		Egypt			Indonesia			Iran			Kazakhstan			Malaysia			Pakistan			Turkey		
		A	D	U	A	D	U	A	D	U	A	D	U	A	D	U	A	D	U	A	D	U
All		64	17	20	33	44	22	58	22	20	11	62	27	38	50	12	67	21	11	66	26	8
Gender	Male	63	16	22	34	44	23	58	21	21	10	63	26	44	45	10	68	20	11	71	24	5
	Female	66	21	13	33	46	21	60	22	18	12	60	29	31	55	15	62	21	14	60	29	12
Age group	Under 26	67	18	15	38	39	23	60	21	20	10	55	35	34	50	15	59	24	1	64	26	10
	26–40	62	16	22	33	45	23	58	25	17	11	60	30	43	46	11	68	21	10	63	29	8
	41–55	65	18	17	32	46	22	600	19	21	10	68	23	36	56	8	71	18	10	72	24	4
	56 and over	64	19	18	32	46	22	54	11	34	14	64	22	35	53	12	67	16	15	84	11	5
Education group	<High school	66	17	18	29	49	22	46	21	33	10	64	26	34	53	13	68	20	12	75	19	6
	High school	75	6	19	35	40	25	61	20	19	11	61	28	34	53	13	68	16	12	64	28	8
	Tertiary	55	19	27	33	48	19	5	23	18	4	88	8	42	45	12	67	21	11	57	33	10

Key: **A** = Agree Percentages are rounded to the nearest 0.5 whole number; **D** = Disagree; **U** = Uncertain

Another indirect way to ascertain the support for jihadi activism may be through the attitudes of Muslims towards war and the place of war in conflict resolution. In a recently concluded study of seven Muslim countries over 6 000 Muslim respondents were asked the following question: 'Is war is justified when other ways of settling international disputes fail?' The results of the survey, reported in Table 3, show an interesting divide among Muslim countries.

The agreement rates in the four South Asian and the Middle Eastern countries ranged from 58 per cent in Iran to 63 per cent in Egypt and 66 per cent in Pakistan and Turkey. The agreement rates for the respondents in the two Southeast Asian Muslim countries, namely Indonesia and Malaysia, were significantly lower and ranged from 37 per cent in Malaysia to 33 per cent in Indonesia. The Kazak Muslims had the lowest agreement rate with only 11 percent agreeing with the statement. In Indonesia, Malaysia and Kazakhstan the disagreement rates were also significantly higher compared with the other countries.

The analysis of data by gender, age and education shows that university educated respondents in Egypt, Iran, Kazakhstan and Turkey were least inclined to agree that war was justified even when other ways of settling disputes had failed. In Pakistan education had no effect on the disagreement rate but in Indonesia and Malaysia the higher the education the higher the rate of agreement. In Malaysia, Pakistan and Turkey men had higher agreement rates than women. Perhaps the most significant variable, relative to the lower level of support for war as a vehicle to resolve international issues, was the level of education (see Table 3).

What are the implications of these findings for jihadi activities? It is difficult to draw definitive and firm conclusions. It is perhaps reasonable to suggest that the prevalence of lower educational levels in the populations of Muslim countries probably would be more conducive to generating support for jihadi activities. The levels of support may vary depending on who the perceived 'enemies' are. In this respect these findings reinforce the importance of the success of the national project for resolving religious, political and social conflicts through peaceful means.

Concluding Remarks

Jihad in Islamic history has served as an ideology of personal striving to achieve superior piety and collective struggle in order to establish an Islamic moral and social order to 'command good and forbid evil'. In the centuries following the rise of Islam the meaning of jihad was expanded to legitimise the Muslim conquests of non-Muslim lands. After the

European colonisation of Muslim territories, jihad became an ideology of resistance against colonial rule (and its rulers). For militant Islamic groups in the contemporary Islamic world jihad has become an ideology of resistance and armed struggle allegedly against 'oppressive' and 'apostate' Muslim regimes and their 'infidel imperialist' supporters. Increasingly it has come to symbolise the armed struggle for the establishment of an Islamic State and a 'purer' Islamic identity. In recent years, the strategy of armed struggle has been replaced by acts of national, sectarian and international terrorism. I have argued that the nature of jihad doctrine and its expression have been profoundly shaped by historical and material conditions prevailing in Muslim societies.

The sponsorship of jihad has ranged from individual Muslims to umma, Islamic rulers and 'private' jihadi organisations funded by Muslim charities. The privatisation of jihadi activities appears to be evolving into 'businesses'. The sponsorship of jihad also has been shaped by the historical conditions. The chapter has noted that while all jihadis are Muslims not all Muslims are jihadis. In fact only a very small fraction of Muslims actively support jihadi organisations and their activities. The lack of public interest and support in the trials and subsequent convictions of the Bali Bombers in Indonesia is just one illustration of that. The jihadi organisations are cellular and secretive and run by charismatic leaders who command intense loyalty among their followers.

The evidence reviewed in the chapter shows that the attitudes towards war, as a vehicle for resolving international disputes, vary significantly in Muslim countries. While South Asian and the Middle Eastern Muslims show greater proclivity towards using war as an instrument for resolving international disputes, Muslims in the Southeast and Central Asian countries of Indonesia, Malaysia and Kazakhstan are less likely to share that view. More educated Muslims are less likely to support war as an instrument of conflict resolution. In this respect, these findings reinforce the significant role of education as a moderating influence on attitudes towards violence and terrorism.

The chapter has also indicated that there is increasing and substantial evidence that the Muslim world is undergoing a religious renaissance. Does this mean that this development will increase support for jihad among Muslims? The evidence suggests that that is not what may be happening. Religious piety in Muslim countries appears to be associated with a decline in support of militant organisations. Most of the Muslims do not belong to jihadi movements. Religiosity, in fact, appears to be positively associated with democratic and tolerant attitudes. This may be a reason contributing to the increasing militancy of jihadi movements because declining support increases their isolation, which in turn makes them more secretive, assertive and violent. The ruthlessness of their violence reflects a desire to gain public attention and is symptomatic of their desperation.[31] As Kepel has observed the September 11 attack on the US was a desperate symbol of the isolation, fragmentation and decline of the jihadi movement not one of its strength and irrepressible might.[32]

It is also possible that jihadi organisations will have a degree of passive support among Muslims. That may be due not to the efficacy of their message but due to the imperialistic policies, what Michael Mann has called 'The New Militarism', being followed by Western powers, especially the US.[33] These include the 'War on Terrorism', which is viewed by many in the Muslim world as 'War on Islam'. Jihadi groups also receive support from their coreligionists' concerns with Muslim sufferings resulting from a long list of transgressions against Muslims over the past fifty years. These include:

- The destruction of Palestine and continued dehumanisation of the Palestinian people;
- The million or so Afghans killed in the war with the Soviets and the tens of thousands more through US bombing;
- The million Iraqi dead from the 1991 Gulf War and subsequent Western inspired sanctions;
- Over 100 000 Iraqis killed since the 2003 Iraqi invasion, and
- Thousands killed in the Balkans, Chechnya and Kashmir conflicts, as well as in Algeria following the overturning of democracy at the prospect of an Islamist victory.

The scale of Muslim suffering-called by some a holocaust[34] – provide those who espouse jihad against the perpetrators with moral stature and justifiable rectitude. This development can severely affect the legitimacy of secular and modernist Muslim leaders and their reform agenda, which would have serious long-term implications.

APPENDIX A
QURANIC FOUNDATIONS OF THE DOCTRINE OF JIHAD

S2.190   Fight in the cause of Allah those who fight you but do not transgress limits; For Allah loveth not transgressors.

S2.191   And slay them wherever ye catch them, and turn them out from where they have turned you out; For persecution is worse than slaughter but fight them not at the sacred mosque unless they (first) fight you there; But if they fight you, slay them. Such is the reward of those who reject faith.

S2.193   And fight them on until there is no more persecution and the religion becomes Allah's. But if they cease, let there be no hostility except to those who practice oppression.

S2.195   And spend of your substance in the cause of Allah, and make not your own hands contribute to (your) destruction; But do good; For Allah loveth those who do good.

S2.216   Fighting is prescribed Upon you, and ye dislike it. But it is possible that ye dislike a thing which is good for you. And that ye love a thing which is bad for you. But Allah knoweth, and ye know not.

S2.217   They ask thee concerning fighting in the prohibited month. Say: 'Fighting therein is a grave (offence); but graver is it in the sight of Allah to prevent access to the path of Allah to deny him, to prevent access to the Sacred Mosque, and drive out its members.' Tumult and oppression are worse than slaughter. Nor will they cease fighting you until they turn you back from your faith if they can. And if any of you turn back from their faith and die in unbelief, their works will bear no fruit in this life and in the Hereafter; They will be companions of the Fire and will abide therein.

S2.244   Then fight in the cause of Allah and know that Allah heareth and knoweth all things

S3.157   And if ye are slain, or die in the way of Allah, forgiveness and mercy from Allah are far better than all they could amass.

S3.158   And if ye die, or are slain, Lo! It is unto Allah that ye are brought together.

S3.169   Think not of those who are slain in Allah's way as dead. Nay, they live, finding their sustenance from their Lord.

S3.170   They rejoice in the bounty provided by Allah: And with regard to those left behind, who have not yet joined them (in their bliss), the (martyrs) glory in the fact that on them is no fear, nor have they (cause to) grieve.

S3.171   They rejoice in the Grace and the Bounty from Allah, and in the fact that Allah suffereth not the reward of the Faithful to be lost (in the least).

S3.172   Of those who answered the call of Allah and the Messenger, even after being wounded, those who do right and refrain from wrong have a great reward;

S4.74   Let those fight in the cause of Allah who sell the life of this world for the Hereafter. To him who fighteth in the cause of Allah, – whether he is slain or gets victory – soon shall We give him a reward of great (value).

S4.75   And why should ye not fight in the cause of Allah and of those who, being weak, are ill-treated (and oppressed)? – Men, women, and children, whose cry is: 'Our Lord! Rescue us from this town. Whose people are oppressors; And raise for us from Thee one who will protect; And raise for use from Thee one who will help!'

S4.76   Those who believe fight in the cause of Allah, and those who reject Faith fight in the cause of Evil (Tagut): So fight ye against the friends, of Satan: feeble indeed is the cunning of Satan.

S4.84   Then fight in Allah's cause – Thou art held responsible only for thyself – and rouse the Believers. It may be that Allah will restrain the fury of the unbelievers; For Allah is the strongest in might and in punishment

S8.39   And fight them on until there is no more persecution, and religion becomes Allah's in its entirety but if they cease, verily Allah doth see all that they do.

S8.61   But if the enemy incline toward peace, do thou (also) incline towards peace, and trust in Allah: for He is the One that heareth and knoweth (All things).

S8.65   O Prophet! Rouse the Believers to the fight. If there are twenty amongst you, patient and persevering, they will vanquish two hundred: if a hundred, they will vanquish a thousand of the Unbelievers: for these are a people without understanding.

S9.5   But when the forbidden months are past, then fight and slay the Pagans wherever ye find them, and seize them, beleaguer them, and lie in wait for them in every strategem (of war); But if they repent, and establish regular prayers. And pay Zakat then open the way for them: For Allah is Oft-forgiving, Most merciful.

S9.13   Will ye not fight people who violated their oaths, plotted to expel the Messenger, and attacked you first? Do we fear them? Nay, It is Allah Whom ye should more justly fear, if ye believe!

S9.14   Fight them, and Allah will punish them by your hands, and disgrace them help you (to victory) over them, Heal the breasts of Believers.

S9.15   And still the indignation of their hearts. For Allah will turn (in mercy) to whom He will: and Allah is All-Knowing, All-Wise.

S9.20   Those who believe and emigrate and strive with might and main, in Allah's cause, with their goods and their persons, Have the highest rank in the sight of Allah: They are the people who will achieve (salvation)

S9.29   Fight those who believe not in Allah nor the Last Day, nor hold that forbidden which hath been forbidden by Allah and His Messenger, nor acknowledge the Religion of Truth, from among the People of the Book, until they pay the Jizya with willing submission, and feel themselves subdued.

S9.81   Those who were left behind (n the Tabuk expedition) rejoiced in their sitting back behind the Messenger of Allah: they hated to strive and fight, with their goods and their persons, in the Cause of Allah: they said, 'Go not forth in the heat.' Say, 'the fire of Hell is fiercer in heat,' If only they could understand!

S9.91   There is no blame on those who are infirm, or ill, or who find no resources to spend (on the Cause), if they are sincere (in duty) to Allah and His Messenger: No ground (of complaint) can there be against such as do right: and Allah is Oft-forgiving, Most Merciful.

S9.123   O ye who believe! Fight the Unbelievers who are near to you and let them find harshness in you: and know that Allah is with those who fear Him.

S22.39   To those against whom war is made, permission is given (to fight), because they are wronged; – and verily, Allah is Most Powerful for their aid; –

S22.40   (They are) those who have been expelled from their homes in defiance of right, – (For no cause) except that they say, 'Our Lord is Allah'. Did not Allah check one set of people by means of another, there would surely have been pulled down monasteries, churches, synagogues, and mosques, in which the name of Allah is commemorated in abundant measure. Allah will certainly aid those who aid His (cause); – for verily Allah is Full of Strength, Exalted in Might, (Able to enforce His Will).

S22.41   (They are) those who, if We establish them in the land, establish regular prayer and give Zakat, enjoin the right and forbid wrong: With Allah rests the end (and decision) of (all) affairs.

S22.78   And strive in His cause as ye ought to strive (with sincerity and under discipline). He has chosen you, and has imposed no difficulties on you in religion; it is the religion of your father Abraham. It is He who has named you Muslims, both before and in this (Revelation); That the Messenger may be a witness for you, and ye be witnesses for mankind! So establish regular Prayer, give zakat and hold fast to

Allah! He is your Protector – the best to protect and the Best to help!

S25.52   Therefore listen not to the Unbelievers, but strive against them with the utmost strenuousness, with the (Qur-an).

S29.69   And those who strive in Our (Cause), – We will certainly guide them to Our Paths: For verily Allah is with those who do right.

S47.4   Therefore, when ye meet the Unbelievers (in fight), smite at their necks; At length, when ye have thoroughly subdued them, bind (the captives) firmly: therefore (is the time for) either generosity or ransom: until the war lays down its burdens. Thus (are ye commanded): but if it had been Allah's Will, he could have certainly exacted retribution from them (Himself); but (He lets you fight) in order to test you, some with others. But those who are slain in the way of Allah, – he will never let their deeds be lost.

S48.16   Say to the desert Arabs who lagged behind: 'Ye shall be summoned (to fight) against a people given to Vehement war: then shall ye fight, or they shall submit. Then if ye show obedience, Allah will grant you a goodly reward, but if ye turn back as ye did before, He will punish you with a grievous Chastisement.'

S48.17   No blame is there on the blind, not is there blame on the lame, nor on one ill (if he joins not the war): But he that obeys Allah and His Messenger, – (Allah) will admit him to Gardens beneath which rivers flow; And he who turns back, (Allah) will punish him with a grievous Chastisement.

S61.11   That ye believe in Allah and His Messenger, and that ye strive (your utmost) in the Cause of Allah, with your wealth and your persons: That will be best for you, if ye but knew!

APPENDIX B
THE CALL TO JIHAD BY THE ISLAMIC MOVEMENT OF UZBEKISTAN

Source: Rashid, 2002, pp.247–249, emphasis in original.

In the Name of Allah the Most Compassionate the Most Merciful

A Message from the General Command Of the Islamic Movement Uzbekistan

'And fight them until there is not more fitnah and the religion is all for Allah' Al Anfaal: 39

The Amir (commander) of the Harakatul Islamiyyah (Islamic Movement) of Uzbekistan, Muhammad Tahir Farooq, has announced the start of the Jihad against the tyrannical government of Uzbekistan and the puppet Islam Karimov and his henchmen. The leadership of the Islamic Movement confirm the following points in the declaration:

This declaration comes after agreement by the major ulema and the leadership of the Islamic Movement.

This agreement comes based on clear evidence on the obligation of Jihad against the tawagheet as well as to liberate the land and the people.

The primary objective for this declaration of Jihad is the establishment of an Islamic state with the application of the Shari'a, founded upon the Koran and the Noble Prohphetic sunnah.

Also from amongst the goals of the declaration of Jihad is:

The defense of our religion of Islam in our land against those who oppose Islam.

The defense of the Muslims in our land from those who humiliate them and spill their blood.

The defense of the scholars and Muslim youth who are being assassinated, imprisoned and tortured in extreme manners – with no rights given to them at all.

And the Almighty says:

'And they had no fault except that they believed in Allah, the All Mighty, Worthy of all praise!' Al Buruj: 8

Also to secure the release of the weak and oppressed who number some 5,000 in prison, held by the transgressors. The Almighty says:

'And what is the matter with you that you do not fight in the way of Allah and the weak and oppressed amongst men, women and children' An Nisaa: 75

And to reopen the thousands of mosques and Islamic schools that have been closed by the evil government.

The Mujahedeen of the Islamic Movement, after their experience in warfare, have completed their training and are ready to establish the blessed Jihad.

The Islamic Movement warns the Uzbek government in Tashkent from propping up or supporting the fight against the Muslims.

The Islamic Movement warns tourists coming to this land that they should keep away, lest they be struck down upon by the Mujahedeen.

The reason for the start of the Jihad in Kyrgyzstan is due to the stance of the ruler Askar Akayev Bishkek, in arresting thousands of Muslim Uzbeks who had migrated as refugees to Kyrgyzastan and were handed over to Karimov's henchmen (i.e., Uzbek regime).

The Most High says:

'Verily the oppressors are friends and protectors to one another'

The Islamic Movement shall, by the will of Allah, make Jihad in the cause of Allah to reach all its aims and objectives.

It is with regret that Foreign Mujahedeen (Al Ansaar) as of yet have bit entered our ranks.

The Islamic Movement invites the ruling government and Karimov leadership in Tashkent to remove all items from office – unconditionally, before the country enters into a state of war and destruction of the land and the people. The responsibility for this will lie totally on the shoulders of the government, for which it shall be punished. Allah is Great and the Honour is for Islam.

Head of the Religious Leadership of the Islamic Movement of Uzbekistan
Az Zubayr Ib 'Abdur Raheem
th Jumadi Al Awwal (ah)
25th August, 1999

9

HIZBUT TAHRIR IN INDONESIA
Seeking a 'Total' Islamic Identity
Greg Fealy

I have been involved in many different Islamic organisations in the past. But I was always dissatisfied. They called themselves 'Islamic' but in many ways they weren't very Islamic at all ... Their kind of Islam was mainly symbolic or confined to certain aspects of life. I wanted Islam to be at the centre of my life. When I came to Hizbut Tahrir, this was exactly what I found. Everything was based on Islam – a whole system of thinking and behaviour based entirely on God's teachings. It showed me all the answers I needed were within Islam; there is no need to take ideas from outside ... Hizbut Tahrir has given me confidence and certainty in my Islamic-ness.

Hizbut Tahrir member, Jakarta, 9 December 2005.

At first glance, Hizbut Tahrir Indonesia (Liberation Party of Indonesia; HTI) may seem an intriguing but not particularly important subject for study. It is, by Indonesian standards, a relatively small movement, which has remained on the fringe of the Muslim community since its emergence in 2000. Its central ideological goal of re-establishing a global caliphate is often dismissed by other Muslim groups as utopian and of little local appeal. Although it describes itself as a 'party', it is not involved in formal politics and lacks the institutional assets and solid social bases of other, better-established Islamic organisations.

Yet there are several reasons why HTI is deserving of close consideration. To begin with, it represents a new phenomenon in Indonesian Islam. Of the many organisations established in the past few decades that draw inspiration from the Middle East or South Asia, HTI is the only one that is directed by a foreign leadership, which draws its ideology strictly from a Middle Eastern source, and whose agenda is fundamentally transnational. Arguably, it is also less subject to indigenising processes than most other foreign-derived Islamic movements. This makes it an illuminating case study of globalised religiosity within an Indonesian context. Much has been written about globalisation and Islam in other parts of the world, particularly the Middle East, Europe and South Asia, but little research has been undertaken of this relationship in Southeast Asia. In particular, the appeal of transnational over localised forms of Islamic identity has not been studied in depth.

A second reason is that Hizbut Tahrir internationally and to a lesser extent in Indonesia has been accused of having violent, subversive and even terrorist inclinations. Zeyno Baran from the Nixon Center described HT as a 'conveyor belt for terrorists' and 'Islam's Bolsheviks'. She called for the banning of HT and the blocking of dissemination of its literature (Baran 2005). The Heritage Foundation's Ariel Cohen called it a 'totalitarian' organisation that 'shares goals of al-Qaeda and other global jihadi movements'. He singled out Indonesia as one of the countries at direct risk from HT: 'Anti-Americanism, extremism, and preaching the violent overthrow of existing regimes make Hizb ut-Tahrir a prime suspect in the next wave of violent political action in Central Asia and other Muslim countries with relatively weak regimes, such as Pakistan and Indonesia' (Cohen 2003: 5). Two other conservative US writers, Ehrenfeld and Lappen, labelled HT a terrorist organisation 'in the mold of al-Qaeda' and called on the US government to outlaw the party and freeze its assets (Ehrenfeld and Lappen 2005). The Singapore-based terrorism writer, Rohan Gunaratna, referred to the 'links' between Southeast Asian terrorists such as Jemaah Islamiyah's Hambali and local Hizbut Tahrir groups (Gunaratna 2004: 124–5). Other writers, however, have cast doubt on these claims, pointing out that while individual Hizbut Tahrir members (usually referred to as *hizbiyyin*) or small groups within the organisation have been involved in violent and subversive acts, there is little indication of central HT approval of, or broader *hizbiyyin* support for, extremist behaviour (Mayer 2004: 23; ICG 2003; Swick 2005). Certainly in the case of Indonesia, none of HT's accusers has adduced evidence to support their claims. In this context, a closer examination of HTI may shed light on the character of the organisation, and particularly, whether its ideology and actions are rightly regarded as dangerous to security and social order.

In this chapter, I will examine the history, structure and discourse of Hizbut Tahrir in Indonesia. Particular attention will be paid to how HTI defines Islamic identity and the nature of its appeal to those Muslims who join the organisation. I will argue that HTI's metanarrative or totalising account of the condition of the Muslim world and the remedy for its problems is an essential element in understanding Hizbut Tahrir's appeal. Lastly, I will compare HTI with other radical Islamist groups in Indonesia and contend that the party, despite its sometimes strident rhetoric, has not been disposed to violence or subversion. The term 'radical' is used here to denote those people or groups seeking sweeping or dramatic social and political change; it is not intended to imply violent behaviour. My narrative and analysis are based on preliminary field research into transnational Islamist groups in Indonesia and is intended as an initial contribution to discussion of HTI.

History and Ideology of Hizb ut-Tahrir

Hizb ut-Tahrir[1] was founded in Jerusalem in early 1953[2] by the Palestinian intellectual and jurist, Taqiuddin an-Nahbani (1909–1977). An-Nahbani had trained in law at al-Azhar University, Cairo, before becoming a clerk and then judge in Amman, Jordan. He had been a sympathiser, if not a member, of the Muslim Brotherhood, and was well versed in the literature produced by that organisation's intellectuals and activists. Brotherhood thinking, regarding the completeness of Islam as a social, political and cultural system, appeared to have a considerable impact upon him as he sought solutions to the problems faced by both the Palestinian and global Muslim communities. According to some writers, he was also attracted to leftist ideologies, as were many other younger Muslim intellectuals of this period. In her detailed study of HT history and ideology, Suha Taji-Farouki credited an-Nahbani as being one of the first Arab thinkers to blend a specifically Islamic agenda with the popular revolutionary discourse of the time.[3]

The distinguishing feature of an-Nahbani's thought was the necessity to resurrect the caliphate; the last caliph, the Ottoman sultan Abdul Hamid II, had been removed by Mustapha Kemal Attaturk's secular Turkish government on 3 March 1924. While the aspiration for caliphal revival was not uncommon among Islamic groups at this time, HT was the first to make this demand the centrepiece of its program. For an-Nahbani, there were powerful doctrinal and practical reasons for restoring the caliphate. He stated that Muslims were obliged to establish and uphold the caliphate as this was the system implemented by the companions of the Prophet during the first generations of Islam and it was also the only system capable of carrying out God's teachings. Moreover, he argued that the abolition of the caliphate had left the

Islamic community weak, disunited and susceptible to impiety. This had made it easy for Islam's enemies to dominate and oppress Muslims. An-Nahbani saw the caliphate as more than just spiritual leadership for the *umma*; it was to be a transnational Islamic government with the power to direct the affairs of the global Muslim community. In particular, the caliph would oversee the implementation of a thoroughly Islamic system of laws and values within Muslim societies, a prerequisite for pious living. Undoubtedly, an-Nahbani's thinking on the caliphate and Islamic unity was fired by a deeply held grievance over the occupation of Palestine by the British and particularly the creation of Israel in 1948.[4]

Shortly after having registered Hizb ut-Tahrir as a political organisation, the Jordanian government banned it and arrested an-Nahbani on subversion charges. He was released soon after and went into exile in Syria and then to Lebanon, where he spent most of the rest of his life. Despite its proscription, HT grew steadily in the Middle East through the late 1950s and 1960s, finding particular support from Palestinian communities in Jordan and Lebanon. In the late 1960s and early 1970s, HT members were involved in a series of failed coup attempts in Jordan, Syria and Iraq, which led to a harsh crackdown on *hizbiyyin* in those countries. The remainder of the 1970s and 1980s were a period of decline and drift for HT. An-Nahbani died in 1977 and was replaced as emir by his loyal follower and academic Sheikh Abdul Qadeem Zaloom (d. 1983) and then Ata abu-l-Rushta, both of whom were Palestinians. HT's fortunes began to revive from the early 1990s, with rapid expansion of the party in post-Soviet Central Asia, North Africa, Turkey, Europe and Southeast Asia. This turned HT into a genuinely global movement. Palestinian émigrés and intellectuals became a major vector for its dissemination. HT refuses to discuss the size of its worldwide membership but estimates range from several hundred thousand to more than one million.

Origins, Structure and Membership of HT in Indonesia

HT has been active in Indonesia since the early 1980s and two figures – Mama Abdullah bin Nuh and Abdurrahman al-Baghdadi – have played a seminal role in its development. Abdullah bin Nuh was an Islamic scholar who specialised in Arabic arts and letters. A popular lecturer and preacher, he became disillusioned with existing Islamic movements in Indonesia during the late 1970s, believing that they had failed to address the problems facing the Muslim community. In his search for alternative paradigms of Islamic thinking and activism, he developed an increasing attraction to HT. He would later tell followers that it was the 'totality of the Hizbut Tahrir approach' that persuaded him of its superiority compared to other Islamic movements. During visits to Sydney, where his son was being educated, bin Nuh became acquainted with *hizbiyyin* there, many of whom were Palestinian Lebanese who had migrated to Australia in the early 1960s to escape persecution. Among the activists he met was a charismatic young teacher, Abdurrahman al-Baghdadi. Despite his surname, al-Baghdadi was Lebanese.[5] A tall and imposing figure, he had joined the Palestinian armed struggle against Israel and, according to some accounts, had been captured and tortured by Israeli soldiers. He appears to have become a member of HT in the Middle East before coming to Australia, though the details remain murky.[6]

At the invitation of bin Nuh, al-Baghdadi went to Indonesia in 1982 to disseminate HT teachings. He used bin Nuh's *pesantren* (Islamic boarding school) al-Ghazali in Bogor, West Java, as his base and soon became a familiar figure preaching to campus Muslim groups, particularly in the larger state tertiary institutions such as the Bogor Agricultural Institute (IPB), the Bandung Institute of Technology (ITB) and the University of Indonesia, as well as at mosques across Java. As al-Baghdadi's following grew, he and bin Nuh began arranging more systematic education and recruitment measures. *Halaqah* (study circles) and *dauroh* (training programs) became the main means to propagate teachings and to draw students into more intensive activities. During these early stages, bin Nuh and al-Baghdadi avoided mention of HT, lest they attract the attention of Indonesia's security services. Publications and training courses did not bear the name Hizbut Tahrir, but key elements of the organisation's doctrine, such as the need for comprehensive implementation of shari'a and a caliphate, were widely disseminated. Indeed, some early recruits to HT recalled that they had several years of involvement in al-Baghdadi's programs before they realised his connection to HT. A HTI executive board chaired by bin Nuh was established clandestinely by the mid-1980s, presumably with the approval of the central HT leadership. The first recruits were formally inducted into HTI around 1987–1988, though the organisation remained 'underground' and members were warned against openly discussing HT's existence in Indonesia (Salim 2005: 130–1).[7] HT's organisational structures and experience of repressive authoritarian regimes in the Middle East proved useful during the remaining years of the Soeharto regime in ensuring that the movement continued to grow without arousing much scrutiny or interference from the intelligence services. Indeed, HTI activists were adept at using state-sponsored religious bodies for recruitment and organisational purposes. For example, HTI student leaders played a prominent role in the Campus Proselytisation Institute (LDK), the main national body for university-based *dakwah* (proselytisation) groups. They also featured in the various Islamic religious boards (often called Rohis or Islamic Religious Bodies) within tertiary and secondary schools. West Java remained the centre of HTI activities. Bin Nuh's *pesantren* became a site for high-level training of cadre and the Bogor Agricultural Institute, in particular, became a *hizbiyyin* stronghold, with HTI members dominating the student council from the early 1990s.[8]

The downfall of the Soeharto regime in May 1998 led to HTI's emergence into public view. In early 2000, the organisation's weekly pamphlet, *Buletin al-Islam* (Islamic Bulletin), which had been published in various guises since 1994, began bearing the attribution 'Syahab Hizbut Tahrir' (Hizbut Tahrir Youth). Then in May of that year, the organisation held an international conference in Jakarta under the banner of Hizbut Tahrir, which attracted extensive media coverage.[9]

Since 2000, HTI's membership, scope of operations and public profile have grown rapidly. As with branches elsewhere in the world, Hizbut Tahrir in Indonesia refuses to release information on the size of its membership, but it does say that it has branches in 27 of Indonesia's 33 provinces. Judging by the size of Hizbut Tahrir rallies in large cities like Jakarta, and the print runs of its various publications, it is reasonable to assume a membership of at least several tens of thousands. One writer has stated that Indonesia and Uzbekistan have the two largest HT memberships in the world, but there is little publicly available evidence to support this. The majority of *hizbiyyin* are tertiary students, particularly from science and technical fields such as economics, accounting and engineering, or middle-class professionals from urban areas; rural and lower class membership appears small.[10]

HT's two most important methods of recruitment are the *halaqah* and *dauroh*. *Dauroh* is usually used to introduce basic HTI principles to new recruits and the most common course runs for 32 hours. *Halaqah* can be at various levels, but the emphases in these study groups are not only on more intensive learning about HTI thinking but also about inculcating correct behaviour. The students participating in an *halaqah* are referred to as *daris* and are always overseen by a *musyrif* or mentor – usually a senior HTI figure. Those intending to be inducted into HT must undergo intensive *halaqah* preparation, often requiring demonstrated commitment over several years.[11] In this sense HT is not a mass organisation seeking to maximise its membership; only recruits of proven commitment are invited to join and great stress is placed on maintaining discipline and doctrinal conformity.

In terms of structure, HTI follows the pattern used by HT internationally. It has a central board, known internally as *majlis wilayah*, but publicly given the title, Dewan Pimpinan Partai (Party Leadership Council, DPP). The number and names of DPP members is uncertain, but information in HTI publications identifies at least five members. Below the DPP are provincial boards, known as Dewan Pengurus Wilayah (DPW), and at the district level are branches. Branches require at least 50 members, 10 of which must have sufficient knowledge of HT doctrine and practices to supervise the newer members. It also has a large women's wing, Perempuan Hizbut Tahrir, which organises separate training and branch activities for women, in keeping with HT's strict segregation policy.[12]

The public face of HTI is its official spokesperson, Muhammad Ismail Yusanto (b. 1962), a geological engineer by training, but now a businessman and part-time lecturer at Jakarta's Syarif Hidayatullah State Islamic University. Yusanto is an experienced and engaging media figure. He has an affable manner and previously hosted a morning television program on Islamic issues. He issues HTI's public statements and conducts virtually all interviews with journalists and researchers regarding the organisation. Two other key figures, though less well known outside HTI and Islamist circles, are Muhammad al-Khaththath and Hafidz Abdurrahman. Al-Khaththath (b. 1964), an agricultural engineer from East Java, is one of bin Nuh's and al-Baghdadi's most favoured early recruits. A resourceful organiser, he used campus and broader Islamist networks to recruit new members and expand the range of HTI activities. He served as HTI general chairman until 2004 and is also secretary-general of the conservative Islamic Community Forum (FUI) and the Dakwah Committee of the Indonesian Ulama Council (MUI). Hafidz Abdurrahman (b. 1971), a Arabic-language teacher, replaced him as chairman in 2004. Interestingly, Yusanto, al-Khaththath and Hafidz all come from a traditionalist Nahdlatul Ulama background, which runs counter to the perception that Islamist groups such as HTI draw their activists mainly from the modernist or reformist side of the Muslim community. Al-Baghdadi, despite being the spiritual leader of HTI, seems to have had no formal role in the DPP in recent years, though he is undoubtedly an influential figure behind the scenes.[13]

As with many other radical groups, HTI has proved adept at disseminating its message, using both traditional means and new technologies. It has two *hizbiyyin*-owned publishers, al-Izzah in Bangil,

East Java, and Pustaka Thariqul al-Izzah in Bandung, which produce many of its translations of foreign HT works as well as locally authored texts. By far the most important publications for HTI are *Buletin al-Islam* and *al-Wa'ie* (*The Light*). *Buletin al-Islam* is a four-page pamphlet distributed free at Friday prayers every week by HTI members and sympathisers. The current print run exceeds 400,000. *Al-Wa'ie* is a higher quality monthly magazine of which about 15 000 copies are printed each edition. HTI has a Bahasa Indonesia website since March 2004 (hizbut-tahrir.or.id), which is well designed, regularly updated and allows interaction between subscribers and HTI officials. The organisation also has two radio production companies, al-Syafi'iyah and DAKTA, which produce programs for syndication across Indonesia.[14]

One thing that sets HTI apart from almost all other Indonesian Islamist groups which have strongly transnationalist tendencies, is its strict subordination to the central Hizb ut-Tahrir leadership. Although many details of this relationship are kept confidential by HTI, it is clear that the central HT board, which is probably based in Amman,[15] closely oversees the activities of the Indonesian branch. The emir sends delegates at least once a year to Indonesia to meet local leaders and observe first hand HTI's activities; it is not clear whether Abu-l Rushta has ever visited Indonesia.[16] Prior to publication, HTI sends all manuscripts to the central leadership for vetting. Particular attention is paid to the doctrinal content to ensure conformity with centrally sanctioned views and policies. Furthermore, HTI's spokesman, Ismail Yusanto, was appointed by the central board, not by the Indonesian branch, and it seems as if he was required to complete intensive training in order to take up the position.[17]

HTI's Program for Creating a Caliphate

A distinguishing feature of Hizb ut-Tahrir, globally, is the high level of adherence to the central board's prescribed ideology. While local branches have some latitude in adapting rhetoric to in-country conditions, the broad conceptual framework, aims and language of HT branches is substantially the same across the world.

As mentioned above, HT believes that only with the creation of a pure transnational Islamic state headed by a caliph can Muslims be assured of living in a just, pious and secure society. It specifically rejects the nation-state as subverting the divine command for a unified community of believers and also dismisses thinking and systems not derived from Islam. Western doctrines such as humanism, communism, democracy and secularism are denounced as inimical to Islam. Particular stress is laid on the incompatibility of liberal democracy with Islamic principles. HT regards the principle of popular sovereignty as inherently flawed because a virtuous state must be based on God's law, not the will of people, especially when much of the electorate lacks a 'true Islamic consciousness'. Thus, although HT is a 'party', it does not involve itself in elections. Another hallmark of HT doctrine is its rejection of gradualism, which it sees as a dilution of the purity of Islamic teachings. It regards compromise as an 'error' that forestalls, rather than facilitates, the creation of a caliphate.

HT sets out a three-stage program for creating a caliphate. The first stage is known as 'culturing' (*tatsqif*), and involves the cultivation and recruitment of Muslims into HT who are prepared to struggle to achieve the party's ideals. The second phase is 'interaction' (*tafa'ul*) with the broader Islamic community in order to make Islam central to the activities of the state and society. The final stage, 'accepting power' (*istilamu al-hukmi*), involves gaining control of government and 'totally implementing Islam' across the world.[18] Hizb ut-Tahrir rejects the use of violence in reaching the third stage and asserts that the caliphate can only be achieved when the majority of Muslims have the correct religious attitudes and actively seek an Islamic state. Such attitudinal change can only brought about through preaching, education and other non-coercive means. HT does allow, however, for 'outside assistance' (*nusrah*) in gaining power. This assistance can be from strategic groups within the community, particularly sections of the elite, which join with HT in installing a caliph. *Nusrah* is seen as a way of accelerating the the achievement of the third stage. HTI describes the period from the mid-1980s to 2000 as its culturing phase and it is now in the second phase of openly promoting its ideas within Indonesia's Muslim community.[19]

In reality, HT, both in Indonesia and elsewhere in the world has shown more flexibility than its formal policies would suggest. While the party has not directly contested elections as an organisation, it has in the past allowed prominent individual members to stand as candidates in elections in Jordan and Yemen. HTI gave its members the freedom to participate in the 2004 general elections, provided they only voted for candidates with explicit pro-shari'a agendas – anecdotal evidence suggests a small minority of *hizbiyyin* exercised this right to vote. Some informants claimed that various groups within HTI pushed for the right to stand as candidates in the election, but this is denied by the executive board. The board does hold open the possibility, however, that in future members might nominate for the Regional Representatives Council (DPD), as this does not require a party affiliation.

The issue of *nusrah* and the use of coercion to achieve an Islamic state is also open to question. In the late 1960s and early 1970s, HT branches were involved in attempted coups in Jordan, Syria and Iraq, in several cases, acting with sections of the military elite. In Indonesia, seemingly as part of its *nusrah* agenda, HTI has recently been cultivating a number of senior military and political figures. The former Army commander, Tyasno Sudarto, appeared at several HTI rallies in early 2006 and retired general Wiranto, has also accepted invitations to speak at functions. The former leader of Muhammadiyah and chairman of the People's Consultative Assembly, Amien Rais, has also been meeting with senior HTI leaders and attended several events. This is not to suggest any reprehensible activity on HTI's part, but rather that the party is becoming more ambitious in its efforts to expand its network of sympathisers within elite circles.

HTI and Militancy

The reputation for violence and subversion that HT has acquired, somewhat exaggeratedly, in other parts of the world, has also led to assumptions among foreign observers about the nature of the party in Indonesia. While little has been written about HTI in English, Western intelligence agencies and security research centres have closely scrutinised the organisation's Indonesian activities, looking for signs of militancy or connections with terrorist groups.

To date, there is no evidence in the public domain to suggest that HTI is a violent organisation. No *hizbiyyin* has been arrested for involvement in terrorist activity in Indonesia and HTI members are far less likely than the supporters of most other radical groups to behave in a physically intimidating or violent way. HTI is one of the few radical groups not to have a formal militia wing or 'security' units, and its rallies and protest meetings are usually well marshalled and orderly. HTI leaders have also not called upon their members to engage in physical jihad, either in Indonesia or abroad. Most of the party's endeavours are directed towards propagation, particularly through preaching and education, rather than mass mobilisation. While HTI does occasionally join with other groups in organising large demonstrations, its primary focus is upon recruitment and development of a solid cadre base.

It is true, nonetheless, that some of HTI's rhetoric is strident and at times inflammatory. Party spokespeople often stereotype and vilify Islam's perceived enemies, particularly Western governments and corporations, but are careful not to call for attacks upon them. The answers, they argue, lie in peaceful systemic change, which must be achieved by 'enlightening' the Islamic community rather than confronting foes.

HTI's Worldview and Islamist Metanarrative

In analysing HT's discourse, it is useful to draw on post-modernist notions of metanarrative. A metanarrative is literally a 'big story', a grand all-encompassing account that purports to explain everything that happens in society. Lyotard and Foucault both critiqued the metanarratives of modernism which they saw as smothering the multiple realities found across time and place. Metanarratives claim to present universal elements in social life and thus are seen by their proponents as superior to more particularistic stories. While giving the impression of having a rigorous scientific basis, metanarratives are, according to post-modernists, inherently political. They require a selective construction of the past and are driven more by the need to establish normative rules than historical facts. Metanarratives can serve as powerful instruments in moulding community identity and consciousness, as well as in legitimising mechanisms of social control and mobilisation. Foucault noted that metanarratives could be used by a particular religious, political or social groups to ascribe dominance over other groups in society.[20]

Fundamentalist religious groups have a strong attraction to metanarratives. Encompassing and absolutist accounts of history and society complement their tendency to dichotomise the world into that which is good and evil, permissible and forbidden. Uncertainty, discursive pluralism or contestation run counter to the fundamentalist mindset, and Muslim fundamentalists are no exception to this. Many of the discourses of radical groups see a single reality, often of an oppressive nature, and construct metanarratives that reflect this. Common themes are that Muslims are victims of exploitation and subjugation by Christians and Jews, that these infidel forces are bent on destroying Islam and that those Muslims who are liberal-minded or given to compromise are contributing to the undermining of their own faith.

Hizbut Tahrir's discourse is more driven by metanarrative than those of most other Islamic groups. The theme of Islam in decline and under constant assault from its enemies pervades HT's literature, as does the accompanying claim that Islam's fate is tied to the restoration of the caliphate. For the *hizbiyyin*, this is the 'big picture', the 'fundamental truth' confronting Muslims today. Those who believe that less drastic or partial solutions will suffice fail to grasp the magnitude of the problem. HTI publications stress this point at every opportunity. In an editorial in a recent edition of *al-Wa'ie*, it was stated:

Now, after more than 80 years without a caliphate, the suffering of the Islamic community is worsening. Islamic states are split into tens of countries which are controlled by Western occupiers. Imagine, they [Islamic nations] can't save Palestine which is occupied by tiny Israel or Iraqi citizens who are being butchered. The blood of Muslims is so easily spilt by US occupiers and their allies, who are helped by traitorous agents from the Islamic community itself. Even though the Islamic community has more than 1.5 billion people. Poverty, ignorance and conflict are synonymous with Islamic states. This is the result of secularisation. This is the result of the collapse of the Islamic Caliphate.[21]

As with other Hizb ut-Tahrir branches elsewhere, HTI weaves contemporary Indonesian issues into its metanarratives in order to bring greater immediacy to the call for radical change. For example, a widely distributed PowerPoint presentation called 'Indonesia cries', listed the following problems in Indonesia:

- Indonesia is again a poor country
- Indonesia's debt is more than Rp1400 trillion [US$140 billion] (foreign debt Rp742 trillion [US$74 billion]
- Tens of millions of people in poverty
- Millions of people losing their jobs
- 40 million unemployed; 3.5 million graduates
- 4.5 million children have dropped out of school
- Millions of malnourished people
- Criminality has increased by 1000%
- Divorce has increased by 400%
- Psychiatric hospital occupancy up 300%[22]

The document then goes on to argue that these are the adverse consequences of secularist Western influence and that all of these problems will be rectified once a caliphate has been restored.[23] Similar lists citing all manner of social, economic, political and cultural ills can be found in other HTI works, giving a sense that nearly everything that afflicts Muslim life derives from non-Islamic sources while the hope for amelioration can only be found within Islam. In effect, HTI is creating what Farish Noor, in another context, refers to as 'chains of moral equivalences'[24]: that is, all that is Islamic (as defined by HT) is good, and all that is not is harmful. This moral dichotomisation and xenophobia is typical of many fundamentalist metanarratives.

In another PowerPoint presentation by Ismail Yusanto to Abu Bakar Ba'asyir's al-Mukmin *pesantren* in Ngruki, Central Java, in December 2005, 'Western Ideology' is equated with 'Capitalism, Satan's Ideology, War mongering, extractor of wealth and coloniser [sic]'. It goes on to state that 'The West' has intervened in the affairs of other nations on 378 occasions between 1758 and 2001, has 'masterminded bloody coups' in 11 countries, including Indonesia, Iran, Brazil and Greece, and has supported repressive regimes in another 11 nations. It then declares that: 'the 11 September Incident was deliberately engineered to become the justification for the launch of a new US foreign policy: the doctrine of 'pre-emptive strike'' and that the 'War on Terror' is really a 'war against Islam'. Such views are not unusual among Islamist groups but HTI's presentation is notable for (1) its clever use of Western source material, albeit of dubious reliability, to convey a sense of careful research and credibility to its claims, and (2) its placing of 9/11 in the context of the need for a pan-Islamic state.[25]

Despite the fact that HTI's material is largely aimed at a well-educated, urban audience, there is remarkably little rigorous or open-minded analysis in its publications. For example, the portrayal of the caliphal tradition in Islam borders on the ahistorical. It is rare for any HTI text to refer to the obvious limitations and failures of the caliphate as an institution, particularly to ensure the political unity, stability and prosperity of the global Muslim community. To read HTI literature is to gain an idealised and romanticised account of how the caliphate operated throughout history.

It is precisely the radical and uncompromising nature of HT's agenda that attracts members to the organisation. As Bobby Sayyid has noted, fundamentalists seek to put religion at the very centre of their lives and to exclude those other elements seen as threatening or alien.[26] Viewed in this way, HT provides a more enveloping Islamic identity for its followers than other movements. To quote from another HT sympathiser:

> I am interested in Hizbut Tahrir because I can see that Islam in Indonesia is in a pitiable state. My own experience shows this. I used to be a student at a big *pesantren* (Islamic boarding school) in Sukabumi and all the time students from our *pesantren* were fighting with people from other *pesantren*. Imagine, we are supposed to be pious students learning about Islam but we are brawling with each other. I came to the UI [University of Indonesia] campus in Depok [West Java] and you know what? People kept on stealing my shoes from the steps of the mosque

when I was praying. What kind of society are we living in that this happens? Unless there is fundamental Islamic change, this will not improve. We need a society and culture that is totally Islamised and this is what HT can give us.[27]

The desire to commit oneself self to, and to being seen as committed to, a 'total' Islamic system of thought and action is a key element in the appeal of Hizbut Tahrir. What HTI's detractors see as the utopianism and millenarianism of the caliphal aspiration, *hizbiyyin* regard as a signifier of their Islamic-ness. It arises out of deep disillusionment with local manifestations of Islamic politics and culture and a concomitant receptiveness to new, globalised forms of Islamic identity.

Prospects

HTI has grown quickly in the past decade, both in terms of size of membership and organisational structure. In most major cities of Indonesia that have a large Muslim population, active HTI branches can now be found. The organisation is now penetrating into rural areas, traditionally places of low support, and also establishing solid footholds in both the corporate sectors and semi-government institutions such as the Indonesian Ulama Council. While HTI leaders are confident of continued rapid expansion, there are grounds for caution. The Hizbut Tahrir ideology, though appealing to particular sections of the Islamic community, does not strike a wide resonance and many mainstream Muslims regard the organisation with some scepticism. Unlike many other Islamist groups, HTI only has limited career and economic opportunities available to its members and this may limit its longer term prospects for consolidation and expansion of influence.

10

BETWEEN 'JIHAD' AND 'MCWORLD'

ENGAGED SUFISM IN INDONESIA

Julia Day Howell

Perhaps having in mind the image of Sufism as pacificist and otherworldly, my colleagues have asked that I address the question: 'To what extent is Sufism being used by Muslims to reclaim a sense of spiritual well-being in the face of challenges on two flanks, from the West on one side and Islamic radicals on the other? An earlier generation of Orienalists[1] took a dim view of the prospects for Islam's Sufi heritage (tasawuf) having very much, if any, relevance in today's world, and so to speculate on how Sufi spiritualities might help people confront global challenges of any sort, whether of 'jihad' or 'McWorld',[2] would have seemed ludicrous. Nonetheless, Sufism has successfully re-established itself among sophisticated urbanities. It has done so in Muslim-majority countries from Indonesia to Morocco, and amongst Muslim diasporas and New Agers from Birmingham to San Francisco.[3] Since 'Sufism' is rendered in so many different forms in all these places and must address highly varied social and political imperatives, searching for a single cause for these successful negotiations of social change is unlikely to be a productive exercise. However, by focusing on a limited social field, we may be able to see how in particular circumstances certain institutional potentials carried through Sufi traditions are seized upon and adapted to meet perceived contemporary needs.

Adopting that strategy, I focus in this chapter on the Sufi revival amongst Indonesia's new middle-class and upper class Muslims. Elsewhere I have described how the recent enthusiasm for Sufism has developed within the larger Islamic revival there, including and even especially amongst city people keen to 'get serious' about their faith.[4] The movement is thus not confined to, nor even primarily based in the circles of old-time 'syncretists' (the problematic Geertzian *abangan* and *priyayi*)[5] looking for a plausible Islamic cover for supposed unorthodox interpolations of locally sourced ritual and mystical practices (In. *bid'ah*; Ar. *bid'ah*). Rather, it draws heavily on the urban middle classes with ties to the Modernist Muhammadiyah movement and upwardly mobile *santri* ('strict' Muslims from modest rural and old trading class backgrounds). This new '*Sufisme perkotaan*' ('urban Sufi') movement is also widely documented in Indonesian publications.[6]

Scattered through these publications on 'urban Sufism' and through the multitude of journalistic accounts of the phenomenon in the Indonesian media is a variety of speculation as to what personal needs Sufism (or *tasawuf*) now meets for well-heeled city folk. A common theme (echoing the supposition implicit in the question quoted above) is that Sufism, involving as it often does, supererogatory devotions, rouses the emotions, especially of regret for sin and love for the merciful God, and thereby provides a gratifying release for anxieties and a ritually-induced sense of assurance.[7] One feature of the contemporary Muslim scene in Indonesia is often cited as evidence (not infrequently dismissively) of the presumed easy emotional 'fix' well groomed urbanities can obtain from refurbished Sufi practices. This is the mass *dzikir* (rituals of remembrance of God through the repetition of His names and Qur'anic passages) led by celebrity preachers like Arifin Ilham in the vast halls of the nation's grandest mosques and broadcast during Ramadan and other holidays on major TV channels.

Another new feature of the Indonesian urban scene might also be taken as evidence that *tasawuf* is being served up commercially as an emotional salve to the modern housewife, business executive and bureaucrat battered by rapid and, these days, chaotic social change. This is the extraordinary popularity of a style of sermonising performed by mega-preachers like Abdullah Gymnastiar ('Aa Gymn') and by spiritualised personal development trainers like Ary Ginanjar Agustian. They encourage loosely 'Sufi' ethical reflection in aid of spiritual cleansing (*taskiya*), leading to the public shedding of tears. In bygone years such public displays of emotion were very much *not* the done thing in most Indonesian cultures.[8]

Other speculation about the psychological value of Sufism centres on less visible, but potentially more enduring spiritual succour found in private by dedicated members of *tarekat* (Sufi orders). Members may use Sufi practices to move into states of peace and ecstasy such as celebrated by Jalaluddin Rumi and other great Sufi mystics. Urban branches of the major orders now accommodate Indonesia's city dwellers.

I am not going to belabour the ambiguous evidence for the presumption that revamped urban forms of Sufism provide emotional or psychological props for the new middle classes in times of challenging changes (positive or negative) in society. There is little systematic research on the issue, but the most popular causal arguments rest on weak cases. Thus the increasing popularity of Sufism over the last twenty years does not correlate neatly with upswings and downturns of the economy, nor with moments of intense political upheaval and relative quiescence. In any case, all forms of religious expression can offer emotional and psychological refuge, not just Sufism. Even scripturalism, emotionally dry as it may be, nonetheless can provide the comfort of familiar convention or smug certainty for exclusivists who style themselves as the vanguard of world-saving reform.

Instead of speculating here on what psychological gratifications the general public have found in Sufism, I will examine the way leading Muslim public intellectuals associated with the progressive Muslim think-tank Paramadina have promoted constructions of Islam that revalorise aspects of the Sufi tradition and recommended them as vital means of addressing contemporary social challenges. Paramadina was established in 1986 as a charitable foundation for the promotion of the highly contextualist and inclusivist Neo-Modern exegesis pioneered by the late Professor Dr Nurcholish Madjid (1939–2005) and his associates.[9] Paramadina became one of the most influential vehicles for renewed reform of modernist Islamic thought. Paramadina's influence has been projected through its scholarly book publishing program (disseminating both the translated works of foreign authors and books by its own scholars), its public lectures and seminars (such as the popular Klub Kajian Agama held monthly in a major hotel), and its short, university-style commercial courses for adults mounted by its Islam Study Centre (Pusat Studi Islam Paramadina).

By no means are all of the scholars who have been associated with Paramadina sympathetic with the new interest in Sufism, particularly in its new individualised and socially engaged forms. And amongst Paramadina scholars there is a diversity of views on Sufi metaphysics, most notably on the orthodoxy or otherwise of the Unity of Being (*wahdat al-wujud*) metaphysics associated with Ibn al-'Arabi and the use of *tasawuf* to justify the view that other religions are reliable guides to salvation. Nonetheless, amongst those Paramadina scholars most influential with the wider public are a number who have encouraged an appreciation of Sufism as a basis for religious tolerance. Several have even appropriated the concept of Sufi 'perennialism,' famously promoted by the Iranian Muslim scholar Seyyed Hossein Nasr,[10] as a support for full appreciation of other faiths in Indonesia's precariously pluralist society.[11] Paramadina scholars who have actively promoted an appreciation of *tasawuf* as a basis for religious tolerance include such prominent figures as Komaruddin Hidayat, Nasaruddin Umar, Kautsar Azhari Noer and Budhy Munawar-Rachman. Each of these thinkers has reached a substantial and influential segment of the Jakarta Muslim public through his books published by Paramadina's publishing house, through Paramadina's public forums, and, importantly, through its adult education courses. Each figure has held teaching posts at the major Jakarta universities, and has contributed to leading newspapers and news magazines. They also appear on radio and TV as commentators on Islam. Komaruddin Hidayat and Nasaruddin Umar have held important positions in government,[12] and both are particularly prominent in the electronic media. They have also developed careers as public speakers at such places as the major mosques, major corporations that hold religious upgrading activities, and private social functions on religious or family occasions.

Each of these prominent Sufi-oriented public intellectuals has some personal form of direct practical involvement in promoting the kind of progressive Islam for which they believe *tasawuf* can be a support and resource. Thus, each has become involved in interfaith activities and acts in various ways in support of gender fairness in the interpretation and practice of Islam. Nasaruddin Umar, in particular, is known for his progressive scholarship on gender issues in Islam, having written his doctoral dissertation in that field. He is able to disseminate his views through his many lecture appearances at major mosques, like Mesjid Sunda Kelapa in the affluent Jakarta suburb of Menteng, and through his television appearances. Finally, each has some kind of personal spiritual practice, inspired in part by his study of *tasawuf*, which both feeds his own philosophical and social reflections and connects him with particular innovative, highly inclusive spiritual movements in the city.

The focus of this chapter, then, is progressive scholarly interpreters of Islam well known for their use of Sufism to advocate religious pluralism in the face of rising Islamic extremism and to champion gender equality in the name of Islam. Heretofore little attention has been paid to the value that these influential younger-generation Paramadina public intellectuals have found in Sufism as a vital element in progressive social engagement.

On this occasion a brief sketch of the career of just one of the Paramadina progressives, long-time director of the Paramadina

Foundation Professor Dr Komaruddin Hidayat, will exemplify the ways Indonesian intellectuals are drawing on Islam's Sufi heritage to both enhance orthodox piety and realise a liberal vision of social good in a modern, Muslim majority nation-state. Features of Komaruddin's career that parallel others of the perennialist circle of Sufi-inspired progressive intellectuals will be discussed thereafter.

Case Study: Professor Dr Komaruddin Hidayat

In 1990, when I was doing a project on an Australian New Religious Movement of Indian origin, the Brahma Kumaris (BKs), I went to the BKs' international spiritual center at Mt Abu, India, on a non-members 'VIP retreat'. Much to my surprise, I saw at one of the gatherings prominent Muslim neo-Modernist and later State Secretary under the Presidency of Abrurrahman Wahid, Djohan Effendi. I had met him in Indonesia some years previous while working on another project. Djohan was himself an early pioneer of Neo-Modernist Islam alongside Nurcholish Madjid. There in Mt Abu he introduced me to his young Muslim associates, who had also come as guests: Dr Komaruddin Hidayat and Mrs Amanda Suharnoko. Amanda Suharnoko was embarking on a period of multi-faith engagement, and had also begun a deeper study of Islam through the Pusat Studi Islam Paramadina (the adult Islamic education center). These activities would eventuate in her founding and running with support from Djohan, Komaruddin, Nasaruddin Umar, Budhy Munawar-Rachman and other leading Muslims and Christians in their circle, an interfaith dialogue NGO called MADIA or Masyarakat Dialog Antar Agama (Society for Inter-Religious Dialogue).[13] Komaruddin described the new kind of Muslim intellectual powerhouse and educational foundation, Paramadina, which he had recently joined as Executive Director, and of which he would later become Chairman.

Djohan, Komaruddin and Amanda's presence at the Brahma Kumaris' Mt Abu retreat was indicative of their openness to the authenticity of spirituality in other faith traditions, just as their involvement in MADIA has shown their commitment to concrete social action in support of religious pluralism at home in Indonesia. Komaruddin's enthusiasm for Paramadina and the social space he was helping to open up there for a new breed of university educated Muslim scholars and middle-class Muslims learners was indicative of his passionate commitment to re-enlivening Islamic scholarship to meet the new challenges of Indonesia's rapidly modernising society. He later had another major opportunity to promote modern Muslim scholarship as

Director of the section of the Ministry of Religion charged with oversight of Islamic post-graduate studies.

Where did Komaruddin's impressive openness to other faith traditions, combined with enthusiasm for Paramadina's agenda of strengthening Islam through rational-critical scholarship come from? Komaruddin, born in 1953, came through the *pesantren* system in his Central Javanese hometown of Magelang. This kind of education can generally be characterised as parochial, however demanding its regime of classical Islamic studies. However Komaruddin went on to tertiary studies at Indonesia's leading State Islamic Institute (IAIN), Syarif Hidayatullah (now a full university, a UIN), in Jakarta. In the 1970s the eminent Islamicist Harun Nasution was Rector of the Institute. He broke open the prevailing normative approach to Indonesian Islamic studies by promoting long neglected Greek-influenced Islamic philosophy of the rationalist Mu'tazilla school and by introducing Western social sciences into the curriculum.[14]

Joining Syarif Hidayatullah in 1978, Komaruddin embarked on a rather obscure field of study, Bahasa Islam (Islamic Hermeneutics) which in his hands nonetheless became a valuable tool for greatly extending historically contextualised and socially relevant exegesis. Following his undergraduate studies, he honed this analytical tool and extended his intellectual horizons through masters and doctoral studies in Philosophy at the Middle East Technical University, Ankara, Turkey, completing his doctorate in 1990. His thesis, which explicated his method, was published in 1996 by Paramadina as *Memahami Bahasa Agama: Sebuah Kajian Hermeneutik* (*Understanding the Language of Religion: A Hermeneutic Study*). It was shortly followed in 1998 by *Tragedi Raja Midas: Moralitas Agama dan Krisis Modernisme* (*The Tragedy of King Midas: Religious Morality and the Crisis of Modernism*), a work that demonstrated how historically contextualised exegesis can reveal an authentic Islamic morality capable meeting pressing contemporary social problems. Dawam Raharjo, in his introduction to the book, hailed Komaruddin as a unique thinker, but also as an outstanding representative of a broader social phenomenon: the educational formation of rural *santri* youths in a way that enabled them to break out of the world of the local *pesantren* and connect with the world of global scholarship, both Islamic and secular.

So far, we have a picture of intellectual flexibility plus finely honed classical Islamic and Western scholarship, but where does Sufism come in? Returning from his doctoral studies to his alma mater, the IAIN Syarif Hidayatullah in Jakarta, Komaruddin assumed a position as lecturer in Philosophy and Islamic Philosophy. In this capacity Komaruddin was able further to explore the social sciences of religion as well as *tasawuf*, which was by tradition included in the Islamic Philosophy program at the IAIN Jakarta. According to Dawam Raharjo, this is what gave Komaruddin the opportunity to develop an appreciation of how potentially valuable elements of the Sufi tradition, entangled in the past with unacceptable practices, could be recovered and rearticulated to help Muslims meet the demands of today's world. In essence, he developed the conviction that an inner sense of connection to God is the heart of religion and necessary to enjoyment of religion as a blessing to, rather than a burden upon, the believer. He also became committed to the idea that such an inner sense of God's presence is necessary to the proper social expression of religion.

Just how 'Sufis' and Muslims in general cultivate such an inner sense of connection with God is, of course, various. When asked about his personal practice,[15] Komaruddin said, 'I'm not a Sufi in the conventional sense'. Indeed he is actually critical of the slick packaging of much popular 'urban Sufism'. But after he returned from his doctoral studies in Turkey and began teaching about Sufism in his courses at the State Islamic Institute in Jakarta, he did look into a Naqsyabandi *tarekat* and a few other Sufi orders. The avant-garde intellectual debate of the time, both Muslim and secular, left him feeling flat. And none of it seemed to make much difference to how the bright young contributors to those debates behaved after they got their degrees and assumed responsible positions in public life. Many of them seemed to care about nothing but their promotions, increasing their departments' budgets and the like. Therefore, he began visiting a number of Sufi orders to investigate what practitioners of Sufism had to offer. At some of the *tarekat* he accepted spiritual direction, participating in their rituals, but he resisted initiation that binds the seeker to the master (*syech*) of the order. 'I was happy to be prayed for', he said, 'but I wasn't going to be loyal...Having studied philosophy, I couldn't be loyal [to a *syech*]'. 'I participated', he explained. 'I took something and I gave something...we shared [Eng.]. I could come and go and get the essence [Eng.]'.

What he has taken includes a habit of remembrance of God (*dzikir*) in the midst of everyday life, as recommended in the Qur'an but less formulaic than *tarekat* ritual practice. He also has his own regime of reciting each morning multiples one popular dzikir phrase (*subhanallah, alhamdulillah, la ilaha illaha, Allahu Akbar, hawalah, shawalat* for the Prophet Muhammad, and *astaghfirullah*). For him, however, these are not intended as investments in a ritual account book or ecstatic practices, as they might be for some traditionalists. Rather, they are opportunities for momentarily stepping aside from the fray and getting perspective. As he describes it,

> I feel that I suddenly become an observer ... of this life. When I remember God, I come to God through His name, The Merciful, the Beneficent ... Then I have compassion for others.

Since Komaruddin moved into lecturing on religion and 'spirituality' in the mass media and to private groups, he has used engaging personal stories reflecting his own practice to enliven his talks. He is now a well-known personality on the public lecture circuit and on TV. He has also combined his personal spiritual insights with reading in the management and psychology literatures to craft a distinctive Islamic approach to management consulting, which has been particularly attractive to executives in the banking sector.

His ideas about the importance of a rich inner life, especially as something that all the major religions foster, have developed recently through the selective appropriation of the concept of 'perennialism'. Perennialism was first introduced into Muslim public discourse in the widely-read pages of *Ulumul Qur'an*, a magazine of the Muslim Neo-Modernist movement founded in 1989 and published by LSAF (Lembaga Studi Agama dan Falsafat or Institute for the Study of Religion and Philosophy) and ICMI (Ikatan Cendekiawan Muslim se-Indonesia or Association of Indonesian Muslim Intellectuals).[16] But the idea for some time gained little traction, despite the inclusion in the magazine's pages of an article by Persian perennialist Seyyed Hossein Nasr, and references in numerous of its other articles to the work of Nasr and Western perennialists who became converts to or deeply sympathetic with Islam. However, that situation has begun to change. Ibn al-'Arabi scholar and Professor of Comparative Religion at Syarif Hidayatullah Islamic University (UIN, formerly IAIN) Kautsar Azhari Noer now promotes a construction of Sufism he calls '*tasawuf* perennial'.[17]

For Komaruddin, as for Munawar-Rachman and Kautsar, perennialism provides a conceptual framework through which the inner spiritual life, which in Islam is the particular focus of *tasawuf*, can be recognised as underlying the different social and ritual conventions of other religions as well. All three argue that cultivating the heart's natural attraction to God through love, as Sufis have done, is not mere indulgence in private spiritual gratifications but potentially of great social value as a support for religious pluralism in a democratic society.

Komaruddin, working with colleague Muhamad Wahyudi Nafis, set out his understanding of perennialism for the public in 2003 in a in a book called *Agama Masa Depan, Perspektif Filsafat Perenial* (*Religion of the Future: A Perennial Philosophy Perspective*). In it, Komaruddin and Nafis explain that the Perennial Philosophy endeavors to trace through a community's symbols, rituals and religious expressions to their source.[18] This source is 'God, Absolute Being' ('Tuhan, Wujud yang Absolut'), from which arises the entire phenomenal world ('sumber dari segela wujud').[19] All religions, according to their account of the Perennial Philosophy, originate in 'The One' (Yang Satu).[20] They seek to clarify this by distinguishing 'Agama (Religion)' from 'agama (religion)': there is only one Agama (Religion), but this has come down to humanity through 'a spectrum of historical and sociological [circumstances]' like sunlight shining off leaves, flowers, water and so on as so many different colors.[21]

Sociology of religion, history (but not 'historicism'), and 'transcendental psychology' are thus all tools that contemporary perennialist scholars can use to explore the relations of the many to the One, and thereby to improve interfaith understanding. Further, Komaruddin and Nafis make explicit the connection between *tauhid*, the core Islamic belief in the Oneness of God, and the lived experience of faith that Islam recommends, but to which the Sufi tradition has given particular attention:

> Dalam pandangan Islam, konsep tauhid bukan hanya terletak pada pengakuan adanya Tuhan yang Esa – sebab jika di situ intinya maka Iblis pun percaya – tetapi yang lebih pokok dari itu, penerimaan dan respons cinta kasih dan kehendak Tuhan yang dialamatkan kepada manusia.

> In the Islamic view, the concept of *tauhid* is not located just in the acknowledgement of the One God – because if that were all, even Satan believes – but more importantly than that, [*tauhid* resides in] the receiving [of God's love] and loving response [to] God's desire [to be loved] which he projects to humanity.[22]

From this Muslim perennialist position, which Komaruddin and Nafis call 'radical monotheism' ('*monoteism radikal*'), Plato and Pythagoras can be numbered amongst the monotheists ('*orang-orang yang bertauhid [muwuh-hidun]*') since they are included in the universalism of Islam ('*termasuk dalam keuniversalan Islam*').[23]

Nonetheless, Komaruddin and Nafis stress that it is important to respect the particular faith traditions that carry the variously colored understandings and modes of responding to the One God.[24] The distinctive characteristics (*keistimewaan partikular*) of each religion should be valued and utilised as the material out of which we construct our spiritual lives. But by this they do not mean to recommend 'parokialism', according to which the exoteric aspects of a religion are taken as absolutes, and, as it were, 'reified' (*reifikasi*) and idolised.[25] Perennialism expressed through 'tradition' (*tradisi*) is thus is an authentic expression of *tauhid* (the Oneness of God, monotheism), whereas, parochialism (the scripturalist absolutising of particular, socially shaped religious rules) is an impoverishment of *tauhid*.

Here, as elsewhere in Komaruddin's writings and addresses, use of social science terminology to discuss matters of theology and interfaith relations is noteworthy (e.g., 'partikular', as in 'local particularisms', 'parokial', 'reifikasi' and the like). This exemplifies the openness of some of Indonesia's leading Muslim religious thinkers to Western (or better, 'international') scholarship and their confident use of it to articulate their own, authentically Muslim and Indonesian understandings of Islam and democratic society. Komaruddin's popularity as a public speaker and TV personality attests to the value much of the public place on this kind of intellectual reconciliation of 'the West' and 'Islam'.

The practical expression of Komaruddin's 'radical monotheism' in relations with other religions can be seen in his work with the interfaith dialogue NGO MADIA, as well as in his work as an educator. Most of his career he has worked at the tertiary level and in the Islamic education sector (teaching at the UIN Syarif Hidayatullah, Jakarta, serving as Director of the Islamic Higher Education section of the Ministry of Religion and, more recently, serving as Director of Postgraduate Studies at the UIN Jakarta). But in the mid 1990s Komaruddin saw a need to create new options in quality primary and secondary schooling. Together with Nurcholish Madjid and other Paramadina associates frustrated with the quality of public secular schooling and anxious to create an educational environment actively supportive of religious pluralism alongside an emerging new breed of elite Muslim schools, he developed the concept for the Madania primary and secondary schools. Having secured a site in Parung, outside Jakarta, they opened the Madania high school in 1996 and the Madania primary school in 1998. Komaruddin became their first Director. Madania students are overwhelmingly Muslim (80–90%), but Christian, Hindu and Buddhist students also attend, and provision is made for religious education in all the students' religions. Moreover, students study not only their own religion, but thirty percent of the curriculum space devoted to religion is dedicated to combined activities that help the students understand the religions of their other classmates. The school promotes these multi-faith studies as part of its program for building attitudes supportive of a healthy civil society ('masyarakat madani', as suggested by the school's name, Madania) and an open attitude to the larger international community. Strong emphasis is put on best international practice in pedagogy, curriculum offerings and foreign language training (especially English) to enable students to function as confident Indonesians in a culturally diverse and technologically challenging global environment.

Komaruddin has also been personally supportive of individual spiritual leaders who have championed non-denominational and multi-faith activities. Not only has he repeatedly offered sympathetic public comment on talks given by visiting Brahma Kumaris sisters (following his initial exposure at the headquarters of the Brahma Kumaris World Spiritual University in Mt Abu, mentioned earlier), but he has spoken in support of the controversial but best-selling spiritual book author Anand Krishna. Anand himself has promoted a kind of perennialism through his books and spiritual centers.[26] Anand, born in Indonesia to Indian Hindu parents, began writing 'appreciations' of the spiritual teachings of all the major faith traditions in the 1990s and opened two centers, the Anand Ashram and the One Earth One Sky center, where he teaches a variety of personal development and meditation techniques. Komaruddin maintained his warm relationship with Anand through the difficult time when Muslim conservatives attacked Anand for presuming to write about Islam as an outsider and for purportedly distorting the teachings of Islam by just talking about its 'spirituality'. Major bookstores temporarily withdrew Anand's books from the shelves at the height of the controversy in 2000.

More recently, Komaruddin has become an enthusiastic participant in and endorser of an ecumenical but strongly Islamic colored movement: the ESQ (Emotional Spiritual Quotient) training programs of former Management Science lecturer and self-made businessman Ary Ginanjar (alluded to above). 'ESQ' is a trademarked brand of personal development offered to the public in four-day intensives at facilities like the Jakarta Convention Centre. It is also offered at major firms and departments of federal and provincial bureaucracies. As explained in Ginanjar's best-seller book,[27] the brand name references the concepts of 'emotional quotient' and 'emotional intelligence'[28] and 'spiritual quotient' or 'spiritual intelligence'.[29] The training programs are promoted to individuals as ways to develop their personal potential (*potensi dasar manusia*) and social contribution in career, family and study. The programs are sold to major corporations like Garuda Airlines, Krakatoa Steel, and Pertamina (state-owned oil company) and departments of the national and regional civil service as ways to minimise corruption and pump up the efficiency of workers through the reinforcement of a sense of gratitude and responsibility towards God. To inspire commitment to personal change, the seminars use growth movement motivational techniques and 'lecturettes' with statistics on the social harm done by moral weakness (e.g., Transparency International's corruption charts where Indonesia features among the highly corrupt). Ginanjar also impresses program participants with statistics on the improved performance of companies and government departments that have commissioned ESQ workshops for their employees. These motivational techniques are combined with American mega-church-style evocations of the glory and wrath of God to inspire deepened faith and surrender to the Almighty. The emphasis on spiritually-inspired purification of the heart[30] and cultivation of general principles of ethical behavior rather than obedience to specific religious laws give the programs and associated teaching material (books, DVDs, etc) a loosely 'Sufi' feel. Komaruddin, in his occasional guest appearances at the workshops, reinforces the gestures towards other faiths that Ginanjar makes throughout the workshop program, but the predominant theme of the programs is the truth of Qur'anic revelation and the piety that such a realisation requires of participants.

Conclusion. Sufism, Perennialism and Social Action in the Work of Paramadina Intellectuals

Komaruddin's career illustrates how 'Sufi' approaches to contemporary Islamic piety are being promoted by scholars with *pesantren* backgrounds and current teaching positions in Indonesia's leading Islamic universities. These credentials testify to their firm grounding in Islamic scholarship. Komaruddin's career also illustrates the intimate familiarity that the younger generations of Indonesian Muslim public intellectuals (including those sympathetic with Sufism) have with Western philosophy and social sciences. Old stereotypes of Sufism as a decaying tradition, popular mostly amongst the religiously poorly educated of the countryside and fatally compromised by local cultural accretions, are clearly belied by the life and work of these Sufi-oriented Paramadina intellectuals. In their hands Sufism is, rather, a vital heritage, fully adapted to the modern social context and firmly based in rigorous Islamic scholarship.

As Komaruddin's career shows, the facility of these Paramadina intellectuals in both classical Islamic scholarship and the Western social sciences and philosophy has been important in enabling them to build intellectual justifications for (selectively) re-valorising Sufism. It has also supported their intellectually adventurous reconnoitring of perennialism and, in some cases like Komaruddin's, Munawar-Rachman's and Kautsar's, their use of perennialism to promote highly inclusivist constructions of Islamic spirituality in the public arena.

Komaruddin's career also illustrates the important role of the progressive Muslim 'think tank' Paramadina in providing both an intellectual environment sufficiently permissive to support bold readaptations of Sufism, and a platform for public engagement for a younger generation of Muslim intellectuals. Paramadina's adult Islamic education program, developed under the leadership of Budhy Munawar-Rachman, has been a springboard for them to careers as commentators, consultants, workshop leaders and TV and lecture circuit personalities with wide audience exposure. It is true that from around 2004 to 2005, during the final illness of Paramadina's key figure, Nurcholish Madjid, a number of public intellectuals, including the Sufi-oriented intellectuals discussed here, diminished their involvement in Paramadina and built up their bases in other institutions (including the Paramadina University recently established by Paramadina Foundation). Nonetheless, the personal networks established through the original Paramadina think-tank and adult Islamic education centre in Pondok Indah remain important.

Reviewing the kinds of social issues that Komaruddin and his 'Sufi-oriented' Paramadina associates have taken up, it is evident that they have focused primarily on domestic social problems associated with rapid economic development and modernisation (especially corruption), rather than on outside 'threats' from the West such as agitate the jihadist Muslim fringe. Nonetheless, they are far from uncritical of the effects of US policy on the Islamic world. Komaruddin, who assumed the chairmanship of the 2004 Election Supervisory Committee (Panwaslu) and was thus thrust into the centre of the political arena, has voiced such criticism publicly on numerous occasions.

The Sufi-oriented Paramadina public intellectuals have been concerned with Islamic radicalism, but more with the narrow scripturalism that corrodes relationships within the Muslim community as well as between religious communities, and impoverishes the spiritual lives of its promoters. They have had to face fierce public criticism for the progressive stands they have taken on issues like interfaith marriages (for which Paramadina has provided a unique facility), wishing Christians 'happy Christmas' and visiting the services of other faith communities.

Kautsar Azhari Noer has received personal threats for his advocacy of friendly interchange with other faith communities.

All the Paramadina proponents of *tasawuf* mentioned here have chosen to build on various forms of 'this-worldly' Sufism (sometimes called 'neo-Sufism' or *tasawuf positif* in the contemporary Indonesian context) in their personal practice and as a basis for social action. This suggestively parallels 'engaged Buddhist' movements in Sri Lanka, China, Vietnam and elsewhere that have adapted Buddhism's esoteric tradition to a new social action agenda.[31] 'Engaged Buddhism' identifies those movements through which, as Queen and King observe, Buddhism has come to mean 'energetic engagement with social and political issues and crises at least as much as it means monastic or meditative withdrawal'.[32] We might then say that the Paramadina scholar-activists have developed a kind of 'engaged Sufism' similar in several respects to 'engaged Buddhism'.

Like engaged Buddhism, the 'engaged Sufism' of the Paramadina reformists transforms an esoteric religious heritage, using sophisticated religious scholarship, into a mandate for compassionate action in a rapidly urbanising and modernising society. Both movements have been strongly ecumenical, albeit with different emphases. Thus while engaged Buddhists have envisioned a unity of Buddhism in 'World Buddhism', engaged Sufism in Indonesia focuses on religious tolerance, both within Islam and amongst religions, rather than mounting a project of religious unification.

Further parallels between engaged Buddhism and engaged Sufism can be found in the socio-historical contexts that have given birth to them and in the social profiles of their leaders. Both movements have emerged from urban elites keen to participate in the reassertion of the value of their faith in the midst of societies challenged by the cultural and political power of Western societies, and both have been led by 'high profile personalities whose careers straddled ... East and West'.[33]

Not surprisingly then, both Buddhist and Sufi engaged piety emphasise the importance of rationality in charting one's spiritual course. However, unlike engaged Buddhism, which, according to Pittman,[34] counter poses rationality to experiential religiosity, 'devaluing' all mysticism, emotion and devotionalism, Indonesia's Sufi-inspired scholar-activists consider that experiential religiosity too has its place when cultivated properly. Indeed, because Sufi-style devotions and mystical practices exercise the spiritual centre of the 'heart' (*qalbu*), they are understood to positively energise and colour social action.

11

NO RESPECT

FORGING DEMOCRACY IN BOSNIA AND KOSOVO

Lynne Christine Alice

Despite the enormous global Islamic population, second only to Christianity in its numerous variations and locations, ignorance and xenophobia about Islam's basic teachings and lifestyle norms is widespread. Justifications of anti-terrorism legislation in Australia and in other western democracies are the most recent context for the elision of Islam and political extremism. Yet even as commentators describe the complexity of Islamic culture and its political dynamism in the face of the post-9/11 construction of the 'threat by Islamic militancy', the variety in Islamic history and politics remains relatively unknown.[1] This chapter reviews aspects of Balkan Islam. I argue that the development of its counter-discourses challenges the democratisation project since the Dayton Accord and provides some insights about the heterogeneity of current Islamic politics in the region. It is commonly held that democratisation contributes to the overall security of a state, and the persistence of discourses that position Islam as incompatible with democracy, in effect undermine human security.[2] The approach taken in this chapter, and discussed through an overview of history and politics, is that much is to be learnt from the complex relationships of indigenous Islamic culture and political consciousness and this is particularly evident in the multi-ethnic Balkans region.

In the former Yugoslavia, the conflating of Islam and terrorism is typically expressed from a mindset that views the entire Balkan region as caught between extremes. On the one hand, the Balkans are portrayed as a civilisational 'terra nullius', where persistent ancient hatreds combine with social problems marking the fall of communism, and the legacy of the Ottoman Empire is summarily dismissed as a dark history of religious barbarism. The fall of communism, military intervention in the 1990s and the panic resulting from 9/11, have certainly shaped the local capacity in Bosnia and Kosova to embed democracy and human rights in appropriate homegrown institutions for transitional justice. However the persistence of 'the age-old ethnic hatred in the Balkans' myth is now frequently refigured in post-9/11 writing that assumes where there is Islam there is terrorism, a view eliding religious culture with political extremism.[3] A more formal example of this can be seen in the concept of *Eurabia*, which denotes the inter-penetration of Arab Islam and European culture, in the latest book by Egyptian-born Jewish historian Bat Ye'or. Bat Ye'or argues that the Muslim world relates to European culture 'in the frame of jihad' leading non-Muslim states eventually to total subjection to Islamic values. She argues, 'We cannot defend ourselves; democracies cannot defend themselves against terrorism.'[4] Joel Starr, a US military commentator working with USAID in Bosnia takes this much further in a recent article titled, 'How to Outflank al-Qaeda in the Balkans'.[5] He writes that in the Balkans, 'Islamic fundamentalism has been halted ... by a strange combination of secularism, pro-Americanism and regional xenophobia.' This suggests to him that recruitment of Balkan Muslims by the US could deliver a strategic outflanking manoeuvre against the threat of al-Qaeda, enabling the US military to 'infiltrate and help disrupt the planning and execution of future terrorists' attacks abroad from Indonesia to the US to Europe'. Both Starr's and Bat Ye'or's writing are examples of over-inscribed discourses about terrorism that interpolate images from computer gaming, team sports and blockbuster movies. In their writing, liberal use of anonymous sources and alleged common knowledge become authoritative and add a 'secret service' ask-no-questions authority to the discourse. For example, Starr ends by stating that his proposed 'bold action in the Balkans' would not only add allies to Bush's 'War on Terror', but it will also boost local economies, and 'begin to defuse the age-old ethnic hatred in the Balkans'. Perhaps unsurprisingly, the imposed democratisation project in post-conflict Bosnia and Kosovo is also dependent upon the 'combination of secularism, pro-Americanism and regional xenophobia' that Starr hopes will provide a bulwark to Islamic extremism and it is for this reason also that the distinctiveness of Balkan Islam merits attention.

As indicated, xenophobic attitudes towards Islam are essentially a conflating of Islam and terrorism. This is reliant on three inter-connecting themes: a xenophobic positioning of Muslims as 'other'; lack of historical understanding of the heterogeneity of Islam; and cultural silences around the contribution of Islam to the potentiality of a political culture to 'grow' democracy (a capacity arguably integral to human security and able to resist the threat posed by xenophobia in the Balkans).[6]

In reviewing the significance of Balkan Islam, I argue that the development of its counter-discourses challenges the democratisation project in Bosnia and Kosovo. Not only does this provide some insights about the heterogeneity of current Islamic politics in the region but it may also counteract the persistent elision of Islam and terrorism that politicizes fears about Islam into what I have elsewhere argued to be a 'politics of hatred'.[7]

Democracy, Security

The end of 2005, and the beginning of 2006, have witnessed some momentous events in the Balkans as Bosnia meets a ten year milestone, Montenegro breaks away from Serbia and Kosovo leaders enter 'final status talks with international representatives. This transition period began in late November 2005 when the tripartite presidency from Bosnia Herzegovina (BiH) representing Serb, Croat and Muslim populations, attended events in Washington marking the anniversary of the Dayton Accord, signed on 21 November 1995. The week's talks included meetings with US defence and World Bank officials, intended to assist BiH's bids to join the European Union and the North Atlantic Treaty Organization (NATO) as part of its democratisation.

In Kosovo, preliminary talks begun in late November sought to determine the final status of the country, which remains legally a province of Serbia although jointly administered by the United Nations (UN) and an interim national assembly since the NATO led intervention against Milosevic's Yugoslav forces in 1999. On Monday the 21st, the Serbian Legislature voted in favour of a resolution that outlined Serbia's policy towards Kosovo's final status. Premier Kostunica stated that any solution for Kosovo must preserve the sovereignty of Serbia Montenegro as well as provide meaningful autonomy for the Kosovo Albanians and autonomy for Serbs still living in the province. On the same day, the Belgrade *Daily News* reported Vice Premier Labus' comment that while Serbia was seeking an historical agreement with the Albanians on the final status of Kosovo and Metohija, they also intended that 'the message being sent to the Albanian side is that the road to Brussels does not go through Tirana, but through Belgrade.'

In Kosovo, a resolution was passed in the National Assembly to be presented to the Special envoy on his arrival for the talks. It stated that Kosovars would not accept internationally imposed preconditions for independence, or in fact any version of conditional independence, including the continued sovereignty authority of Serbia or the decentralisation of government in favour of establishing autonomous ethnic cantons. The letter stated that the will of the Kosovar people was clear and that the continuing presence of the civil and military international presence was hereafter to become dependent on the declared will of the citizens as expressed through the country's legitimate political institutions. The Organisation for Security and Cooperation in Europe (OSCE) reported that in an attempt to quell the rising defiance, the UN Interim Administration (UNMIK) SRSG, Soren Jessen Petersen, cryptically stated that the arrival of UN's Special Envoy Ahtisaari marked the beginning of a process to place the last pieces of the Western Balkans jigsaw puzzle and solve the status of Kosovo. Reiterating the 'standards before status' demands of the UN, he said that the international community had taken more than six years to consider Kosovo's status because it was simply too difficult and attention had been diverted to the situations in Iraq and Afghanistan. Ending controversially, he told Kosovars that 'the Security Council, the Contact Group, the European Union (EU) Foreign Ministers have all clearly confirmed on numerous occasions that there will be no partition of Kosovo'. While these deliberations are most often attributed to the resolution of issues around sovereignty and security, their outcome rests upon issues of cultural difference and representation in which the historical relationships of Islam, Serbian Orthodoxy and Catholicism in the region are central.

The current tensions have a long history in which Islamic culture, and external views of it, are shaped by widely varying interpretations and it is to this I now turn.

Divergent Local and Outsider Accounts of Islamic Cultural History in the Balkans

In both BiH and Kosovo, the ending of what is usually regarded as inter-ethnic wars in the 1990s led to ongoing democratisation projects organised by the UN, the OSCE and lately the EU. These are intended to assist citizens to resolve past conflicts and to determine the institutions that will shape their political future. Although in the popular imagination BiH and Kosovo are often confused or considered two sites of essentially the same conflict resulting from communist Yugoslavia's disintegration, there are distinct differences, and no easy camaraderie between citizens in the two countries. The Balkans have long been a crossroads for religions and the crucible for the rise and fall of civilisations.[8]

Linking the two countries are aspects of a shared history and religion, dominated by mostly Turkish Islam. Yet what makes the region distinctively different as a Muslim population is that Islam originated from both the East and the West, that is, from the Ottoman Empire as well as from North Africa, via Spain and Central Europe. One could say that in Kosovo in particular, Islam exhibits *European* as well as Ottoman influences.[9] In BiH, Bosnians, Croats, and Serbs are religious and cultural identities constructed over several centuries and in the expanding and contracting of empires in the region. Notably, all three Slavic groups speak a language, called either Serbo–Croatian or Bosnian that has only minor variations. Nevertheless, the 'politics of language' has become a trope for identity politics with the emergence of new borders. In Kosovo, Albanian is the major language, although following 1999, Serbian and English are also official languages.

Even the sharing of language, religion and history is too large a claim for commonality; there are shared myths and confessional allegiances, and a great deal of disagreement about the rest. The significance of the spread of the Ottoman Empire through the Balkans is much contested. What is undeniable is the depth and breadth of the Turkish Islamic cultural, political and religious influence in both BiH and Kosovo. The battle of Kosovo at (Kosovo Polje) the 'field of blackbirds' in 1389 is the pivotal although contested point for understanding much of the mythology that continues to shape national identities in the region. The Turks defeated the Serbs at the famous battle after the Serbian prince, in a heavenly vision, refused a divine option to capitulate and live under Turkish rule. The Turks had comprehensively conquered all of Bosnia–Herzegovina and Serbia including Kosovo, by 1483. The Ottoman Empire was vast by then, yet spawned significant pockets of resistance. For example, feted in his time by three Popes, the Christian warrior, Gjerg Kastrioti Skenderbeg, remains the icon of resistance to real and potential oppressors throughout the Albanian Muslim world, most particularly and clearly in Kosovo today, where his statue or bust is displayed in most city centres and public buildings.[10] Similarly, the Christian saint, Mother Teresa, is another cultural icon whose Christian faith and works are held in as much high esteem as her nationality amongst Albanians in Kosovo, where a main street in the capital is named Nanë Tereza Rruga.

During the 450 years of Ottoman rule over the Balkans, most of its population lived more or less peacefully. Many Christian Slavs in BiH became Muslim, and in what is now Albania and Kosovo the syncretism inherited from earlier Illyrian culture meant that Islam, Roman

Catholicism and emerging forms of Orthodoxy from both the east and west, co-existed. In most regions of the Ottoman Empire, local intellectual and political elites developed to rule on behalf of their Turkish overlords. Some pro-Serbian historians record the period as one of servitude and suffering under Islamic rule, in which Serbian Christians and Jews were protected under Ottoman rule subject to taxes and forfeiture of property rights. The treaty of Khaybar allegedly became a model contract for protection of non-Islamic citizens under Ottoman rule. It originated in the seventh century, when the Jews at Khaybar in Arabia accepted a treaty offered to them by Muhammad, detailing how they would live under the Shari'a law. However, from the late fifteenth century to the nineteenth, the signifier 'Bosnian' denoted a multi-ethnic inter-faith identity since the region was heavily populated by Muslims, Jews (who had escaped Spain in 1492), and many confessions of the Christian faith, and intermarriage, if not common, was not forbidden.

The shrinking of the Ottoman Empire in the nineteenth century provoked many Muslims to migrate from its borders to Bosnia. The war against the Ottomans waged in Serbia and Montenegro was aided by the Russians and prompted the annexing of Bosnia by the Austro–Hungarian Empire in 1908. Ostensively, the annexation was meant to limit Russia's influence in the Balkans, and give Serbia control over the northern areas of what is now Kosovo (the areas around Prishtina and Mitrovica). The formation of 'The Prizren League' (*Lidhja e Prizrenit*) in 1878, which included Muslim leaders from BiH, Albania and what is now Macedonia, although initially supported by the weakening Ottoman state, became an increasingly nationalist quest to re-unite Albanian and Muslim occupied lands. The League intersected peripherally with the rise of the 'Young Turks' and in Kosovo for a time supported direct resistance to the growing Slavic population in the region. However, when the 'Young Turk Movement' (Committee of Union and Progress (CUP), in Turkish *Ittihad ve Terakki Cemiyeti*) came to power in 1908, and demanded that all eligible voters have a knowledge of Turkish language, the bulk of both Albanian or Serbian populations in Kosovo were disenfranchised. The Prizren League was caught between the Young Turks' attempts to contain Albanian moves towards autonomy and Serbia's political ambitions for the province, further stimulating Albanian nationalism. Becoming evident was the divorcing of Kosovar Albanian religiosity from any compulsory adherence to Turkish Islam, arguably an organic development from the coexistence of a multi-confessional based culture.[11]

In the ensuing first Balkan War of 1912, Albania was attacked by Montenegro, Serbia, Bulgaria and Greece, while the Albanians allied again with the Ottomans. Within Kosovo, the population divided as Serbs joined the allied army in large numbers, in what was widely regarded as a revisiting of the 1389 Serbian defeat by the Turks at the Battle of Kosovo Polje. Kosovar Albanians rose to support Albania and their Kosovo lands, as Serbs demolished Turkish and Albanian houses and atrocities were committed on both sides. At the Conference of Ambassadors in London in 1912, presided over by Sir Edward Grey, the British Foreign Secretary, Serbia was given sovereignty over Kosovo. A programme of settlement by Serb peasants followed the occupying army as Kosovo came under Serbian authority, where it remained until 1999.

In Bosnia–Herzegovina, the Berlin mandate allowing the Austro–Hungarian powers to annex the countries to Serbia's north and northwest contradicted Serbia's own intentions to occupy BiH. The ensuing clash led to the assassination by a Serbian nationalist, Austrian archduke, Franz Ferdinand, in Sarajevo on 28 June 1914. This event precipitated the start of World War I, but in Albanian-occupied lands seemed a potential solution to the problem of Serbian domination in Kosovo, despite the devastation on both sides and an unprecedented flow of Albanian refugees into Albania. The Western allies met in 1915, in the secret Pact of London, and agreed to divide Albania between Greece and Italy leaving only a small autonomous state in the central region. Austro–Hungarian and Bulgarian troops advanced into Kosovo, beating back the Serb armies in a disastrous wintry trek of soldiers and frightened civilians across the snowy mountains to safety in Serbia. Many Kosovar Albanians joined the Austro–Hungarian and Bulgarian forces that occupied Kosovo until 1918, when fortune turned against Austro–Hungarian politics and the Serb army swept back into Kosovo to take revenge. The retaliatory guerrilla warfare against the invading Serbs probably set up a model for civilian militias in the 1990s. Following the peace settlement, Bosnia and Herzegovina were annexed to Serbia as part of the newly formed Kingdom of Serbs, Croats, and Slovenes on 26 October 1918, and the region became Yugoslavia in 1929.

Ten years later, Italian forces occupied Albania. The Yugoslav government reluctantly joined the Tripartite Pact (Germany, Italy and Japan) on 25 March 1941, and was occupied by Germany on 6 April 1941. Croatia and Bosnia–Herzegovina then allied with Germany, and Italy annexed Slovenia and occupied Montenegro, while German forces occupied Serbia, Macedonia, Greece and the northern mining region of Kosovo. Albanian forces under Italian command occupied the rest of

Kosovo and about 100 000 Albanians moved back to Kosovo, displacing Serbs. However from 1943, British support for the resistance led by Croat Communist Party boss Josip Broz, enabled a consolidation of post-war communist rule over Yugoslavia.

After the war, as thousands of Albanians returned to Kosovo, their numbers increased to seventy-five per cent of the population. The alleged brutalising of Serbian civilians by Albanians under German command during the war, coupled with a resurgence of Albanian nationalism, contributed to Yugoslav attempts to disarm and contain the Albanian population in the late 1940s. Although in 1940 the Yugoslavia Communist Party had promised an autonomous 'Peasant Republic of Kosovo', this was denied in the 1946 Yugoslav constitution, which not only failed to grant territorial autonomy to Kosovo but also refused to recognise Albanian as a nationality within the Federation. Instead, five Slavic nationalities were recognised: Serb, Croat, Slovene, Montenegrin and Macedonian. Kosovo was defined as an autonomous region under Federal rather than Serbian jurisdiction. Tito's break with Stalin in 1948 ended diplomatic relations between Yugoslavia and pro-Moscow Albania. Kosovar Albanians were now labelled 'Stalinists' rather than fascists, and following further reductions to their autonomy in the 1953 Yugoslav constitution, were subjected to considerable repression. From 1956, resurgent Albanian nationalism was savagely policed until in 1963 a new constitution ended any vestiges of Kosovo autonomy by placing the province under Serbian rather than Federal control. Although concessions were made by Tito in 1967 to increase Kosovar Albanian representation in the Federal parliament, this prompted demands for autonomy and the increase in the immigration of Albanians to the province was mirrored in the emigration of Serbs. Finally, the 1974 constitution gave Kosovo provincial autonomy and like Serbia, equal constitutional agency under the Federation, as one of the eight units comprising Yugoslavia

By Tito's death, on 4 May 1980, Albanian nationalism had stimulated the renaissance of a Second Prizren League, who advocated a variety of agendas towards independence, including incorporation within a greater Albania. Within a year, riots became widespread in Kosovo, sparked by numerous causes including the under-funding of and over-crowding at the state university. Serbian nationalism flared within the province, fanned by intellectuals in the Serbian Academy of Arts and Sciences, who called for a complete revoking of Kosovo autonomy. An increasing sense of threat in the province resulted in the attempt, in February 1987, by the Serbian government to dissolve Kosovo's autonomy, although they lacked the authority to do so since the province was under Federal not Serbian authority.

The thirteen years from 1974 until Milosevic's Serbian presidency in 1987 enabled considerable administrative and cultural autonomy for Kosovar Albanians, but emerging debates about ethnic pluralism and nationalism began to reshape the basis of all the federated states. At the end of 1990, and again in 1992, Milosevic was reinstalled as president of the Serbian Republic. Kosovar Albanians largely boycotted the elections amidst the increasing furore of nationalism resulting from the collapse of communism, which also saw Slovenia and the Croatia elect nationalist leaders. The eight-member Presidency of Socialist Yugoslavia tended to support Milosevic's ideas, but stalemates were common. In mid-June 1991, Slovenia and Croatia seceded from the Federation, followed by Macedonia and Bosnia and Herzegovina in early 1992. Serbian minorities in Croatia and Bosnia argued for the right to remain in Yugoslavia. Arguing from the right of self-determination that had won Croats and Slovenes independence, Serbs in Croatia and then Bosnia–Herzegovina began to organise autonomously and this resulted in war against Croatia in 1992. In 1992, the Yugoslav People's Army moved into Bosnia and Herzegovina.

In the Bosnian wars of 1992–1995 Muslim, Catholic Croat, and Orthodox Serb factions fought for control of predominantly Muslim Bosnia. Eventually, the US intervened decisively with air power on the side of the Muslims. The result was the peace agreement, negotiated in Dayton, Ohio, and signed in Paris on 14 September 1995. Milosevic negotiated on behalf of the Bosnian Serbs and was lauded in the US. The Dayton Peace Accord was signed by the Republic of Bosnia–Herzegovina, the Republic of Croatia, and the Federal Republic of Yugoslavia and set up a Republic of Bosnia and Herzegovina consisting of two entities: a Croatian–Muslim Federation and a Republika Srpska. Structural difficulties in administering the separate entities have involved billions of dollars of international aid, US and European efforts to establish models for governance, and thousands of NATO and UN troops. The resettlement of about half the population, displaced during the 1992–1995 wars, remains an unresolved priority of the Dayton Accord. It is fair to say that the Dayton Accord was successful in stopping the conflict, but in re-inscribing the cultural differences accentuated by the rise of Milosevic's nationalist agenda, it continues to undermine the long history of multi-ethnic and multi-confessional co-existence, to the extent that currently 'the words tolerance, hate, co-existence and fear are all equally applicable'.[12]

In Kosovo, an agreement to end the NATO bombing campaign against the infrastructure of Serbia was formalised by UN Security Council Resolution 1244, adopted 10 June 1999. Key elements of this resolution included the right of all Kosovo refugees to return home; the commitment of member states to the sovereignty and territorial integrity of Yugoslavia and a framework for a political solution to the Kosovo crisis. The framework included the ending of hostilities in Kosovo, the withdrawal of Serbian forces, the deployment of UN forces and the establishment of an interim administration. The safe return of refugees and displaced persons and access to Kosovo by humanitarian aid organisations to support their resettlement as part of the general economic stabilisation of the economy, had vestiges of the Dayton Accord in its intent, but it was bound to alienate Milosevic and provide a basis for NATO military intervention. Since Dayton in 1995, and the 1999 NATO intervention over Kosovo, both countries have undergone a version of democratisation that is an hierarchically organised and imposed process that has proved to be more divisive than unifying.

History, said Voltaire, is little else than a long succession of useless cruelties. However, few locals in Kosovo or BiH would agree either that the cruelties, the war crimes, the atrocities, the inter-cultural miscommunications about prospects for democracy, and the extremes of xenophobia have been for nothing, or that the divisiveness emerging within democratisation is a re-emergence of 'ancient hatreds'. A key issue is whether all this has damaged the potential for human security in the region that is central to the democratisation projects in Bosnia–Herzegovina and Kosovo, and in turn underpins both the current episode and the historical development of Islamic democracy and human rights.

Democratisation in Bosnia–Herzegovina and Kosovo is patterned roughly on the same model, but differs in significant ways. Embedded in the model and its problems of 'fit' are assumptions by the intervening foreign forces about the potential of the local populations to be democratised, which reflect common myths and often xenophobic reactions to an homogenised 'Islamic culture'. As Ruth Siefert also argues, the persistence of the 'ancient hatreds' discourse and view of Islam as problematically positioned within European culture, fundamentally ignores the *European* slant to the region's Islamic history and the ways in which populations in Balkan countries often already view themselves as European.

The principles of democratisation in BiH were set in place by the Dayton Accord in 1995, which sought to achieve peace and then to restore order and justice. Essentially, Dayton set up a four-part series of agreements comprised of the consolidation of the cease-fire and territorial settlements; constitutional and election arrangements, economic reconstruction plans, and implementation arrangements for human security. The extent to which the Dayton Peace Accord divided territories into governing political entities along ethnic lines should not be under-stated, and much of the fear of Islamism in the region is influenced by local angst arising from Dayton's inability to deliver democracy, justice and conflict resolution as a package for citizens of all the region's ethnicities. Clearly, the region's conflicts had more complex causes and divisions than can be explained by the social marker of ethnicity, or could be resolved by political structures built upon fear of religious-inflected ethnic differences.[13] However, given the many-sided problems of reconstructing peace through multi-ethnic power sharing in BiH, the democratisation project appears successful to outsiders less aware of the degree to which citizen input is severely constrained, that accountability frameworks at municipal to national level are dysfunctional, and that elected representatives have, as yet, little autonomy.

The principles of democratisation in Kosovo were pre-figured at the unsuccessful peace settlement at Rambouillet, then comprehensively imposed by the UN interim joint administration initiatives in 1999 that involved the UNMIK (United Nations Interim Administration in Kosovo), OSCE (Organisation for Security and Cooperation in Europe) and the EU (European Union), together with a myriad of international non-governmental organisations throughout Kosovo. Although the four pillars of reconstruction were claimed to be 'the first such ever established by the UN' (OSCE, 2005), in fact they correspond closely with the overall format of the principles and operations of Dayton in BiH. Kosovo's democratisation is supported by a civil administration orchestrated by the United Nations with humanitarian assistance mediated by the UNHCR, institution-building established by the OSCE, and economic development overseen by the EU. To reinforce this, UNMIK relies upon NATO forces (Kosovo Forces of Reconstruction, KFOR) to support their joint efforts. This effectively authorises new modes of military humanitarianism and introduces issues of military-civilian relations that are unfortunately too complex to include here. Operating under the mandate of the UN Security Council Resolution 1244, which empowered the UN interim joint administration, the OSCE's task of 'institution building, focus[es] on governance at central and local level, media, human rights, elections, political parties, and rule of law and judicial system'.

Conventional outsider histories of the Balkans almost invariably concentrate on the political crises and social problems rather than on coexistence, and democratic forerunners such as local leadership, authority and modes of organisation. From there, they often generalise about trends and populations in ways that construct and reinforce dominant Islamophobic discourses and conceptual frameworks. Left out of these grand narratives are counter discourses that argue positive future prospects for indigenous democracy and human security in the Balkans. In order to discuss these, I turn now to a few examples of Balkan resistance to what is locally considered Islam extremism.

Counter Discourses from Balkans Islam

Stephen Schwartz has commented that 'the alleged clash of civilisations and its resulting Islamophobia are powerfully answered by the traditional pluralism of Turkish Islam found in the Balkans'.[14] He points to the work of the Bosnian Party of Democratic Action (SDA) incorporating Islamic cultural values with European political norms; to the election of Prime Minister Abdullah Gul in Turkey, representing the Justice and Development Party and to the opposition amongst indigenous Balkan Muslims to the rise of Islam extremism, particularly neo-Wahhabism. Although recent commentators such as Dragomir Andan, the Chief of Police for Republika Srpska, would have us believe that Bosnia Herzegovina is a hotbed for Islamic terrorism[15], there is little evidence to suggest this. Andan claims that three extremist groups infiltrating the Balkans are working 'towards [the] destruction of the existing secular governments in certain Muslim countries and towards creation of countries on the principle of strict Shari'a law'. Like many pro-Serbian nationalists, Andan interprets the Muslim leadership of the SDA party as excluding non-Muslims and like Bat Ye'or and Joel Starr, simply asserts connections with extremist Islam. As evidence, he points to the use of Mujahedin mercenaries in the Bosnian wars and alleges that the current Bosniak leadership is complicit in enabling Mujahedin to stay in Bosnia and Herzegovina following the signing of Dayton Peace Agreement. The fact that only a handful of these mercenaries remained, married into communities and took up Bosnian citizenship does not appear to contradict allegations of an ever present threat of Islamic terrorism offered by popular commentators happy to elide Islam in the Balkans with terrorism. A consideration of alternative viewpoints may be useful and I turn to this now.

Describing the historical formation of Albanian culture, Ismail Hasani quotes Gani Bobi who said, 'Situated between the East and the West they adopted the values of the Orient and Occident.'[16] Both these sociologists view the distinctiveness of Albanian cultural identity as emerging from 'religious pluralism [that has] resulted in mostly harmonious social relationships and a valuing of inter-cultural cohesion based on respect for differences.' Hasani stresses three factors as central: the common basis of monotheism in the region, the syncretic pluralism of Illyrian mythology, which he says was 'directly transliterated into Albanian traditions and cultural stories' that persist today, and thirdly, the shared valuing of cultural difference as a marker of ethnic identity. He maintains Kosovar Albanians have peacefully adhered to three religions: Catholic, Orthodox and Islam from the fifteenth century to the present.[17] While this view of the cultural pluralism of Kosovar Albanians is contested, it is evident that religious influences remain diverse and heavily secularised in Kosovo. There is, for example, little tolerance of Arab Islamic values, despite the money the United Arab Emirates government and independent Saudi groups have poured into the rebuilding of mosques and the funding of women to return to the home and *hijab*.

Few in Kosovo and Bosnia can forget that Iraq and Libya condemned the NATO intervention in Kosovo as aggression against Serbia's sovereignty, with Syria's and Lebanon's connivance, or that the Palestinian Authority invited Milosevic to celebrate the Orthodox Christmas in Bethlehem in 1999. Overall, Arab states were silent about genocidal actions against Muslims in Bosnia and Kosova. It is most likely that the long tradition of inter-faith coexistence and religious pluralism of Bosniaks and Kosovar Albanians is anathema to Wahabism and this is certainly the general view of Kosovar Albanians. Before the Ottoman conquest of the region, followers of Serbian Orthodoxy, Catholicism and Judaism practiced alongside each other in mixed communities. While Turkish Islam added another layer to this mix, including political institutions, it never equalled the religious repression of the Taliban regime in Afghanistan. In Kosovo, before and after the 1999 conflict, Catholicism publicly and privately supported Muslims displaced by Serbian police and militia and that respectful relationship remains between Muslims and Catholics. Clearly, the relationship between Serb Orthodoxy and Kosovar Muslims remains unresolved.

In contrast, the contribution of the Mujahideen to the army of the Republic of Bosnia–Herzegovina, over-stated in many commentaries, was always locally regarded with ambivalence. As Schwartz has pointed out ,'the Mujahideen did not influence the course of a single battle in the Bosnian conflict ... [they] were largely Saudi adventurers who loved war'. When Bosnians fought, it was for their country, not for God or the opportunity for martyrdom. When the Bosnian war ended in 1995, no Bosnians followed the Mujahideen to battle in Chechnya or Central Asia'. In 1995, the imposition of the Dayton Accord ended Arab-Islam's intervention in Bosnia, and those who stayed became part of the Bosniak community.[18] There is no evidence that the remaining Arab Muslims were or are an operational cell for potential terrorism and they are probably not the recipients of the substantial Saudi money for relief and reconstruction operations. In both Bosnia and Kosovo, Wahhabism attracts more attention for the architectural styles insisted upon by the Saudi- and Gulf-financiers of new mosques, than for their sectarian ideas. Bosniaks and Kosovar Albanians prefer the ornate Ottoman architecture, but the Saudis will pay only for the erection of austere Wahhabi-style mosques. Attempts in 2001 by Saudi-sponsored reconstruction programmes in Kosovo included plans to demolish the undamaged seventeenth century Carshi Mosque in Rahoveç, in order to build a much larger Arab style complex that would dwarf the town's buildings. Similarly, the Saudi Joint Relief Committee for the People of Kosovo and Chechnya began to pressure local authorities in Prizren to renovate its numerous historic mosques that had survived the war unscathed. Possibly only news from other villages in Kosovo where so-called restorations had been completed saved the most ancient mosques and village graveyards from demolition by the Saudi operations.

Wahhabi-oriented aid groups operating in Kosovo view the locals as having lost their commitment to Islam and maintain that the establishment of 'true' Islamic symbols are required. The precinct of local mosques in Kosovo, typically have village graveyards with distinctive Ottoman era tombstones, decorated with delicate carvings and Qur'anic verses, which Wahhabis consider idolatrous. In smaller towns heavily damaged by Serb militias, where there is widespread unemployment and little if any money to rebuild, the work of Islamic aid groups, first to supply food and shelter and then to rebuild mosques was greeted with enthusiasm. In the past five years as Saudi groups have funded young women to wear hijab and men to return to daily prayers the initial enthusiasm is turning to indignant rejection of Arab-Islamic intentions for the province. Kosovo's grand Mufti Rexhep Boja responded to the post-war influx of Arab Islamists: 'We have been Muslims for more than 600 years and we do not need to be told what Islam is. We have our own history and tradition here, our own Islamic culture and architecture. We would like to rebuild our community and to rebuild our mosques, but we want to do it our way'.[19] Although Kosovars have so far refused the imposition of Arab Islam and what they regard as its associations with terrorism, this does not necessarily mean that Balkan Muslims regard the 'War on Terror' as their fight. Many social demographic features of Kosovo and Bosnia are similar: high unemployment, comparatively young, male-dominated, literate populations, significant, rural–urban drift and so on. In both cases, the effect of democratisation is disappointingly uneven and remains the top priority for citizens in the region.

Faking Democracy? Counter-Discourses, Everyday Living, and Possible Futures

The complex conflicts in the Balkans demonstrate how the two predominant approaches to human security inevitably intertwine. The 'freedom from fear' approach typically focuses upon humanitarian intervention, the creation of international regimes and renewed relationships between citizens and state, to alleviate harm to individuals threatened by violence, repression and conflict. The 'freedom from want' approach focuses upon ameliorating the social, political, and economic conditions arising from both humanitarian emergencies and longer-term inequalities. Typically, the latter perspective offers a broad horizon on human security factors including longer-term development issues, and impacts of environmental change. Human security in the Balkans is a necessary part of the development of democracy, and inevitably influenced by Balkan Islam. Triggered by the collapse of communism, democratisation was on one hand a series of political transitions from communist ideology towards western-style governmental and economic policy development, driven by rising socioeconomic standards and competitive pressures in the global marketplace. On the other hand, democratisation intends to deliver frameworks for resolving the emergence of nationalism, and the likely re-assertion of ethnic, religious and cultural identities in the Balkan states. Balkans democratisation is depicted as 'faking democracy'[20] because instead of an organic development over time, it is entirely the contrivance and imposition of humanitarian intervention.

The development of democracy relies fundamentally on a sovereign state securing the consent of its people and governing within the Rule of Law. The instigation of elections, the finer details of electoral systems and the protection of human rights are secondary to these basic principles, but none of these fundamentals exists straightforwardly within BiH and Kosovo. In Bosnia, the Dayton Accord established a comprehensive bureaucracy that convinces few citizens about its viability because of the over-riding authority of the High representative and resulting impotence of local politicians. High unemployment and falling industrial production discourages foreign investment. Like Kosovo, destroyed or partially wrecked buildings dot the Bosnian countryside, mass graves and evidence of poor living conditions are inescapable. While the cities are fashionable and comparatively well resourced, capitalism remains skin-deep. Six years after humanitarian intervention and the oversight of international institutions, Kosovo still has erratic water and electricity services and massive unemployment. The average wage of less than $US12 000 has not improved in a decade. Health, education, social services and communications infrastructures have improved, but public services remain below European standards.

Although the bulk of the Balkan population struggles with poverty, there is no evidence that 'they do not understand democracy', said David Chandler four years ago when observing the first national elections in Kosovo.[21] According to Chandler, rather than ensuring peace and decent living standards, the democratisation process in BiH and Kosova has three main outcomes. First, it deploys a 'White Man's Burden', colonial methodology, to deliver rights-based political institutions modelled on western liberal democracies. Second, the process heavily regulates rights and freedoms amongst selected ethnic groups and thereby exaggerates social, cultural and religious differences. Third, the magnitude of international intervention is more about major powers maximising the scope of their foreign policy than about achieving stability in the region. Subsequent writing by Chandler and others, and indeed from the many sides of the debate about Balkan democratisation, exhaustively illustrate his criticisms. Overtly at stake, in whether democratisation will achieve its objectives in Bosnia and Kosovo, are the impacts of western discourses that, in bringing 'peace', dislodge self-determination struggles and ignore the counter-discourses of democracy, human rights and open society evident from liberal Islamist thinkers, not just in the Balkans but further afield.[22]

Conclusion

So far, the imposition of democracy on the back of military intervention in Bosnia and Kosovo has failed to clarify what self-determination means for ethnic groups there. The political futures of BiH and Kosovo are prescribed by peace agreements that are bureaucratically unwieldy and dependent on a continued and convincingly strong international military presence to safeguard both security and democratic process. In both Bosnia and Kosovo, the best hope for human security is seen by internationals to lie in consolidating economic progress to ensure not only closer cooperation with neighbouring countries but to also enhance societal and community opportunities. For locals, the promise of human security lies in more mundane evidence; employment, education, good and services and the peace to enjoy them. Since international intervention, the future political viability of Bosnia and Kosovo is sometimes said to depend on Balkan Muslims remembering earlier times when ethnic and religious groups peacefully co-existed. The irony of this idea should also serve as a reminder to non-Muslims of their limited grasp of contemporary Islamic political thinking.

ENDNOTES

Chapter 1

1 The term 'Neo-Islamism' was first coined by Faleh Jabar in Jabar, Faleh. 'Origins and Ideology of Neo-Islamism: A Few Landmarks' (in French), *Pensée*, vol. 299, (1994), pp. 51-58; Robert Snyder has taken up on this point by arguing that Osama bin Laden has positioned himself as a 'civilizational revolutionary' by 'externalizing regional conflicts', see Snyder, Robert S. 'Hating America: Bin Laden as a Civilizational Revolutionary', *The Review of Politics*, vol. 65, no. 4, (2003), pp. 325-350.

2 In Europe, the estimated number of Muslims is 20,000,000. In the US, the estimated number of Muslims is 7,000,000. In Australia, the estimated number of Muslims is 300,000.

3 Huntington, Samuel P. 'The Clash of Civilizations?', *Foreign Affairs*, vol. 72, no. 3, (1993), pp. 22-49; Lewis, Bernard. *What Went Wrong? Western Impact and Middle Eastern Response* (Oxford: Oxford University Press, 2001).

4 Lapidus, Ira M. A *History of Islamic Societies* (Cambridge: Cambridge University Press, 2001).

5 Shahrani, Nazif M. 'War, Factionalism and the State in Afghanistan', *American Anthropologist*, vol. 104, no. 3, (2002), pp. 715-722

6 In a classified 'National Intelligence Estimate' report released in September 2006, the US intelligence community declared that the Iraq war has exacerbated the terrorist threat faced by the US as the conflict had become a "cause celebre" for many extremist Muslims. See Mazzetti, Mark. 'Spy Agencies Say Iraq War Worsens Terrorist Threat', *New York Times*, 24 September, (2006), www.nytimes.com/2006/09/24/world/middleeast/24terror.html?pagewant ed=1&_r=1.

7 For a useful overview, see Fuller, Graham E. *The Future of Political Islam* (New York: Palgrave Macmillan, 2003).

8 Ayubi, Nazih N. *Over-Stating the Arab State: Politics and Society in the Middle East* (London: I.B. Tauris, 1996).

9 Eickelman, Dale F. & Piscatori, James. *Muslim Politics* (Princeton: Princeton University Press, 2004), pp. 22-45.

10 Wiktorowicz, Quintan. 'Introduction: Islamic Activism and Social Movement Theory' in Wiktorowicz, Quintan. *Islamic Activism: A Social Movement Theory Approach* (Bloomington: Indiana University Press, 2004), pp. 1-36.

11 The definitive work on the origins of the Muslim Brotherhood (al-Ikhwan al-Muslimun) is: Mitchell, Richard P. *The Society of Muslim Brothers* (Oxford: Oxford University Press, 1993).

12 Joshi, Pooja. *Jama'at-i Islami: The Catalyst for Islamicization in Pakistan* (Karachi: Kalinga Publications, 2003).

13 Takeyh, Ray. 'Iran: from Reform to Revolution?', *Survival,* vol. 46, no. 1, (2004), pp. 131-143.
14 Junt, Tony and Denis Lacome. 'The Banality of Anti-Americanism', in Tony Junt and Denis Lacome (eds.) *With Us or Against Us: Studies in Global Anti-Americanism* (New York: Palgrave Macmillan, 2005).
15 Roy, Olivier. 'Europe's Response to Radical Islam', *Current History,* Vol. 104, No. 685 (2005), p. 361.

Chapter 2

1   An-Na`im, Abdullahi Ahmed, *Toward an Islamic Reformism: Civil Liberties, Human Rights, and International Law* (New York: Syracuse University Press, 1990), pp. 57.
2   For a detailed discussion, see Amin Saikal, *Modern Afghanistan: A History of Struggle and Survival,* London: I.B. Tauris, 2004, Ch. 9, Steve Coll, *Ghost War: The Secret History of the CIA, Afghanistan and Bin Laden, From the Soviet Invasion to September 10, 2001*, Penguin, 2004.
3   www.islam-online.net/English/News/2002-09/15/article17
4   Roberts, Les et al. 'Morality Before and After the 2003 Invasion of Iraq: Cluster Sample Survey' *The Lancet* (29 October 2004).
5   globalsecurity.org/military/ops/iraq_casualties.htm
6   BBC News (12 February 2005).
7   Saikal, Amin. *Islam and the West: Conflict or Cooperation?* (London: Palgrave, 2003)., p.15
8   Lewis, Bernard, *The Crisis of Islam: Holy War and Unholy Terror* (London: Weidenfeld & Nicolson, 2003).
9   news.bbc.co.uk/go/pr/fr/-/2/hi/middle_east/4188216.stm
10 See Lobe, Jim, 'Gap Grows Between U.S., World Public Opinion' *Inter-Press Service* (16 March 2004); Telhami, Shibley, 'Arab Public Opinion: A Survey in Six Countries' *San Jose Mercury* (16 March 2003); Page, Susan 'Poll: Muslim countries, Europe Question U.S. Motives' *USA Today* (24 June 2004); 'Poll: Majority of Muslims Think U.S. "Ruthless", "Arrogant"' www.islamonline.net/english/News/2002-02/27/artucke05.shtml
11 Kinzer, Stephen, *All the Shah's Men: An American Coup and the Roots of Middle East Terror* (New Jersey: Wiley, 2003); Saikal, Amin, *The Rise and Fall of the Shah* (Princeton: Princeton University Press, 1980).
12 Saikal, Amin 'Securing Afghanistan's Border', *Survival,* vol. 48, no. 1 (2006), pp. 129–142; Jones, Seth G. 'Averting Failure in Afghanistan' Survival, vol. 48, no. 1 (2006), pp. 111–128.

Chapter 3

1   In this chapter I have drawn on my Elie Kedourie Memorial Lecture, 'Imagining Pan-Islam: Religious Activism and Political Utopias', *Proceedings of the British Academy*, 131 (2005), pp. 421–42.
2   For the argument that Muslim politics is principally a contest over the production and meaning of symbols in Muslim societies, see: Eickelman, Dale and James Piscatori, *Muslim Politics*, 2nd edn. (Princeton: Princeton University Press, 2004), chapter 1.

3   For the standard treatment of this subject, see: Landau, Jacob *The Politics of Pan-Islam: Ideology and Organization* (Oxford: Clarendon Press, 1990), especially chapters 1 and 2.

4   Robinson, Francis 'Islam and the Impact of Print in South Asia' in N. Crook (ed.) *The Transmission of Knowledge in South Asia; Essays on Education, Religion, History, and Politics* (Delhi: Oxford University Press, 1996), p. 74.

5   Ibid.

6   Rida, Muhammad Rashid *al-Khilafa aw'l-imama al-'uzma* (Cairo: Matba'at al-Manar, 1341A.H./1923).

7   'Abd al-Raziq, 'Ali *al-Islam wa usul al-hukm; bahth fi' l-khilafa wa' l-hukuma fi' l-islam* (Sousse/Tunis: Dar al-Ma'arif li'l-Tiba'a wa'l-Nashr, 1999), especially pp. 21–48.

8   Sanhoury, A. *Le Califat: son évolution vers une société des nations orientale* (Paris: Paul Geuthner, 1926), pp. 255–87, 569–607.

9   Al-Ghazali, Muhammad al-Fasad *al-siyasi fi'l-mujtama'at al-'arabiyya wa'l-islamiyya* (Cairo: Nahdat Misr, 2005), pp. 119–21.

10 Cited in Kramer, Martin, *Islam Assembled: The Advent of the Muslim Congresses* (New York: Columbia University Press, 1986), p. 117. This section on the Muslim congresses draws on Kramer's analysis.

11 See, for instance: Depont, Octave and Xavier Coppolani, Les confréries religieuses musulmanes (Algiers: A. Jourdan, 1897 [reprinted 1986]).

12 Gibb, H.A.R. *Modern Trends in Islam* (Chicago: The University of Chicago Press, 1947), pp. 112–13; Gibb, *Whither Islam?* (London, Victor Gollancz Ltd, 1932), p. 379. .

13 Gibb, *Modern Trends in Islam*, p. 113.

14 Nallino, C.A. *Notes on the 'Caliphate' in General and on the Alleged 'Ottoman Caliphate'*, trans. from the 2nd edn. (Rome: Direzione Generale degli Affari Politici, 1919); Arnold, Thomas Walker, *The Caliphate* (Oxford: Oxford University Press, 1924).

15 Gibb, *Modern Trends in Islam*, pp. 113–14.

16 Arnold, *op cit.*, p. 183.

17 Abushouk, Ahmed Ibrahim 'Muslim Unity; Lessons from History', *International Journal of Muslim Unity*, 1, no. 1 (June 2003), pp. 1–20.

18 Article II B(4 and 5) of the Charter of the Organisation, the text of which can be found in Annexure I of S. A. Khan, *Reasserting International Islam: A Focus on the Organization of the Islamic Conference and Other Islamic Institutions* (Karachi: Oxford University Press, 2001), pp. 316–23, quotation at p. 317. The Charter of the OIC can also be found on-line: www.oic-un.org/about/Charter.htm

19 For the full text of Bin Ladin's speech, see: http://news.bbc.co.uk/1/hi/world/south_asia/1585636.stm Also see The Times [London], 8 October 2001.

20 These are common arguments of Hizb al-Tahrir. See, for example, its website, www.1924.org , or its magazine, al-Khilafah.

21 In Bin Ladin's *fatwa* against Americans: *al-Quds al-'Arabi* [London], 23 February 1998.

22 This was said, for example, in his speech before Congress after the
    September 11th attacks:
    http://www.whitehouse.gov/news/releases/2001/09/20010920-8.html
    (accessed 25 April 2006).

23 Al-Jazeera Channel, 15 April 2004; 29 October 2004.

24 Al-Qaradawi, Yusuf Fi *fiqh al-aqalliyat al-muslima; hayat al-muslimin wasat
    mujtama'at al-ukhra* (Cairo: Dar al-Shuruq, 2001).

25 Al-Qaradawi was the chief signatory to a fatwa of 10 Rajab 1422 A.H./27
    September 2001 that American Muslims could participate in the
    forthcoming war in Afghanistan because to do otherwise would bring their
    patriotism into question. For the text of this *fatwa* in Arabic, see:
    http://www.unc.edu/~kurzman/Qaradawi_et_al_Arabic.htm (accessed on
    30 June 2003). But, after considerable opposition was expressed throughout
    the Muslim world, he, along with other senior scholars, issued a second
    fatwa in late October 2001 that abrogated the first one and banned
    American Muslim soldiers from fighting in the war. See *al-Sharq al-Awsat*, 30
    October 2001.

26 See, for example, the Iraqi Coalition Provisional Authority translation of his
    early 2004 (released in February 2004) letter:
    www.state.gov/p/nea/rls/31694.htm (accessed 29 June 2006).

27 Cole, Juan *Sacred Space and Holy War: The Politics, Culture and History of Shi'ite
    Islam* (London: I.B. Tauris, 2002), pp. 69–70.

28 *Majallat al-Azhar*, supplement, 30, no. 8 (Sha'ban 1378/February 1959), no
    page numbers indicated.

29 Enayat, Hamid *Modern Islamic Political Thought: The Response of the Shi'i and
    Sunni Muslims to the Twentieth Century* (London: Macmillan, 192), pp. 48–51;
    Zebiri, Kate *Mahmud Shaltut and Islamic Modernism* (Oxford: Clarendon Press,
    1993), pp. 24–26.

30 Hallaq, Wael B. 'Can theShari'a Be Restored?', in Haddad, Yvonne Yazbeck
    and Barbara Freya Stowasser (eds), *Islamic Law and the Challenge of Modernity*
    (Walnut Creek, California: AltaMira Press, 2004), pp. 21–26, quotations (in
    order) at pp. 25, 22.

31 Mandaville, Peter 'Toward a Virtual Caliphate', *YaleGlobal Online*, 27 October
    2005. See: http://yaleglobal.yale.edu/display.article?id=6416 (accessed 23
    January 2006).

32 See, for example, al-Khateeb, Muhibbudeen *Al-Khutoot al-'Areedah': An
    Exposition and Refutation of the Sources Upon Which the Shi'ite Religion is Based*,
    trans. by Mahmoud Murad (Burnaby, British Columbia: Majlis of al-Haq
    Publication Society, 1983).

33 Algar, Hamid *Wahhabism: A Critical Essay* (Oneonta, New York: Islamic
    Publications International, 2002), p. 3.

34 Anderson, Benedict *The Spectre of Comparisons: Nationalism, Southeast Asia and
    the World* (London: Verso, 1998), chapters 1–3.

35 Bhabha, Homi K. 'DissemiNation: Time, Narrative and the Margins of the
    Modern Nation', in Bhabha (ed.), *Nation and Narration* (London: Routledge,
    1990), p. 317.

Chapter 4

1 For more details see Mandaville, Peter. *Transnational Muslim Politics* (London: Routledge, 2004).

2 Clifford Geertz and other anthropologists do not consider the distinction between (local) culture and (cross-cultural) civilisation. On the unity of Islamic civilisation see the authoritative history of Islam by. Hodgson, Marshall G.S *The Venture of Islam. Conscience and History in a World Civilization.* 3 volumes (Chicago: University of Chicago Press, 1977).

3 The term was coined by Robertson, Roland. *Globalization, Social Theory and Global Culture* (London: Sage, 1992), pp. 8–31.

4 See my chapter on Islam and the religionisation of politics as a source of tension in Isar Y. Raj and Anheier, Helmut. (eds.) *Culture, Conflict, Globalization* (London: Sage, 2007).

5 Tibi, Bassam. 'From Islamist Jihadism to Democratic Peace? Islam at the Crossroads in Post-Bipolar International Politics', *Ankara Paper 16* (London: Taylor & Francis, 2005), pp. 1–41.

6 See Haqqani, Hussain. *Pakistan. Between Mosque and Military* (Washington/DC: Carnegie Endowment, 2005).

7 Herzog, Roman et al., *Preventing the Clash of Civilizations* (New York: St. Martin's Press, 1999).

8 See Tibi, Bassam. *The Challenge of Fundamentalism. Political Islam and the New World Disorder* (Berkeley: University of California Press, 1998, updated edition 2002).

9 For more details see Marty, Martin and Appleby, Scott. (eds.) *The Fundamentalism Project*, five volumes (Chicago: Chicago University Press, 1991–1995). Islamic fundamentalism and its jihadism are not an expression of traditionalism in that Islamists draw on modern technology and make adoptions from it for waging their irregular war. On this see Tibi, Bassam. 'The Worldview of Sunni–Arab Fundamentalists: Attitudes towards Modern Science and Technology' in: vol. 2, *Fundamentalisms and Society* (Chicago: Chicago University Press, 1993), pp. 73–102.

10 Juergensmeyer, M. *Terror in the Mind of God. The Global Rise of Religious Violence* (Berkeley: University of California Press, 2000). For a case study on jihadist Islamism see B. Tibi, Jihadism as a Religious Legitimation of Terrorism in the Path of God: Irregular War, in *Interntaional Security Today*, edited by Mustafa Aydin and Kostas Ifantis (Ankara: Center for Strategic Research, SAM Papers, 2006).

11 See my contribution to van Creveld, Martin and von Knop, Katharina. (eds.) *Countering Modern Terrorism* (Bielefeld: Bertelsmann, 2005), pp. 131–172.

12 See my article 'Jihad' in Powers, Roger and Vogele, William B. (eds.) *Protest, Power and Change. An Encyclopedia of Nonviolent Action* (New York: Garland Publishers, 1997), pp. 277–281.

13 In an early contribution to this subject by Wordlaw, Grant. *Political Terrorism* (Cambridge: Cambridge University Press, 1982, 2nd edition 1989), we find, for instance, no reference to Islam or to jihad. In contrast, recent books like the one by Hoffman, Bruce. *Inside Terrorism* (New York: Columbia University Press, 1998) deal with this issue. Among the recent contributions are

Whittacker, David J. (ed.) *The Terrorism Reader* (London: Routledge, 2001)
Pillar, Paul R. *Terrorism and US Foreign Policy* (Washington/DC: Brookings
Inst., 2001).

14 In overcoming classical realism Nye, Joseph. *Bound to Lead. The Changing
Nature of American Power* (New York: Basic Books, 1990) distinguishes
between state related, and not-state challenges/challengers; he notes 'private
actors … have become more powerful': 182. In so arguing, Nye draws our
attention to new challenges and challengers related to the rise of non-state
actors. Back in 1990 the jihadist private actors were not yet visible in the
West as an example and therefore Nye does not refer to them.

15 On this politicisation see the contributions to the special issue of
Millennium, *Journal of International Affairs*, vol. 29, no. 3 (2000) on Religion
and International Relations, including Tibi, Bassam. 'Post-Bipolar Order in
Crisis: The Challenge of Politicized Islam', pp. 843–859. See also Haynes,
Jeff. *Religion in Global Politics* (London: Longman, 1998) herein in particular
chapter 7 on the Middle East.

16 In his work, Hedley Bull strongly puts the study of order at the center of
International Relations; see *The Anarchical Society. A Study of Order in World
Politics* (New York: Columbia University Press, 1977), herein in particular
part one. For an appreciation of Bull, see: Hoffmann, Stanley. 'Bull and the
contribution to International Relations' in *World Disorders. Troubled Peace in the
Post-Cold War Era* (New York: Rowman & Littlefield, 1998), pp. 13–34.

17 Aron, Raymond. *Paix et guerre entre les nations* (Paris: Calmann-Lévy, 1962).

18 On this see Jackson, Robert H. *Quasi-States: Sovereignty, International Relations
and the Third World* (Cambridge: Cambridge University Press, 1990). On the
concept of 'the nominal nation-state' see Tibi, Bassam. 'Old Tribes and
Imposed Nation-States' in Khoury Philip S. and Kostiner, Joseph. (eds.)
Tribes and State Formation in the Middle East (Berkeley: University of California
Press, 1990), pp. 127–152.

19 On these conflicting visions see first on democratic peace Russet, Bruce.
Grasping Democratic Peace (Princeton/NJ: Princeton University Press, 1993).
The origin of the concept is Kant, Immanuel. *Zum ewigen Frieden* (Frankfurt:
Suhrkamp, 1979), pp. 37–82. On the other vision, i.e. the Islamic concept of
peace, see Tibi, Bassam. 'War and Peace in Islam' in Nardin, Terry. (ed.) *The
Ethics of War and Peace* (Princeton/NJ: Princeton University Press, 1996 and
1998). The reference to this classical concept of calling for an 'Islamic world
revolution for achieving Islamic world peace' can be found in Sayyid Qutb's
work.

20 See the respective chapters in the part 'Remaking the World through
Militancy' in volume 3 of *The Fundamentalism Project: Fundamentalisms and the
State* (Chicago: Chicago University Press, 1993).

21 On this concept of divine order see the analysis based on the authentic
Islamist references in Tibi, Bassam. *Fundamentalismus im Islam. Eine Gefahr für
den Weltfrieden* (Darmstadt: Wissenschaftliche Buchgesellschaft 2000, 3rd
edition 2002) chapters 2, 4 and 5. The origin of this concept is the holy book
of the Islamists by Qutb, Sayyid. *Ma'alim fi al-tariq/ Signs along the Road*,
published in millions of copies in Arabic as well as in diverse translations

into other languages. I use the 13th legal edition (Cairo: Dar al-shuruq, 1989).

22 On the basic difference between Islam and Islamism from a perspective of security studies see Tibi, Bassam. 'Islam and Islamism: A Dialogue with Islam and a Security Approach vis-à-vis Islamism' in Jacoby, Tamy A. and Sasley, Brent. (eds.) *Redefining Security in the Middle East* (Manchester and New York: Manchester University Press, 2002), pp. 62–82.

23 Hobsbawm, Eric and Ranger, Terence. (eds.) *The Invention of Tradition* (Cambridge: Cambridge University Press, 1983).

24 Hoffer, Eric. *The True Believer. Thoughts on the Nature of Mass Movements* (New York: Perenial Library, 2002, reprint of the original 1951).

25 Holsti, Kalevi. *The Dividing Discipline* (London: Allen and Unwin, 1985).

26 Bull, Hedley. 'The Revolt against the West' in Bull, Hedley and Watson, Adam. (eds.) *The Expansion of International Society* (Oxford: Clarendon, 1984), pp. 217–228

27 Bull, Hedley, *The Anarchical Society,* note 16, pp. 273. On this simultaneity see Tibi, *The Challenge of Fundamentalism,* chapters 1 and 5.

28 Tibi, Bassam. *Islam between Culture and Politics* (New York: Palgrave, 2nd enlarged edition 2005), chapter 4.

29 On this see Curtin, Philip. *The World and the West. The European Challenge* (Cambridge: Cambridge University Press, 2000); see also Scruton, Roger. *The West and the Rest. Globalization and the Terrorist Threat* (Wilmington/Del.: ISI-books, 2002). On the claims and on the failure as well as on the future of universalism of Western civilisation see Gress, David. *From Plato to NATO. The Idea of the West and its Opponents* (New York: The Free Press, 1998), chapter 12.

30 See Tibi, Bassam. 'Culture and Knowledge. The Fundamentalist Claim of de-Westernization' in *Theory, Culture and Society,* vol. 12, no. 1 (1995), pp. 1–24.

31 See the reference in note 8 above and also Ayubi, Nazih. *Political Islam, Religion and Politics in the Arab World* (London: Routledge, 1991).

32 Mitchell, Richard. *The Society of the Muslim Brothers* (London: Oxford University Press, 1969).

33 al-Banna, Hasan. 'Risalat al-jihad/Essay on jihad' in the collected writings of al-Banna, *Majmu'at rasail al-Banna* (Cairo: Dar al-da'wa, 1990), pp. 271–292.

34 See the informative article by Philipott, Daniel. 'The Challenge of September 11 to Secularism in International Relations' in *World Politics,* vol. 55, no. 1 (2002), pp. 66–95. Much earlier, Mark Juergensmeyer gave his pertinent book the title *The New Cold War?* the subtitle: *Religious Nationalism* confronts the Secular State (Berkeley: University of California Press, 1993). On this subject see also Tibi, Bassam, 'Secularization and Desecularization in Modern Islam' in *Religion, Staat, Gesellschaft,* vol. 1, no. 1 (2000), pp. 95–117.

35 Doran, Michael. 'Somebody Else's Civil War' *Foreign Affairs,* vol. 82, no. 1 (2002), pp. 22–42.

36 Qutb, Sayyid. *al-salam al-alami wa al-Islam/World Peace and Islam* (Cairo: Dar al-shuruq, 1992), pp. 172.

37 On the religious legitimization of September 11 see Lincoln, Bruce. *Holy Terrors. Thinking about Religion after September 11* (Chicago: University of

Chicago Press, 2003), on jihad see herein chapter 3. See also Tibi, Bassam. 'Islamism, National and International Security after September 11' in Baechler, Guenther and Wenger, Andreas. (eds.) *Conflict and Cooperation* (Zurich: Neue Zuercher Zeitung Publ., 2002), pp. 127–152. In an earlier book on Middle Eastern wars, I suggested that the rise of Islamic fundamentalism compels to consider a new security approach, see Tibi, Bassam. *Conflict and War in the Middle East. From Interstate War to New Security* (New York: St. Martin's Press, 2nd enlarged edition 1997), chapter 12.

38 Huntington, Samuel P. *Clash of Civilizations and the Framing of World Order* (New York: Simon & Schuster, 1996), the idea was published 1993 in Foreign Affairs. However, I disagree with Huntington and I elaborate on the existing differences in the new edition of my book *Krieg der Zivilisationen. Politik und Religion zwischen Vernunft und Fundamentalismus,* first published 1995 (Munich: Heyne Verlag, 1998, new extended edition 2001), chapter 7.

39 For this pursuit see Tibi, Bassam. *The Crisis of Modern Islam* (Salt Lake City: Utah University Press, 1988); and Tibi, Bassam. *Islam and the Cultural Accommodation of Social Change* (Boulder/Col.: Westview Press, 1990, reprinted 1991).

40 Within the framework of the Geneva-based Security Studies Program the following study was completed before September 11 see Grare, Frédéric. (ed.) *Islamism and Security. Political Islam and the Western World* (Geneva: Program for Strategic and International Security Studies, 1999). It is also worth mentioning that the Swiss Zentralstelle für Gesamtverteidigung / Office Centrale de la Défense back in March 1997 summoned experts on political Islam, including myself, and published the brochure *Islam et l'Islamisme* (Bern 1997), my contribution, pp. 9–20.

41 On de-Westernisation see note 30 above, on Westernisation see van der Laue, Theodore. *The World Revolution of Westernization* (New York: Oxford University Press, 1987). On globalisation and culture see Robertson, Roland. *Globalization, Social Theory and Global Culture* (referenced in note 3). Robertson criticizes those who overlook 'the relative autonomy of culture'.

42 Habermas, Juergen. 'Glauben und Wissen' in Frankfurter Allgemeine Zeitung, October 15, 2001, pp. 9. For a critique see Tibi, Bassam. 'Habermas and the Return of the Sacred. Is it a Religious Renaissance? Political Religion as a New Totalitarianism' in *Religion, Staat, Gesellschaft,* Vol. 3, No. 2 (2002), pp. 265–296.

43 See the proceedings of the Erasmus Foundation/Amsterdam: *The Limits of Pluralism. Neo-Absolutisms and Relativism* (Amsterdam: Praemium Erasmianum, 1994), herein the essay on political Islam as a variety of neo-absolutism by Bassam Tibi, pp. 29–36. This volume also includes the controversy between Clifford Geertz and Ernest Gellner on culture and relativism.

44 See the chapter on the Islamic worldview in Tibi (2005) *op cit,* pp. 53–68.

45 See the allegation of 'Une vaste conspiration judeo-chrétienne' by Kassab, Mohammed Y. *L'Islam face au nouvel ordre mondial* (Algier: Editions Salama, 1991), pp. 75–93. Not only Islamists, also Germans (left and right) claim that September 11 was a conspiracy. This is done in a dozen of German

bestsellers, see the special issue Verschwörung/conspiracy of the news magazine Der Spiegel 37/2003 criticising these bestsellers.

46 Giddens, *Anthony. Beyond Left and Right. The Future of Radical Politics* (Cambridge: Polity Press, 1994).

47 Qutb (1992), *Op Cit*, pp. 167–199.

48 On Qutb see Euben, Roxanne E. *The Enemy in the Mirror. Islamic Fundamentalism and the Limits of Modern Nationalism* (Princeton/NJ: Princeton University Press, 1999), chapter 3.

49 See Miller, Lynne. *Global Order* (Boulder: Westview, 1990), on the Westphalian system see chapter 2.

50 Hedley Bull, *The Revolt against the West*, pp. 223.

51 See the contributions in Lyons Gene M. and Mastanduno, Michael. (eds.) *Beyond Westphalia* (Baltimore: John Hopkins University Press, 1995).

52 See al-Awwa, Salim. *Fi al-nizam al-siyasi li al-dawla al-Islamiyya* (Cairo: al-maktab al-masri, 1975, 6th reprinting 1983).

53 On the discrimination of non-Muslims in the shari'a see the work of the Muslim reformist An-Na'im, Abdullahi A. *Toward an Islamic Reformation* (Syracuse: Syracuse University Press, 1990), chapter 7. See also Ye'or, Bat. *Islam and Dhimmitude* (Cransbury: Associated University Presses, 2002). The Islamic shari'a contradicts individual human rights. On all counts see Tibi, Bassam. 'Islamic Law/ shari'a, Human Rights, Universal Morality and International Relations' *Human Rights Quarterly*, Vol. 16, No. 2 (1994), pp. 277–299.

54 On these movements see Ayubi (1991), *Op Cit*; see also Roy, Olivier. *The Failure of Political Islam* (Cambridge/MA: Harvard University Press, 1994).

55 On this duality see Jansen, Johannes. *The Dual Nature of Islamic Fundamentalism* (Ithaca and New York: Cornell University Press, 1997); see also Tibi (1993), Op Cit.

56 The sources of this approach are in the first place Arnold Toynbee with his multi volume opus magnum, *The Study of History* (New York: Oxford University Press, 1947); and then Will Durant, *The Story of Civilizations*, 11 volumes (New York: Simon & Schuster, 1963–1967); more recent Lipson, Leslie. *The Ethical Crisis of Civilizations* (London: Sage, 1993). Huntington, Samuel P. *Clash of Civilizations and the Framing of World Order* (New York: Simon & Schuster, 1996) introduced this approach to International Relations, however, with an insufficient knowledge of the issue.

57 See Kepel, Gilles. *Jihad-Expansion et le Déclin de l'Islamisme* (Paris: Gallimard, 2000); in contrast to Kepel see my introduction to the updated edition of my book *The Challenge of Fundamentalism*.

58 See Buzan, Barry. *People, States and Fear. An Agenda for International Security Studies in the Post-Cold War Era* (Boulder/Col.: Lynne Rienner Publ., 1991).

59 On the traditional origins of this concept and its current relevance see Kelsay, John. *Islam and War* (Louisville/KY: John Knox Press, 1993), chapter 5. See also Johanson, James T. *The Holy War Idea in Western and Islamic Tradition* (University Park/PN: Pennsylvania State University Press, 1997) and notes 12 and 19 above.

60 See Gibb, Sir Hamilton A.R. *Studies on the Civilization of Islam* (Princeton/NJ: Princeton University Press, 1962, reprint 1982).
61 See Cockburn, Andrew and Cockburn, Patrick. *Out of the Ashes. The Resurgence of Saddam Hussein* (New York: Harper and Collins Publ., 1999).
62 Kelsay (1993), *Op Cit*, pp. 117.
63 See Lincoln (2003), *Op Cit.*
64 Martin, Leonore. (ed.) *New Frontiers in Middle Eastern Security* (New York: St. Martin's Press, 1999).
65 See on this the pioneering works by Holsti, Kalevi J. *The State, War, and the State of War* (Cambridge: Cambridge University Press, 1996); and earlier van Creveld, Martin. *The Transformation of War* (New York: The Free Press, 1991); as well as part five on 'new security', in Tibi (1997), *Op Cit.*
66 For more details see Ulfkotte, Udo. *Der Krieg in unseren Städte. Wie radikale Islamisten Deutschland unterwandern* (Frankfurt/M: Fischer, 2004).
67 I borrow the term 'gated diaspora' from Papastergiadis, Nikos. *The Turbulance of Migration* (Cambridge: Polity Press, 2000).
68 See AlSayyad Nezar and Castells, Manuel. (eds.) *Muslim Europe or Euro-Islam?* (Lanham: Lexington Books, 2002), this volume includes Tibi, Bassam. 'Muslim Migrants in Europe: Between Euro-Islam and Ghettoization', pp. 31–52.
69 See Tibi, Bassam. 'Europeanizing Islam or the Islamization of Europe? ' in Katzenstein, Peter and Byrnes, Tim. (eds.) *Religion in an Expanding Europe* (Cambridge: Cambridge University Press, 2006), pp. 204–224.
70 See Tibi, Bassam. *Der neue Totalitarismus* (Darmstadt: Primus, 2004); Tibi, B., 'The Totalitarianism of Jihadist Islamism and its Challenge to Islam and Europe, *Totalitarian Movements and Political Religion*, vol 1, 8 (2007) pp., 35–54.
71 Popper, Karl. *The Open Society and its Enemies*, 2 volumes (London: Routledge and Paul Kegan, 1945).
72 On this see Revel, Jean-François. *Democracy Against Itself* (New York: Free Press, 1993), on Islamic terrorism see chapter 12.
73 Tibi, Bassam. 'Les conditions d'Euro-Islam' in Bistolfi, Robert and Zabbal, François. (eds.) *Islam d'Europe. Intégration ou insertion communitaire* (Paris: Editions de l'Aube, 1995), pp. 230–234. See also Tibi, Bassam. 'Between Communitarism and Euro-Islam. Europe, Multicultural Identities and the Challenge of Migration' in Docker, John and Fischer, Gerhard. (eds.) *Adventures of Identity. European Multicultural Experiences and Perspectives* (Tübingen: Stauffenberg, 2001), pp. 45–60 and notes 68 and 69 above.
74 On Islam's compatibility with democracy and modernity see Watt, William M. *Islamic Fundamentalism and Modernity* (London: Routledge, 1988); and Fazlur, Rahman. *Islam and Modernity. Transformation of Intellectual Tradition* (Chicago: Chicago University Press, 1982). See also Tibi, Bassam. 'Democracy and Democratization in Islam. The Quest of Islamic Enlightenment' in Schmiegelow, Michèle. (ed.) *Democracy in Asia* (New York: St. Martin's Press, 1997), pp. 127–146.
75 See Chasdi, Richard. *Tapestry of Terrorism. A Portrait of Middle Eastern Terrorism 1994–1999* (Lanham: Lexington Books, 2002); and Berman, Paul. *Terror and Liberalism* (New York: Nortion & Company, 2003).

Chapter 5

1 Gilroy, Paul. 'Joined up politics and post-colonial melancholia' in Lash, S. and Featherstone, M. (eds.) *Recognition and Difference: politics, identity, multiculturalism* (London: Sage, 2002), pp. 161–162.

2 Derrida, Jacques. *Of Hospitality* (Stanford: Stanford University Press, 2000).

3 Benvenisti, Emile. *Indo-European Language and Society* (London: Faber, 1973).

4 *Ibid.*

5 *Ibid.*

6 Durkheim, Emile. *The Elementary Forms of the Religious Life* (Beverly Hills, CA: Sage Publications, 1954).

7 Schmitt, Carl. *The Concept of the Political* (Chicago: University of Chicago Press, 1986).

8 Benvenisti, *Op Cit.*

9 Turner, Brian S. 'Warrior charisma and the spiritualization of violence' *Body & Society* Vol. 9, No. 4 (2004), pp. 93–108.

10 Bauman, Zygmunt. *Modernity and the Holocaust* (Cambridge: Polity Press, 1989).

11 Benvenisti, *Op Cit.*

12 Sassen, Saskia. *Guests and Aliens* (New York: New York Press, 1999).

13 Glazer, Nathan. *We Are All Multiculturalists Now* (Cambridge, MA: Harvard University Press, 1997).

14 Bourdieu, Pierre. (ed.) *La Misere du monde* (Paris: Seuil, 1993).

15 See figures by UNHCR at: www.unhcr.org/cgi-bin/texis/vtx/basics/opendoc.htm?tbl=BASICS&id=3b028097c#Numbers

16 Kaldor, Mary H. *New & Old Wars. Organized Violence in a Global Era* (Cambridge: Polity, 2001).

17 See, for instance, Evans, Peter B.; Rueschemeyer, Dietrich & Skočpol, Theda. (eds.) *Bringing the State Back In* (Cambridge: Cambridge University Press, 1985).

18 Sayad, Abdelmalek. *The Suffering of the Immigrant* (Cambridge: Polity Press, 2004).

19 Blackburn, R. *Banking on Death or Investing in Life. The history and future of pensions* (London: Verso, 2002).

20 Anderson, Benedict. *Imagined Communities* (London: Verso, 1983).

21 Corrigan, P. and Sayer, D. *The Great Arch. English State Formation as Cultural Revolution* (Oxford: Basil Blackwell, 1985).

22 Agamben, Giorgio. *Homo Sacer: sovereign power and bare life* (Stanford: Meridian, 1998), pp. 19.

23 Foucault, Michel. *Power. The Essential Works 3* (London : Allen Lane, 2001).

24 Joppke, Christian. 'The retreat of multiculturalism in the liberal state: theory and policy' *British Journal of Sociology* Vol. 55, No. 2 (2004): 237-257.

25 Department of Immigration and Multicultural Affairs. *National Agenda for a Multicultural Australia*, www.immi.gov.au/multicultural/_inc/publications/agenda/agenda89/toc.htm (1989), pp. 50.

26 Barry, B. *Culture and Equality* (Cambridge: Polity Press, 2001); Montgomery, J.D. and Glazer, N. (eds.) *Sovereignty under Challenge* (New Brunswick: Transaction Books, 200); Joppke, (2004); Satori, G. (2000) *Pluralismo, multiculturalismo e estranei* (Milano: Rizzoli, 2000).

27 Shklar, J. N. *Redeeming American Political Thought* (Chicago: University of Chicago, 1998).

28 Levy, J. *The Multiculturalism of Fear* (Oxford: Oxford University Press, 2000).

29 Turner, Brian S. 'Cosmopolitan virtue, globalization and patriotism' *Theory Culture & Society* Vol. 19, No. 1–2 (2002), pp. 45–63.

30 Kaldor, *Op Cit.*

31 von Clausewitz, Karl. *On War* (London: Pelican,.1968).

32 Hirst, P. *War and Power in the 21st Century. The state military conflict and the international system* (Cambridge: Polity, 2001).

33 Kaldor, *Op Cit.*

34 Muenkler, H. *The New Wars* (Cambridge: Polity, 2005).

35 Kaldor, *Op Cit.*

36 Hartman, D. and Gerteis, J. 'Dealing with Diversity: mapping multiculturalism in sociological terms' *Sociological Theory* Vol. 23, No. 2 (2005) pp. 218–240.

37 Hamilton, C. 'Multiculturalism as a political strategy' in Gordon A. and Newfield C. (eds.) *Mapping Multiculturalism* (Minneapolis: University of Minnesota Press, 1996), pp. 167–76.

38 Craig, G. 'Ethnicity racism and the labour market: a European perspective' in Andersen J.G. and Jensen P.H. (eds.) *Changing Labour Markets, Welfare Policies and Citizenship* (Bristol: Policy Press, 2002), pp. 149–182; Kamali, M. *Distorted Integration. Clientization of Immigrants in Sweden* (Uppsala: Uppsala Multiethnic Papers, 1997).

39 Glazer, *Op Cit*, pp. 147.

40 The Institute of Community Cohesion. *Challenging Local Communities to Challenge Oldham* (The Cantle Report), (2001), news.bbc.co.uk/2/shared/bsp/hi/pdfs/25_05_06_oldham_report.pdf, pp. 9.

41 Furnivall, J.S. *Colonial Policy and Practice. A Comparative Study of Burma and Netherlands India* (Cambridge: Cambridge University Press, 1948).

42 Ameli, Saied Reza *Globalization, Americanization and British Muslim Identity*, (London: ICAS Press, 2002); Amelia, Saied Reza and Merali, Arzu *British Muslims' Expectations of the Government. Dual Citizenship: British Islamic or Both? Obligation, RecognitionRespect and Belonging* (Wembley: Islamic Human Rights Commission. Amelia and Merali, 2005).

43 Brubaker, W. R. *Citizenship and Nationhood in France and Germany* (Cambridge, MA: Harvard University Press, 1992).

44 Muenkler, *Op Cit.*

45 Kymlicka, Will. *Multicultural Citizenship* (Oxford: Clarendon Press, 1995).

46 Cooke, M. 'Authenticity and Autonomy: Taylor, Habermas, and the politics of recognition' *Political Theory* Vol. 25, No. 2 (1997), pp. 258–288.

47 Strauss, Leo. *Natural Right and History* (Chicago: University of Chicago Press, 1950).

48 Schmitt, *Op Cit.*
49 Turner, Brian S. 'The erosion of citizenship' *The British Journal of Sociology* Vol. 52, No. 2 (2001), pp. 189–209.
50 Ong, Aihwa. *Flexible Citizenship. The Cultural Logics of Transnationality* (Durham and London: Duke University Press, 1999); Ong, Aihwa. 'Citizenship' in Nugent, D. and Vincent, J. (eds.) *A Companion to the Anthropology of Politics* (Oxford: Blackwell, 2005), pp. 55–68.
51 Glazer, Nathan. 'Dual Citizenship as a Challenge to Sovereignty' in Montgomery, J.D. and Glazer, N. (eds) *Sovereignty under Challenge. How Governments Respond*, (New Brunswick: Transaction, 2002), pp. 33–54.
52 Glazer, Op Cit.
53 Ignatieff, Michael. *The Lesser Evil. Political Ethics in an age of terror* (Princeton: Princeton University Press, 2004).

Chapter 6

1 See: Korten, D *Globalizing Civil Society: Reclaiming our Right to Power*, (Seven Stories Press, New York, 1998).; Salamon, L.; Anheier, H.; List, R.; Toepler, S. & Sokolowski, S. *Global Civil Society. Dimensions of the Non-Profit Sector* (Baltimore: The Johns Hopkins Centre for Civil Society Studies, 1999).; Edwards, M. & Gaventa, J. *Global Citizen Action* (London: Earthscan, 2001).; Howell, Julia & Pearce, J. *Civil Society and Development: A Critical Exploration* (Boulder: Lynne Rienner, 2002).; van Rooy, A. *Global Legitimacy Game. Civil Society, Globalization and Protest* (London: Palgrave, 2004).
2 Dunn, K.; Thomson, S.; Hanna, B.; Murphy, P. & Burnley, I. 'Multicultural Policy within Local Government in Australia', *Urban Studies*, vol. 38, no. 13, Dec. 2001), pp. 2477–2494.
3 This research has involved a number of local and international collaborative studies with Bryan Turner, Kevin Brown, Greg Barton, Jenny Onyx, Terry Burke and Fethi Mansouri.
4 Kenny, Sue; Mansouri, Fethi & Spratt, P. *Arabic Communities and Well-Being: Supports and Barriers to Social Connectedness* (Melbourne: Deakin University, Centre for Citizenship and Human Rights, 2005).
5 This is an Australian Research Council funded grant, undertaken with colleague Greg Barton. It involves case-studies of the views and experiences of participants in NGOs and an analysis of different capacity building funding programs.
6 Islamic NGOs are defined by an explicit reference in their mission to work within an Islamic framework. Whilst there are different conceptions of what is means to 'work within an Islamic framework', discussion of these conceptions is beyond the scope of this paper. For the purpose of research into NGOs it is important to note that Islamist organisations are excluded, because Islamist organisations do not fulfil all the criteria required for categorisation as a NGO, where a civil society sphere, offering a space of free deliberation, and acceptance of a secular state are both required.
7 Roy, Olivier. *Globalised Islam: the search for the new ummah* (London: C.Hurst & Co., 2004).

8   The official figure of American deaths since the invasion of Iraq is just over 2,000. There are no official figures for Iraqi deaths in this period. However estimates range between 26,797 and 30,163 (see www.iraqbodycount.net).

9   Glasser, S. 'Global Terrorism Statistics Debated, New Report Leaves Some Wondering How to Measure the Number of Attacks', *Washington Post*, 29 October, (2005).

10   Following Roy, I use the term Islamism to refer to 'the brand of modern political Islamic fundamentalism hat claims to re-create a true Islamic society, not simply by imposing shari'a, but by establishing first an Islamic state through political action'. Islamists identify Islam as not just religion, but a political ideology that reshapes all aspects of society. Interestingly Islamists also use precepts of modern social science. Roy (2004), *Op Cit*, pp. 58.

11   Beck, Ulrich. & Ritter, M. *Risk Society: Towards a New Modernity* (London: Sage, 1992); Beck, Ulrich. *World Risk Society* (Cambridge: Polity Press, 1999).

12   Beck (1999), *Op Cit*, pp. 137–138.

13   *Ibid,* pp. 141.

14   *Ibid,* pp. 135.

15   *Ibid,* pp. 137–138.

16   Mythen, G. *Ulrich Beck. A Critical Introduction to the Risk Society.* (London: Pluto Press, 2004).

17   Giddens, Anthony. *The Third Way* (Cambridge: Polity Press, 1998).

18   Beck (1999), *Op Cit,* pp. 139.

19   Lupton, D. *Risk* (London: Routledge, 1999).

20   Douglas, M. *Risk and Blame: Essays in Cultural Theory* (London: Routledge, 1992).

21   Beck (1999) *Op Cit;* Mythen (2004), *Op Cit;* Giddens, Anthony. *Beyond Left and Right. The Future of Radical Politics* (Cambridge: Polity Press, 1994).; Turner, Brian. S. 'The erosion of citizenship' *The British Journal of Sociology*, vol. 52, no. 2, (2001), pp. 189–209.

22   Giddens (1994), *Op Cit.*

23   Giddens (1998), *Op Cit.*

24   Slovic, P.; Lichtenstein, S. & Fischhoff, B. 'Perceived Risk: Psychological Factors and Social Implications', *Proceedings of the Royal Society*, (1981), pp. 17–34.

25   Beck (1992), *Op Cit*, pp. 135.

26   Mythen (2004), *Op Cit*, pp. 118.

27   Beck (1999), *Op Cit*, pp. 3.

28   *Ibid*, pp. 75.

29   Klein, Naomi. 'The Rise of Disaster Capitalism', *The Nation*, 23 May, (2005).

30   Osborne, D. & Gaebler, T. *Reinventing Government: How the Entrepreneurial Spirit is Transforming the Public Sector* (New York: Plume, 1993).

31   Lyon, D. *Surveillance after September 11* (Cambridge: Polity Press, 2003).

32   Douglas, M. *Risk Acceptability According to the Social Sciences* (London: Routledge, 1985).

33   Culpitt, I. *Social Policy and Risk* (London: Sage, 1999).

34   Huntington, Samuel P. *Clash of Civilizations and the Framing of World Order* (New York: Simon & Schuster, 1996).

35 Sayyid, Bobby S. *A Fundamental Fear: Eurocentrism and the Emergence of Islamism,* (London: Zed Books, 1997), pp. 3–4.

36 Lupton (1999), *Op Cit*, pp. 123.

37 Douglas (1985), *Op Cit*; Lupton (1999), *Op Cit*; Bauman, Zygmunt. *Modernity and Ambivalence* (Cambridge: Polity Press, 1991).

38 Xenophobia refers to 'morbid dislike or fear of foreigners'. The term xenophobia derives from the Greek xenos or strange/r, and phobia referring to fear or aversion.

39 Huntington (1997), *Op Cit.*

40 Said, Edward. *Orientalism* (New York: Pantheon, 1978), pp. 3–4.

41 *Ibid,* pp. 202–203.

42 Kenny et al (2005), *Op Cit.*

43 Klein (2005), *Op Cit.*

44 Beck (1998), *Op Cit.*

45 *Ibid.*

46 Douglas (1992), *Op Cit.*

47 Wilkinson, I. *Anxiety in a Risk Society* (London: Routledge, 2001).

48 Giddens (1994), *Op Cit;* Franklin, J. (ed.) *The Politics of Risk Society* (Cambridge: Polity Press, 1998).

49 Salamon, L.; Anheier, H.; List, R.; Toepler, S. & Sokolowski, S. *Global Civil Society. Dimensions of the Non-Profit Sector* (Baltimore: The Johns Hopkins Centre for Civil Society Studies, 1999).

Chapter 7

1 Agamben, Giorgi. 'Security and Terror' *Theory and Event*, vol. 5, no. 4 (2002), pp. 290–307.

2 Roy, Olivier. *Globalised Islam: the Search for the New* Ummah (London: Hurst & Co., 2004).

3 *Ibid,* pp. ix.

4 Feldman, Allen. 'Securocratic Wars of Public Safety' *Interventions*, vol. 6, no. 3 (2004) pp. 330–350.

5 *Ibid,* pp. 332.

6 *Ibid,* pp. 335.

7 Herzfeld, Michael. *Anthropology: Theoretical Practice in Culture and Society* (Oxford: Blackwell, 2001), pp. 133.

8 In the case of France North Africans were recruited as unskilled industrial labour as early as 1905.

9 Rosaldo, Renato. *Culture and Truth* (Boston: Beacon Press, 1989), pp. 198–219.

10 Humphrey, Michael. *Islam, Multiculturalism, Transnationalism: from the Lebanese Diaspora* (London: IB Tauris with the Centre for Lebanese Studies, 1998).

11 Roy (2004), *Op Cit,* pp. 103.

12 *Ibid.*

13 *Ibid,* pp. 22–23.

14 *Ibid,* pp. 25.

15 *Ibid,* pp. 41.

16 *Ibid,* pp. 99.

17 *Ibid,* pp. 6.
18 Roy, Olivier. 'A Clash of Cultures or a Debate on Europe's Values? *ISIM REVIEW*, vol. 15, no. 6–7 (2005), pp. 5.
19 See comments by Associate Editor Rohan Jayasekera in November 2004, *Index on Censorship.*
20 Roy (2005), pp. 6.
21 Roy (2004), pp. 68.
22 Agamben (2002), *Op Cit.*
23 Herzfeld (2001), *Op Cit,* pp. 305.
24 Wissam Saad on an Alternate Australian Muslim Religious Leadership, *The Religion Report,* 20 October 2004, ABC Radio National, www.abc.net.au/rn/talks/8.30/relrpt/stories/s1223296
25 www.darulfatwa.org.au/English/
26 Roy (2005), *Op Cit,* pp. 6.
27 Duffield, M & Waddell, N. 'Human Security and Global Danger: Exploring a Governmental Assemblage', *Report for Economic and Social Science Research Council,* (2004) www.bond.org.uk/pubs/gsd/duffield.pdf, pp. 2.
28 *Ibid,* pp. 2.
29 *Ibid,* pp. 35.
30 Corbeil-Essones, Evry. 'An Underclass Rebellion' *The Economist,* 12 November, (2005), pp. 25–27.
31 Duffield (2004), *Op Cit;* Agambem (2002), Op Cit.
32 Agamben (2002), *Op Cit.*
33 *Ibid.*
34 *Ibid.*
35 Feldman (2004), *Op Cit,* pp. 333.
36 *Ibid.*
37 *Ibid,* pp. 335.
38 'Financing terrorists: Looking in the wrong places' *The Economist,* 20 October (2005).
39 *Ibid.*
40 Herzfeld (2001), *Op Cit,* pp. 256.
41 *Ibid,* pp. 270.
42 Buck-Morss, Susan. 'The Cinema Screen as Prosthesis of Perception: A Historical Account' in Seremetakis, C.N. (ed.) *The Sense Still: Perception and Memory as Material Culture in Modernity* (Chicago: The University of Chicago Press, 1996).
43 Feldman (2004), *Op Cit,* pp. 340.
44 Wilkinson, M; Davies, Anne and Clennell, Andrew. 'Muslims unite – it's time to disown terror' *Sydney Morning Herald,* 26 July (2005).
45 Malik, Abdul-Rehman. 'Hear the true voice of Islam' *The Observer* 24 July (2005).
46 *Ibid.*

Chapter 8

1 Al Ghunaimi, Mohammad Talaat. *The Muslim Conception of International Law and the Western Approach* (The Hague: Martinus Nijhoff, 1968), pp. 135–161.;

Hashmi, Sohail H. 'Jihad', in Wuthnow, Robert. (ed.) *Encyclopaedia of Politics and Religion* (Washington, D.C: Congressional Quarterly Inc., 1998).; Lewis, Bernard. *The Encyclopaedia of Islam* (London: Brill, 1960), pp. 538.; Peters, Rudolph. *Islam and Colonialism* (The Hague: Mouton Publishers, 1979).

2 Peters (1979), pp. 3; El Fadl, Khaled Abou. 'Islam and the Theology of Power' *Middle East Report*, vol. 221, Winter (2001).

3 Khadduri, Majid. *War and Peace in the Law of Islam* (Baltimore: The Johns Hopkins Press, 1955).; Peters (1979); Peters, Rudolph. 'Jihad', in Esposito, John L. (ed.) *The Oxford Encyclopaedia of Modern Muslim World* (Oxford: Oxford University Press, 1995).

4 Khadduri (1955); Peters, F.E. *Islam: A Guide for Jews and Christians* (Princeton: Princeton University Press, 2003).; Rahman, Fazlur. *Islam* (London: Weidenfeld and Nicolson, 1966).; Rahman, Fazlur *Islam and Modernity: Transformation of Intellectual Tradition* (Chicago: Chicago University Press, 1982).

5 Rahman (1966), pp. 37.

6 Rahman (1994).

7 Peters (2003), pp. 206; Rahman (1966), pp. 37.

8 *Ibid*, pp. 37; Armstrong, Karen. *Islam: A Short History* (New York: The Modern Library, 2000), pp. 6.

9 Peters (2003); Rahman (1966), pp. 37–38.

10 Khadduri (1955); Hamidullah, Muhammad. *Muslim Conduct of State,* (Lahore: Muhammad Ashraf, 1968).; Peters (1979); Peters (2003), pp. 206–208.

11 Cited in Peters (2003), pp. 212.

12 Peters (1995).

13 Peters (1979), pp 42–44.

14 Kuran, Timur. *Islam and Mammon: The Economic Predicaments of Islamism,* (Princeton: Princeton University Press: 2004).

15 Castells, Manuel. *The Power of Identity* (Oxford: Blackwell Publishers, 2004), pp. 112–115.

16 Rana, M. *A to Z of Jehadi Organizations in Pakistan* (Lahore: Mashal Books, 2004).; Stern, Jessica. 'Pakistan's Jihad Culture', *Foreign Affairs*, vol, 79, no.6 (2000).

17 Kuran 2004, pp. 82–102; Sageman, Marc. *Understanding Terror Networks* (Philadelphia: University of Pennsylvania Press, 2004).

18 Rana (2004), pp. 85.

19 See *Ibid*, Chapter 1.

20 Napoleoni, Loretta. *Modern Jihad: Tracing the Dollars Behind the Terror Networks* (London: Pluto Press, 2003).

21 Butt, SS. 2005. 'Small-time hoodlum being used for terror', *The News*, (January 4, 2005).

22 Khan, Ismail. 'Militants were paid to repay Al Qaeda debt', *Dawn*, Karachi, www.dawn.com/2005/02/09/top1.htm (9 February, 2005).

23 Hassan, Riaz. *Faithlines: Muslim Conceptions of Islam and Society* (Oxford: Oxford University Press, 2002).; Kepel, Gilles. Jihad: *The Trail Political Islam* (Cambridge: Harvard University Press, 2002).

24 *Ibid*; El Fadl (2001); Mann, Michael. *Incoherent Empire* (London: Verso: 2003).; Rashid, Ahmad. *Jihad: The Rise of Militant Islam in Central Asia* (Lahore: Vanguard, 2002).; Sageman (2003).

25 Kepel (2002); Mann (2003); Napoleoni (2003); Ramakrishna, Kumar. 'Jemaah Islamiah: Aims, Motivations and Possible Counter Strategies', www.ntu.edu.sg/idss/Perspectives/research_050221.htm (2002); Rashid (2002).

26 Mann (2003).

27 Sageman (2004).

28 *Ibid*.

29 Rana (2004).

30 See Kepel (2002); Peters (1986); Rashid (2002).

31 Hassan (2002).

32 Kepel (2002), pp. 375–376; Atran, Scott. 'Facing Catastrophe: Risk and Response: The 9/11 and M-11 Commissions' Blind Sides' AEI-Brookings Joint Center, www.aei.brookings.org/policy/page.php?id=207 (2005).

33 Mann (2003).

34 Ali, Imran. 'Islam, Power and Political Legitimacy in Pakistan' Paper presented at the conference on Political Legitimacy in Islamic Asia (Asia Research Institute, National University of Singapore, 25–26 April, 2005).

Chapter 9

1   In most English-language texts, HT uses the transliteration Hizb ut-Tahrir; in Indonesia, Hizbut Tahrir is the official spelling.

2   There is some debate as to the correct year of HT's founding. Although some scholarly sources give the year of 1952, as this was when an-Nahbani first established a group of this name, the organisation itself formally lists 1953 as its foundation date, based on the Jordanian government's initial registration of HT. Interviews with Ismail Yusanto and Muhammad al-Khaththath, Jakarta 2005. See also the Hizbut Tahrir website: www.hizb-ut-tahrir.org.

3   Taji-Farouki, Suha. *A Fundamental Quest: Hizb al-Tahrir and the Search for the Islamic Caliphate* (London: Grey Seal, 1996); International Crisis Group. (2003), 'Radical Islam in Central Asia: Responding to the Threat of Hizb ut-Tahrir', *ICG Asia Report no 58*, 30 June, available at: www.crisisweb.org, pp. 2.

4   Taji-Farouki, Suha. 'Islamists and the threat of Jihad: Hizb al-Tahrir and al-Muhajiroun on Israel and the Jews' *Middle Eastern Studies*, vol. 36, no. 4, October (2000), pp. 21–25.

5   The most detailed account of HTI's early history can be found in Salim, Agus. 'The Rise of Hizbut Tahrir Indonesia (1982–2004): It's Political Opportunity Structure, Resource Mobilization, and Collective Action Frames', MA Thesis, Syarif Hidayatullah State Islamic University, Jakarta (2005). I have gained valuable additional information from interviews in Jakarta with Ismail Yusanto (2 March 2004 and 5 December 2005), Muhammad al-Khaththath (10 December 2005) and Ahmad al-Junaidi (5 and 9 December 2005).

6   As with many aspects of HTI's history, al-Baghdadi's precise status with the organisation is uncertain. Some sources claim that he was a 'senior official' or 'trusted activist' with the HT central leadership in Jordan, while others claim that he held no special position.

7   Interview with Muhammad al-Khaththath, Jakarta, 27 March 2006.

8   Interview with Muhammad Ismail Yusanto, Jakarta, 21 March 2006, and Muhammad al-Khaththath, Jakarta, 27 March 2006.

9   Salim, *Op Cit*, 2005, pp. 145; Sabili, May 2000.

10 Interviews with Ismail Yusanto, Canberra, 3 March 2004 and Canberra, 1 September 2004.

11 Salim, *Op Cit*, 2005; Mayer, Jean-François. 'Hizb ut-Tahrir – The Next al-Qaida, Really?', *PSIO Occasional Paper 4/2004*, Federal Department of Foreign Affairs, Switzerland (2004).

12 Female members are known as nisa and males are called rijal. Salim, *Op Cit*, pp. 145–149; Novikov, Evgenii (2004), 'The Recruiting and Organizational Structure of Hizb ut-Tahrir', *Terrorism Monitor*, The Jamestown Foundation, http://jamestown.org/publications_details.php?volume_id=400&issue_id_3 148, accessed 6 March 2006, pp. 1–5.

13 Interviews with Ismail Yusanto, Jakarta, 2 March 2004; and Muhammad al-Khaththath, Jakarta, 10 December 2005. Salim, *Op Cit*, pp. 152–61.

14 *Ibid*, pp. 138–140 & 175.

15 HT does not reveal the location of its central leadership. The headquarters of the international HT spokesman is Amman, and many observers believe this is also were the executive board and emir are based.

16 When questioned on whether the emir had visited, HTI leaders firmly replied that no answers would be given on such matters.

17 Interviews with senior HTI figures, Jakarta, December 2005 and March 2006.

18 Hizbut Tahrir. *Mengenal Hizbut Tahrir: Partai Politik Islam Ideologis (Introducing Hizbut Tahrir: An Ideological Islamic Political Party)*, Bogor: Pustaka Thariqul Izzah (2002), pp. 34–39; Mayer, *Op Cit*, pp. 15–17.

19 Interview with Ahmad Junaidi, Jakarta, 5 December 2005.

20 Tan, Merlyna. *Islamic Radicalism and Anti-Americanism in Indonesia: The Role of the Internet*, (Washington DC: Policy Studies 18, East–West Center, Washington, 2005), pp. 5–6.; Lyotard, Jean-François. *The Postmodern Condition: A Report on Knowledge* (Minnesota: University of Minnesota Press, 1985).; Foucault, Michel. *The Archeology of Knowledge and the Discourse on Language* (New York: Pantheon Books, 1985).

21 *al-Wa'ie, Edisi Khusus* (Special Edition), March (2005), pp. 4.

22 'Indonesia Menangis', on *al-Wa'ie CD Database* Interaktif, Bonus Edisi Khusus, (2006).

23 HTI has made considerable use of CDs to disseminate its materials. The presentations on this CD are intended not only to inform hizbiyyin but also to be used by HTI preachers.

24 Noor, Farish. 'Mapping out the Political Topography of Political Islam in Malaysia: Actors, Agents and Currents of Thought and Ideas' at CSCAP General Conference, Jakarta, 4 December (2003).

25 HTI, 'Jihad dan Terrorisme: Antara Fakta dan Propaganda' (Jihad and
    Terrorism: Between Facts and Propaganda), December (2005), on al-Wa'ie
    CD Database Interaktif, Bonus Edisi Khusus, 2006.
26 Sayyid, Bobby S. *A Fundamental Fear: Eurocentrism and the Emergence of Islamism*
    (London: Zed Books, 1997).
27 Comments from a participant at a HTI public forum in Kuningan, Jakarta in
    August 2002.

Chapter 10

1   For example, see Arberry, A.J. *Sufism* (London: Allen & Unwin, 1950). See
    also Geertz, Clifford. *The Religion of Java* (Glencoe, Ill.: The Free Press, 1960);
    Geertz, Clifford. *Islam Observed* (Chicago: University of Chicago Press, 1968);
    Gellner, Ernest. *Muslim Society* (Cambridge: Cambridge University Press,
    1981); and Gellner, Ernest. *Postmodernism, Reason and Religion* (London:
    Routledge, 1992).
2   The author borrows here from the catchy phasing and useful schema of
    Benjamin Barber. See Barber, Benjamin R. *Jihad vs. McWorld* (New York:
    Ballentine, 1996).
3   Bruinessen, Martin van & Howell, Julia Day. *Sufism and the 'Modern' in Islam*
    (London: IB Tauris, In Press); Malik, Jamal and Hinnells, John, eds. *Sufism in
    the West* (London: Routledge 2006).
4   Howell, Julia Day. 'Modernity and Islamic Spirituality in Indonesia's New
    Sufi Networks'. In *Sufism and the 'Modern' in Islam*, ed. M. van Bruinessen and
    J.D. Howell (London: I.B. Tauris 2007); Howell, Julia Day. 'Sufism and the
    Indonesian Islamic Revival', *Journal of Asian Studies*, vol. 60, no. 3, (2001), pp.
    701–729.; Howell, Julia D. & Nelson, Peter L. 'New Faces of Indonesian
    Sufism: A Demographic Profile of Tarekat Qodiriyyah-Naqsyabandiyyah,
    Pesantren Suryalaya in the 1990s', *Review of Indonesian and Malaysian Affairs*,
    vol. 35, no. 2, (2001), pp. 33–60.
5   Geertz, *Op Cit.*
6   Burhani, Ahmad Najib. *Sufisme Kota* (Jakarta: Serambi, 2001); Ibrahim, Idi
    Subandy. 'Kesalehan Instan dan Spiritualitas Orang Kota', Pikiran Rakyat,
    vol. 17, Nov. (2001).; Mulkhan, Abdul Munir. *Dari Semar ke Sufi. Kesalehan
    Multikultural Sebagai Solusi Islam di Tengah Tragedi Keagamaan Umat Manusia*
    (Kalasan, Sleman, Yogyakarta: Al-Ghiyats, 2003); Noer, Kautsar Ashari.
    Tasawuf Perenial. Kearifan Kritis Kaum Sufi (Jakarta: Serambi, 2002); van
    Bruinessen, Martin. Kitab Kuning, *Pesantren dan Tarekat, Tradisi-tradisi Islam di
    Indonesia* (Bandung: Mizan, 1995).
7   Burhani, *Op Cit*; Ibrahim, *Op Cit.*
8   Heider, Karl G. *Landscapes of Emotion, Mapping Three Cultures of Emotion in
    Indonesia* (Cambridge: Cambridge University Press, 1991); Siegel, James T.
    'Images and Odors in Javanese Practices Surrounding Death', *Indonesia*, vol.
    3, no. 6, (1983), pp. 1–14.; Wikan, Unni. *Managing Turbulent Hearts, A Balinese
    Formula for Living* (Chicago: University of Chicago Press, 1990).
9   See Barton, Greg. 'Indonesia's Nurcholish Madjid and Abdurrahman Wahid
    as Intellectual 'Ulama: The Meeting of Islamic Traditionalism and
    Modernism in Neo-Modernist Thought', *Studia Islamika*, vol. 4, no. 1, (1997);

Kull, Ann. *Piety and Politics: Nurcholish Madjid and His Interpretation of Islam in Modern Indonesia* (Lund: Lund Studies in History of Religions, 2005); Woodward, Mark R. 'Talking Across Paradigms: Indonesia, Islam and Orientalism'. In *Toward a New Paradigm: Recent Developments in Indonesian Islamic Thought*, ed. by M.R. Woodward. (Tempe: Arizona State University 1996).

10 The perennialist movement has promoted the idea that 'many paths lead to God', particularly by pointing to the esoteric traditions of the major world religions that are understood to facilitate fundamentally similar mystical experiences of the Ultimate. Many of the perennialists, including René Guénon, Martin Lings, Frithjof Schuon, Nasr and others, developed their perennialist orientation via studies of Islam's Sufi tradition.

11 Although almost ninety percent of Indonesians are Muslims, the state was not founded as an Islamic state but on the basis of the religiously neutral 'Panca Sila' or Five Pillars, the first of which is 'Belief in the One High God' (Tuhan Yang Maha Esa). Nonetheless, proponents of an Islamic state of one sort or another have repeatedly challenged the Panca Sila formula for managing religious diversity in Indonesia. The most recent (unsuccessful) challenge was in 2002.

12 On Komariddin's positions, see below. Nasaruddin Umar is presently Director General of Islamic Affairs (Dirjen Bimas Islam) in the Ministry of Religion.

13 The convocation that officially launched MADIA on 10 November 1996 included participants from several Muslim and Christian institutions. The office of a Christian monthly magazine, KAIROS, which had recently folded, was made available for the occasion, and individuals from Paramadina, the State Islamic Institute (IAIN) Jakarta, the Indonesian Bishops' Conference (KWI) and the Centre for Research and Development of the Indonesian Churches Association (PGI) attended in their personal capacities. Later meetings expanded to include Confucianists, Buddhists, Brahma Kumari (BKWSU) sisters and others.

14 Jamhari and Jabali, Fuad. *IAIN dan Modernisasi Islam di Indonesia* (Ciputat, Indonesia: Logos Wacana Ilmu, 2002); Riddell, Peter. *Islam and the Malay-Indonesian World, Transmission and Responses* (Honolulu: University of Hawaii Press, 2001), pp. 231.

15 Interview with the author in Jakarta on 17 September 2003.

16 See, for examples articles like 'Filsafat Perenial: Perspektif Alternatif untuk Studi Agama' by Seyyed Hossein Nasr (*Ulumul Qur'an* vol. III, no. 3, 1992, pp. 86–95) and 'Tradisionalisme Nasr: Eksposisi dan Refleksi. Laporan dari Seminar Seyyed Hossein Nasr' (*Ulumul Qur'an* vol. IV, no. 4, 1993, pp. 106–111) covering Nasr's visit to Indonesia in June 1993, when he gave a number of talks like 'Spiritualitas, Krisis Dunia Moderen dan Agama Masa Depan' (Spirituality, the Crisis of the Modern World and the Religion of the Future') at the Hotel Wisata International, Jakarta, and 'Filsafat Perennial' ('Perennial Philosophy') at the Paramadina Foundation, Jakarta.

17 Noer, *Op Cit.*

18 Hidayat, Komaruddin and Wahyudi Nafis, Muhamad. *Agama Masa Depan, Perspektif Filsafat Perennial* (Jakarta: Gramedia Pustaka Utama, 2003), pp. 40.

19 *Ibid,* pp. 39.
20 *Ibid,* pp. 39.
21 *Ibid,* pp. 39.
22 *Ibid,* pp. 43.
23 *Ibid,* pp. 43.
24 *Ibid,* pp. 53.
25 *Ibid,* pp. 46, 55.
26 Howell, Julia. 'Muslims, the New Age and Marginal Religions in Indonesia: Changing Meanings of Religious Pluralism', *Social Compass,* vol. 52, no. 4, (2005), pp. 473–493.
27 Ginanjar, Ary. *Rahasia Sukses Membangun Kercerdasan Emosi dan Spiritual, ESQ, Emotional Spiritual Quotient, Berdasarkan 6 Rukun Iman dan 5 Rukun Islam* (Jakarta: Arga Publishers, 2001).
28 See Goleman, Daniel. *Working with Emotional Intelligence* (New York: Bantam Books, 1999).
29 See Zohar, Danah & Marshall, Ian. *SQ: Spiritual Intelligence, The Ultimate Intelligence* (London: Bloomsbury, 2000).
30 One of the key personal development tools taught in the ESQ programs is 'Zero Mind Process' which is defined in an ESQ Training brochure as an 'effort to purify the heart [*penjernihan hati*] in order to develop the ability to hear the hidden voice of the heart that is the source of wisdom [kebijaksanaan (*wisdom*)] and motivation [motivasi (*energy*)]' (English glosses as per original).
31 See Gombrich, Richard F. and Gananth Obeyesekere. *Buddhism Transformed: Religious Change in Sri Lanka* (Princeton, NJ: Princeton University Press 1988); Kotler, Arnold, ed. *Engaged Buddhist Reader* (Berkeley: Parallax Press 1996); Pittman, Don A. *Toward a Modern Chinese Buddhism: Taixu's Reforms* (Honolulu: University of Hawai'i Press 2001); and Queen, Christopher S. and Sallie B. King, eds. *Engaged Buddhism, Buddhist Liberation Movments in Asia* (Albany: State University Press of New York 1996).
32 Queen, Christopher S. and Sallie B. King, eds. 'Preface' in *Engaged Buddhism: Buddhist Liberation Movments in Asia* (Albany: State University Press of New York 1996), pp. ix.
33 Queen, Christopher S. and Sallie B. King. 'Introduction: The Shapes and Sources of Engaged Buddhism' in *Ibid.* pp. 23.
34 Pittman, Don A. *Toward a Modern Chinese Buddhism: Taixu's Reforms* (Honolulu: University of Hawai'i Press 2001), pp. 296.

Chapter 11

1 See the informative discussion by Akbarzadeh, Shahram and Saeed, Abdullah. *Islam and Political Legitimacy,* (New York: Routledge Curzon, 2003), pp. 1–14. See also Sadiki, Larbi. *The Search for Arab Democracy Discourses and Counter-Discourses,* (New York: Columbia University Press, 2004).
2 See Lane, Ann. *Yugoslavia, When Ideals Collide,* (London: Palgrave, 2004), pp. 7–34.

3   As evident for example in news items such as Casciani, Dominic. 'UK "Islamophobia" rises after 11 September', BBC News, (29 August, 2002), http://news.bbc.co.uk/1/hi/uk/2223301.stm (accessed Nov. 21st 2005).

4   See Crittenden, Stephen. 'Interview with Bat Ye'or', The Religion Report, www.abc.net.au/rn/talks/8.30/relrpt/stories/s1250346.htm (accessed Nov. 21st 2005).

5   Starr, Joel. 'How to Outflank al Qaeda in the Balkans', *European Affairs,* (Fall 2004), europeanaffairs.org/current_issue/2004_fall/2004_fall_98 (accessed Nov. 21st 2005).

6   See for example, the website of the UN Office for the Coordination of Humanitarian Affairs, The Commission on Human Security (CHS) http://ochaonline.un.org/

7   Alice, Lynne. Hatred and democracy: risks, rights and freedoms. Unpublished paper presented at Eighth International Seminar 'Democracy and Human Rights in Multiethnic Societies', 11–15 July 2005, Konjic, Bosnia & Herzegovina.

8   Ethnically BiH's 4 million people have a 48% majority of Bosniaks (Muslim Slavs), Serbs constitute 37.1%, Croats 14.3%, and 'others' 0.6%. Kosovo's two million people are 90% Albanian, the remaining 10% being Serbs and ten or so ethnic minorities, notably Egyptian, Ashkali and Roma.

9   This is particularly so in the southern Dragash region, where there are remains of mosques that pre-date the Ottoman Empire.

10 Originally a general in the Ottoman military, Skenderbeg deserted the Turkish army in 1443 and took his troops to establish self-rule in his Albanian homeland homelands to prevent the Turkish invasion of Catholic Western Europe.

11 See Bose, Sumantra. *Bosnia After Dayton, National Partition and International Intervention,* (Oxford: Oxford University Press, 2002), pp. 1–38, for an interesting discussion of this historical development in Bosnia, in his. See also Bieber, Florian. *Post-War Bosnia: Ethnicity, Inequality and Public Sector Governance.* (New York: UNRISD, Palgrave Macmillan), 2006.

12 Bougarel, Xavier. 'Bosnia and Hercegovina: State and Communitarianism', in Dyker D.A. and Vejvoda, Ivan. (eds.), *Yugoslavia and After: A Study in Fragmentation, Despair and Rebirth,* Addison (Boston: Wesley Longman, 2006), cited in Bose, (2002), *Op Cit,* pp. 18.

13 The inadequacy of ethnicity as a singular or even key explanation of the conflicts in the Balkans following the fall of communism has been comprehensively described, see for example Markotich, Stan. 'Making Sense of the Deterioration of Brotherly Nations: Why Serbs, Croats, Bosniaks and Albanians Went to War, while the Montenegrins, Voivodinians and Slovenes Did Not' in Alice, Lynne. *Ethno-Politics in the Former Yugoslavia* (Berne: Peter Lang, forthcoming, 2007).

14 Schwartz, Stephen. 'Democracy and Islam After September 11. The case for optimism', *The Weekly Standard,* (December 16, 2002). Paper offered at the 23rd annual convention of the Assembly of Turkish–American Associations, as part of a panel discussion titled 'Reevaluating Democracy and Islam after September 11'. Available at:

www.frontpagemag.com/Articles/ReadArticle.asp?ID=5102 (Accessed Nov.21st 2005). See also Schwartz, Stephen. *The Two Faces of Islam: The House of Sa'ud from Tradition to Terror,* (London: Doubleday 2002).

15 Andan, Dragomir. 'Report: The Development of Islamic Terrorism in Bosnia–Herzegovina to the International Conference on Terrorist Threats in South–East Europe - May 8, 2005', available at: www.slobodan-milosevic.org/news/report050705.htm (accessed November 21st 2005). Andan names the groups allegedly operating in BiH as: al-Gama'a al-Islamiyya form Egypt, Groupe Islamique Armee (GIA: Armed Islamic Group) from Algeria, al-Jihad from Egypt, and al-Qaida from Afghanistan.

16 Bobi, Gani. *Cultural Paradox,* (no date, circa 1979), (Prishtina: University of Prishtina), pp. 47.

17 Hasani, Ismail. 'The Albanians - Culture, Religion and Nationalism' in Lynne (2007), *Op Cit.*

18 Darwish, M. 'The Hidden Face of Extremism – the 'New Wahhabi' Movement' *EastWest Record,* (Oct. 8 2001) at www.eastwestrecord.com/articles/theNewWahhabMovement.asp. Also cited by Schwartz, Stephen. 'The Arab Betrayal of Balkan Islam', *Middle East Quarterly,* vol. 9, no. 2 (Spring 2002).

19 Quoted in Schwartz, Stephen. 'Islamic Fundamentalism in the Balkans', *Partisan Review,* (Summer 2000) available at www.bu.edu/partisanreview/archive/2000/3/schwartz (accessed Nov. 21st 2005).

20 Chandler, David. *Bosnia: Faking Democracy After Dayton,* (London: Pluto Press, 2000).

21 *Ibid,* pp. 200–212; Chandler, David. *Kosovo Elections: Failing The Test Of Democracy?,* British Helsinki Human Rights Group available at: www.bhhrg.org (accessed November 21st 2005).

22 Fuller, (2003) *Op Cit,* pp. 29–33. In addition, see Mousalli, Ahmad. 'Modern Islamist Fundamentalist Discourses on Civil Society, Pluralism and Democracy' in Schwedler, Jillian (ed.) *Toward Civil Society in the Middle East?* (Boulder, Co: Lynne Rienner, 1995); Mardin, Serif. 'Civil Society and Islam' in Hall, John A. (ed.) *Civil Society,* (New York: Polity Press, 1996); Lahoud, Nelly. *Political Thought in Islam: A Study in Intellectual Boundaries,* (London: Routledge, 2005).

NOTES ON CONTRIBUTORS

Shahram Akbarzadeh is Associate Professor of Politics and Director of the Centre for Muslim Minorities and Islam Policy Studies, School of Political & Social Inquiry, Monash University. He is Convenor of the Islam Node in the ARC Asia Pacific Futures Research Network. His research interests include the politics of Central Asia, the Middle East and political Islam. Associate Professor Akbarzadeh has published seven books and numerous book chapters, refereed journal articles and reports. His books include *Islam and Globalization* - 4 volumes (London: Routledge series on Critical Concepts in Islamic Studies, 2006); *Uzbekistan and the United States: Authoritarianism, Islamism and Washington's New Security Agenda* (London: Zed Books, 2005); and *Islam and Political Legitimacy* (London: Routledge Curzon Press, 2003).

Lynne Alice is a Senior Lecturer in International Relations at Deakin University, Melbourne, Australia. Her research interests include human rights and humanitarian law, the politics of military intervention, and ethno-nationalism and feminist political analysis. Dr Alice works with the Kosovo Women's Network and Zene Zenama (Sarajevo) as the international consultant for the monitoring of the UN Security Council Resolution 1325 in Kosovo and Bosnia-Herzegovina.

Greg Fealy is a Research Fellow in Indonesian Politics at the Australian National University, Canberra, Australia. His research interests include Islam and civil society, and the impact of globalization on religion and culture in Southeast Asia. Dr Fealy has been a Visiting Professor at the Johns Hopkins School of Advanced International Studies, Washington D.C.

Riaz Hassan is an ARC Professional Fellow and Emeritus Professor in the Department of Sociology at Flinders University, Adelaide, Australia. His research interests include sociology or religion, social demography, and applied sociology. In June 2006, he was appointed a Member of the Order of Australia.

Julia Howell is Deputy Director of the Griffith Asia Institute at Griffith University, Brisbane, Australia. Assoc Prof Howell's research interests include the sociology of Islam, spiritual practices and religious experiences in Hindu and Sufi traditions, Asian new religious movements in Western societies, Indonesian studies, and religion, society, and modernity.

Michael Humphrey is Chair of the Department of Sociology and Social Policy at the University of Sydney, Australia. His current research interests are in violence, healing, reconciliation and justice. Professor Humphrey has also published widely on Lebanese Muslim immigrant culture and politics, Islamic movements, ethnic conflict, globalization, human rights, violence.

Susan Kenny is Chair of the Institute of Citizenship and Globalisation and Director of the Centre for Citizenship and Human Rights at Deakin University, Melbourne, Australia. Professor Kenny's research interests include comparative studies of civil society, non-government organizations and risk; community development and citizenship, and the sociology of human rights (focusing on refugee research; cross-cultural issues and racism).

Fethi Mansouri teaches history, cultures and ideologies of the contemporary Middle East in the School of International and Political Studies, Deakin University, Melbourne, Australia. Associate Professor Mansouri's recent publications include *Australia and the Middle East: a Front-line Relationship* (Tauris Academic Studies, 2006, London/New York) and (with Michael Leach) *Lives in Limbo* (UNSW Press 2004).

James Piscatori is Professor of Islamic Studies at Oxford University. His research interests include Islam and politics, modern Islamic political thought and movements, modern Middle Eastern, (specifically Arab) history and politics. Professor Piscatori is currently running a research project on *The Transnationalism of Islam*.

Amin Saikal is Professor of Political Science and Director of the Centre for Arab and Islamic Studies (the Middle East and Central Asia) at the Australian National University, Canberra. His research interests include the politics, history, and international relations of the Middle East and Central Asia. Professor Saikal has been a Visiting Fellow at Princeton University, Cambridge University, and the Institute of Development Studies at the University of Sussex. In January 2006, he was awarded the Order of Australia. Professor Saikal's latest books include: *Modern*

Afghanistan: A History of Struggle and Survival (London: IB Tauris, 2006), and *Islam and the West: Conflict or Cooperation?* (London: Palgrave, 2003).

Bassam Tibi is Director of the Centre of International Affairs and Professor of International Relations at the University of Goettingen, Germany. He is also A.D. White Professor at Large in Cornell. Professor Tibi's research interests include international relations and Islamic civilization, the Middle East, and the Mediterranean region. He held various visiting professorships, inter alia, in the United States (Harvard, Princeton, Berkeley, Ann Arbor), Turkey, Sudan, Cameroon, and recently in Switzerland, Indonesia and Singapore. His latest book is *Islam between Culture and Politics*, expanded and updated edition, (Palgrave, 2005).

Bryan Turner is the research leader on religion and globalization at the Asia Research Institute, National University of Singapore. He is currently writing a three-volume study of sociology of religion and editing the *Dictionary of Sociology* for Cambridge University Press. Professor Turner's latest book, *Human Rights and Vulnerability*, is published by Penn State University Press, 2006.

REFERENCES

Abdul Rehman, Malik. 'Hear the true voice of Islam', *The Observer* Sunday July 24, (2005) www.observer.co.uk.

Abdullah, Kurniawan, 'Fenomena Gerakan Politik Islam Ekstraparlementer: Hizbut Tahrir Indonesia', *Dialog: Jurnal Penelitian dan Kajian Keagamaan*, vol. 1, (2005), pp. 31–58.

Agamben, Giorgi. *Homo Sacer: Sovereign Power and Bare Life* (Stanford: Stanford University Press, 1998).

Agamben, Giorgi. 'Security and Terror' *Theory and Event,* vol. 5, no. 4 (2002), pp. 290–307.

Akbarzadeh, Shahram & Saeed, Abdullah. (eds.) *Islam and Political Legitimacy*, (London: Routledge, 2003).

Al Awwa, Salim. *Fi al-nizam al-siyasi li al-dawla al-Islamiyya* (Cairo: al-maktab al-masr, 1975).

Al Banna, Hasan. *Majmu'at rasail al-Banna* (Cairo: Dar al-da'wa, 1990).

Al Ghunaimi, Mohammad Talaat. *The Muslim Conception of International Law and the Western Approach* (The Hague: Martinus Nijhoff, 1968).

Al Sayyad, Nezar & Castells, Manuel. (eds.) *Muslim Europe or Euro-Islam?* (Lanham: Lexington Books, 2002).

Ali, Imran. 'Islam, Power and Political Legitimacy in Pakistan' Paper presented at the conference on *Political Legitimacy in Islamic Asia* (Asia Research Institute, National University of Singapore, 25–26 April, 2005).

Alice, Lynne. *Ethno-Politics in the Former Yugoslavia* (Berne: Peter Lang, forthcoming 2007).

Ameli, Saied Reza. *Globalization, Americanization and British Muslim Identity* (London: ICAS Press, 2002).

Ameli, Saied Reza & Merali, Arzu. *British Muslims' Expectations of the Government. Dual Citizenship: British Islamic or Both? Obligation, Recognition, Respect and Belonging* (Wembley: Islamic Human Rights Commission, 2004).

An Na`im, Abdullahi Ahmed. *Toward an Islamic Reformism: Civil Liberties, Human Rights, and International Law* (New York: Syracuse University Press, 1990).

Andan, Dragomir. *Report: The Development of Islamic Terrorism in Bosnia–Herzegovina*, International Conference on Terrorist Threats in South–

East Europe, 8 May (2005) www.slobodan-
milosevic.org/news/report050705.htm.

Anderson, Benedict. *Imagined Communities: Reflections on the Origin and Spread of Nationalism* (London: Verso, 1983).

Andersen, Jørgen G. & Jensen, Per H. (eds.) *Changing Labour Markets, Welfare Policies and Citizenship* (Bristol: Policy Press, 1985).

Arberry, A.J. *Sufism* (London: Allen & Unwin, 1950).

Armstrong, Karen. *Islam: A Short History* (New York: The Modern Library, 2000).

Aron, Raymond. *Paix et guerre entre les nations* (Paris: Calmann-Lévy, 1962).

Atran, Scott. 'Facing Catastrophe: Risk and Response: The 9/11 and M-11 Commissions' Blind Sides' AEI-Brookings Joint Center, (2005) www.aei.brookings.org/policy/page.php?id=207.

Ayubi, Nazih. *Political Islam, Religion and Politics in the Arab World* (London: Routledge, 1991).

Ayubi, Nazih N. *Over-Stating the Arab State: Politics and Society in the Middle East* (London: I.B. Tauris, 1996).

Baechler, Guenther & Wenger, Andreas. (eds.) *Conflict and Cooperation* (Zurich: Neue Zuercher Zeitung Publishers, 2002).

Baran, Zeyno. (ed.) *The Challenge of Hizb ut-Tahrir: Deciphering and Combating Radical Islamic Ideology*, Conference Report, The Nixon Center, September, (2004) pp. 124–126.

Baran, Zeyno. 'Fighting the War of Ideas', *Foreign Affairs*, November/December, (2005), pp. 68–78.

Barber, Benjamin R. *Jihad vs. McWorld* (New York: Ballentine, 1996).

Barry, Brian. *Culture and Equality* (Cambridge: Polity Press, 2001).

Barton, Greg. 'Neo-Modernism: A Vital Synthesis of Traditionalist and Modernist Islamic Thought in Indonesia', *Studia Islamika*, vol. 2, no. 3, (1995).

Barton, Greg. 'Indonesia's Nurcholish Madjid and Abdurrahman Wahid as Intellectual '*Ulama*: The Meeting of Islamic Traditionalism and Modernism in Neo-Modernist Thought', *Studia Islamika*, vol. 4, no. 1, (1997).

Batscha, Zwi & Saage, Richard. (eds.) *Friedensutopien* (Frankfurt: Suhrkamp, 1979).

Bauman, Zygmunt. *Modernity and the Holocaust* (Cambridge: Polity Press, 1989).

Bauman, Zygmunt. *Modernity and Ambivalence* (Cambridge: Polity Press, 1991).

Beck, Ulrich. & Ritter, M. *Risk Society: Towards a New Modernity* (London: Sage, 1992).

Beck, Ulrich. *World Risk Society* (Cambridge: Polity Press, 1999).

Berman, Paul. *Terror and Liberalism* (New York: Norton & Company, 2003).

Bieber, Florian. *Post-War Bosnia: Ethnicity, Inequality and Public Sector Governance* (London: UNRISD & Palgrave McMillan, 2006).

Bistolfi, Robert & Zabbal, François. (eds.) *Islam d'Europe. Intégration ou insertion communitaire* (Paris: Editions de l'Aube, 1995).

Blackburn, Robin. *Banking on Death or Investing in Life. The History and Future of Pensions* (London: Verso, 2002).

Blomberg, S. Brock; Hess, Gregory D. & Weerapana, Akila. *Terrorism from Within: An Economic Model of Terrorism* (Claremont Graduate University, Claremont, CA: Claremont Working Papers in Economics, 2002).

Bobi, Gani. *Cultural Paradox* (Prishtina : University of Prishtina, circa 1979).

Bose, Sumantra. *Bosnia After Dayton, National Partition and International Intervention* (Oxford: Oxford University Press, 2002).

Bourdieu, Pierre. (ed.) *La Misere du monde* (Paris: Seuil, 1993).

Brubaker, W. Rogers. *Citizenship and Nationhood in France and Germany* (Cambridge, MA: Harvard University Press, 1992).

Bull, Hedley. *The Anarchical Society: A Study of Order in World Politics* (New York: Columbia University Press, 1977).

Bull, Hedley & Watson, Adam. (eds.) *The Expansion of International Society* (Oxford: Clarendon, 1984).

Burhani, Ahmad Najib. *Sufisme Kota* (Jakarta: Serambi, 2001).

Butt, S.S. 'Small-time hoodlum being used for terror' *The News*, 4 January (2005).

Buzan, Barry. *People, States and Fear: An Agenda for International Security Studies in the Post-Cold War Era* (Boulder: Lynne Rienner, 1991).

Casciani, Dominic. 'UK 'Islamophobia' rises after 11 September' BBC News, 29 August, 2002).

Castells, Manuel. *The Power of Identity* (Oxford: Blackwell Publishers, 2004).

Chandler, David. *Bosnia: Faking Democracy After Dayton* (London: Pluto Press, 2000).

Chandler, David. *Kosovo Elections: Failing The Test Of Democracy?* British Helsinki Human Rights Group, 21 November (2005) www.bhhrg.org.

Chasdi, Richard. *Tapestry of Terrorism. A Portrait of Middle Eastern Terrorism 1994–1999* (Lanham: Lexington Books, 2002).

Cockburn, Andrew & Cockburn, Patrick. *Out of the Ashes: The Resurgence of Saddam Hussein* (New York: Harper and Collins, 1999).

Cohen, Ariel. 'Hizb ut-Tahrir: An Emerging Threat to U.S. Interests in Central Asia', *The Heritage Foundation Backgrounder*, no. 1656, 30 May, (2003), www.heritage.org.

Cooke, Maeve. (1997) 'Authenticity and Autonomy: Taylor, Habermas, and the Politics of Recognition' *Political Theory* vol. 25, no. 2, pp. 258–288.

Corrigan, Phillip & Sayer, Derek. *The Great Arch: English State Formation as Cultural Revolution* (Oxford: Basil Blackwell, 1985).

Crittenden , Stephen. 'Interview with Bat Ye'or' *The Religion Report*, 21 November, (2005), www.abc.net.au/rn/talks/8.30/relrpt/stories/s1250346.htm.

Culpitt, I. *Social Policy and Risk* (London: Sage, 1999).

Curtin, Philip. *The World and the West. The European Challenge* (Cambridge: Cambridge University Press, 2000).

Darwish, Mahmoud. 'The Hidden Face of Extremism – the 'New Wahhabi' Movement' *EastWest Record*, 8 October, (2001), www.eastwestrecord.com/articles/theNewWahhabMovement.asp.

Derrida, Jacques. *Of Hospitality* (Stanford: Stanford University Press, 2000).

Docker, John & Fischer, Gerhard. (eds.) *Adventures of Identity: European Multicultural Experiences and Perspectives* (Tübingen: Stauffenberg, 2001).

Douglas, M. *Risk Acceptability According to the Social Sciences* (London: Routledge, 1985).

Douglas, M. *Risk and Blame: Essays in Cultural Theory* (London: Routledge, 1992).

Doran, Michael. 'Somebody Else's Civil War' *Foreign Affairs* vol. 82, no. 1 (2002), pp. 22–42.

Dunn, K.; Thomson, S.; Hanna, B.; Murphy, P. & Burnley, I. (2001) 'Multicultural Policy within Local Government in Australia', *Urban Studies*, vol. 38, no. 13, Dec. 2001), pp. 2477–2494.

Durant, Will. *The Story of Civilizations* (New York: Simon & Schuster, 1967).

Duffield, Mark & Waddell, Nicholas. 'Human Security and Global Danger: Exploring a Governmental Assemblage', *Report for Economic and Social Science Research Council*, (2004), www.bond.org.uk/pubs/gsd/duffield.pdf.

Dyker, David A. & Vejvoda, Ivan. (eds.) *Yugoslavia and After: A Study in Fragmentation, Despair and Rebirth* (London: Addison Wesley Longman, 2006).

Edwards, M. & Gaventa, J. *Global Citizen Action* (London: Earthscan, 2001).

Ehrenfeld, Rachel & Lappen, Alyssa A., 'Terror Rising – Two Islamic terrorist groups launch their bid for a global caliphate', *Free Republic*, 20 February, (2005) freerepublic.info/focus/f-news/1536359/posts.

Eickelman, Dale F. & Piscatori, James. *Muslim Politics* (Princeton: Princeton University Press, 2004).

El Fadl, Khaled Abou. 'Islam and the Theology of Power' *Middle East Report*, vol. 221, Winter (2001).

Esposito, John L. (ed.) *The Oxford Encyclopaedia of Modern Muslim World* (Oxford: Oxford University Press, 1995).

Euben, Roxanne E. *The Enemy in the Mirror. Islamic Fundamentalism and the Limits of Modern Nationalism* (Princeton/NJ: Princeton University Press, 1999).

Feldman, Allen. 'Securocratic Wars of Public Safety' *Interventions*, vol. 6, no. 3 (2004), pp. 330–350.

Foucault, Michel. *The Archeology of Knowledge and the Discourse on Language* (New York: Pantheon Books, 1985).

Foucault, Michel. *Power: The Essential Works 3* (London: Allen Lane, 2001).

Foucault, Michel. *Discipline and Punish, The Birth of the Prison* (London: Allen Lane, 1977).

Franklin, J. (ed.) *The Politics of Risk Society* (Cambridge: Polity Press, 1998).

Fuller, Graham. E. *The Future of Political Islam* (London: Palgrave, 2003).

Furnivall, J.S. *Colonial Policy and Practice. A Comparative Study of Burma and Netherlands India* (Cambridge: Cambridge University Press, 1948).

Geertz, Clifford. *The Religion of Java* (Glencoe, Ill.: The Free Press, 1960).

Geertz, Clifford. *Islam Observed* (Chicago: University of Chicago Press, 1968).

Gellner, Ernest. *Muslim Society* (Cambridge: Cambridge University Press, 1981).

Gellner, Ernest. *Postmodernism, Reason and Religion.* (London: Routledge, 1992).

Gibb, Hamilton A.R. *Studies on the Civilization of Islam* (Princeton/NJ: Princeton University Press, 1962).

Giddens, Anthony. *Beyond Left and Right. The Future of Radical Politics* (Cambridge: Polity Press, 1994).

Giddens, Anthony. *The Third Way* (Cambridge: Polity Press, 1998).

Ginanjar, Ary. *Rahasia Sukses Membangun Kercerdasan Emosi dan Spiritual*, ESQ, Emotional Spiritual Quotient, Berdasarkan 6 Rukun Iman dan 5 Rukun Islam (Jakarta: Arga Publishers, 2001).

Glasser, S. 'Global Terrorism Statistics Debated, New Report Leaves Some Wondering How to Measure the Number of Attacks', *Washington Post*, 29 October, (2005).

Glazer, Nathan. *We Are All Multiculturalists Now* (Cambridge, MA: Harvard University Press, 2007).

Goleman, Daniel. *Working with Emotional Intelligence* (New York: Bantam Books, 1999).

Gordon, Avery & Newfield, Christopher. (eds.) *Mapping Multiculturalism* (Minneapolis: University of Minnesota Press, 1996).

Gottlieb, Anthony. 'An Underclass Rebellion: Corbeil-Essones and Evry' *The Economist*, 10 November (2005).

Grare, Frédéric. (ed.) *Islamism and Security. Political Islam and the Western World* (Geneva: Program for Strategic and International Security Studies, 1999).

Gress, David. *From Plato to NATO: The Idea of the West and its Opponents* (New York: The Free Press, 1998).

Habermas, Juergen. *Frankfurter Allgemeine Zeitung*, 15 October, (2001).

Haenni, Patrick & Roy, Olivier. *L'islam dans les rythmes du temps mondial* (Paris: Karthala Publishers, Forthcoming).

Hall, John A. (ed.) *Civil Society* (New York: Polity Press, 1996).

Hamidullah, Muhammad. *Muslim Conduct of State*, (Lahore: Muhammad Ashraf, 1968).

Haqqami, Hussain. *Pakistan: Between Mosque and Military* (Washington D.C.: Carnegie Endowment, 2005).

Hartman, D. & Gerteis, J. 'Dealing with Diversity: mapping multiculturalism in sociological terms' *Sociological Theory*, vol. 23, no. 2, (2005), pp.218–240.

Hashmi, Sohail. (ed.) *Islamic Political Ethics* (Princeton: Princeton University Press, 2002).

Hassan, Riaz. *Faithlines: Muslim Conceptions of Islam and Society* (Oxford: Oxford University Press, 2002).

Haynes, Jeff. *Religion in Global Politics* (London: Longman, 1998).

Heider, Karl G. *Landscapes of Emotion, Mapping Three Cultures of Emotion in Indonesia* (Cambridge: Cambridge University Press, 1991).

Herzfeld, Michael. *Anthropology: Theoretical Practice in Culture and Society* (Oxford: Blackwell, 2001).

Herzog, Roman & Schmiegelow, Henrik. (eds.) *Preventing the Clash of Civilizations* (New York: St. Martin's Press, 1999).

Hidayat, Komaruddin & Wahyudi Nafis, Muhamad. *Agama Masa Depan, Perspektif Filsafat Perennial* (Jakarta: Gramedia Pustaka Utama, 2003).

Hirst, Phillip. *War and Power in the 21st Century. The state military conflict and the international system* (Cambridge: Polity, 2001).

Hizbut Tahrir. *Mengenal Hizbut Tahrir: Partai Politik Islam Ideologis* (Bogor: Pustaka Thariqul Izzah, 2002).

Hizbut Tahrir. *Seruan Hizbut Tahrir Kepada Kaum Muslim* (Bogor: Pustaka Thariqul Izzah, 2003).

Hobsbawm, Eric & Ranger, Terence. (eds.) *The Invention of Tradition* (Cambridge: Cambridge University Press, 1983).

Hodgson, Marshall G.S. *The Venture of Islam. Conscience and History in a World Civilization* (Chicago: University of Chicago Press, 1977).

Hoffer, Eric. *The True Believer: Thoughts on the Nature of Mass Movements* (New York: Perenial Library, 2002).

Hoffman, Bruce. *Inside Terrorism* (New York: Columbia University Press, 1998).

Hoffmann, Stanley. *World Disorders: Troubled Peace in the Post-Cold War Era* (New York: Rowman & Littlefield, 1998).

Holsti, Kalevi J. *The Dividing Discipline* (London: Allen and Unwin, 1985).

Holsti, Kalevi J. *The State, War, and the State of War* (Cambridge: Cambridge University Press, 1996).

Howell, Julia. 'Sufism and the Indonesian Islamic Revival', *Journal of Asian Studies*, vol. 60, no. 3, (2001), pp. 701–729.

Howell, Julia. 'Muslims, the New Age and Marginal Religions in Indonesia: Changing Meanings of Religious Pluralism', *Social Compass*, vol. 52, no. 4, (2005), pp. 473–493.

Howell, Julia Day. 'Modernity and Islamic Spirituality in Indonesia's New Sufi Networks' in *Sufism and the 'Modern' in Islam*, M. van Bruinesses and J.D. Howell eds (London: IB Tauris, 2007)

Howell, Julia & Nelson, Peter L. 'New Faces of Indonesian Sufism: A Demographic Profile of Tarekat Qodiriyyah-Naqsyabandiyyah, Pesantren Suryalaya in the 1990s', *Review of Indonesian and Malaysian Affairs*, vol. 35, no. 2, (2001), pp. 33–60.

Howell, Julia & Pearce, J. *Civil Society and Development: A Critical Exploration* (Boulder: Lynne Rienner, 2002).

Humphrey, Michael. (1998) *Islam, Multiculturalism, Transnationalism: from the Lebanese Diaspora* (London: IB Tauris, 1998).

Huntington, Samuel P. 'The Clash of Civilizations?', *Foreign Affairs*, vol. 72, no. 3, (1993), pp. 22–49.

Huntington, Samuel P. *Clash of Civilizations and the Framing of World Order* (New York: Simon & Schuster, 1996).

Ibrahim, Idi Subandy. 'Kesalehan Instan dan Spiritualitas Orang Kota', *Pikiran Rakyat*, vol. 17, Nov. (2001).

Ignatieff, Michael. *The Lesser Evil. Political Ethics in an Age of Terror*, (Princeton :Princeton University Press, 2004).

Ingram, Edward. (ed.) *National and International Politics in the Middle East* (London: Frank Cass, 1986).

International Crisis Group, 'Radical Islam in Central Asia: Responding to the Threat of Hizb ut-Tahrir', *ICG Asia Report*, no 58, 30 June, (2003), www.crisisweb.org.

Isar, Y. Raj & Anheier, Helmut. (eds.) *World Cultures Yearbook* (London: Sage, 2007).

Jabar, Faleh. 'Origins and Ideology of Neo-Islamism: A Few Landmarks' (in French), *Pensée*, vol. 299, (1994), pp. 51–58.

Jackson, Robert H. *Quasi-States: Sovereignty, International Relations and the Third World* (Cambridge: Cambridge University Press, 1990).

Jacoby, Tamy A. & Sasley, Brent. (eds.) *Redefining Security in the Middle East* (Manchester and New York: Manchester University Press, 2002).

Jamhari & Jabali, Fuad. *IAIN dan Modernisasi Islam di Indonesia* (Ciputat, Indonesia: Logos Wacana Ilmu, 2002).

Jansen, Johannes. *The Dual Nature of Islamic Fundamentalism* (Ithaca and New York: Cornell University Press, 1997).

Johanson, James T. *The Holy War Idea in Western and Islamic Tradition* (University Park: Pennsylvania State University Press, 1997).

Jones, Seth G. 'Averting Failure in Afghanistan' *Survival* vol. 48, no. 1 (2006)pp. 111–128.

Joppke, C. 'The retreat of multiculturalism in the liberal state: theory and policy' *British Journal of Sociology*, vol. 55, no. 2, (2004) pp. 237–257.

Juergensmeyer, Mark. *The New Cold War?: Religious Nationalism confronts the Secular State* (Berkeley: University of California Press, 1993).

Juergensmeyer, Mark. *Terror in the Mind of God: The Global Rise of Religious Violence* (Berkeley: University of California Press, 2000).

Junt, Tony and Denis Lacome (eds.) *With Us or Against Us: Studies in Global Anti-Americanism* (New York: Palgrave Macmillan, 2005).

Kaldor, Mary. H. *New & Old Wars. Organized Violence in a Global Era* (Cambridge: Polity Press, 2001).

Kamali, M. *Distorted Integration. Clientization of Immigrants in Sweden* (Uppsala: Uppsala Multiethnic Papers, 1997).

Kassab, Mohammed Y. *L' Islam face au nouvel ordre mondial* (Algier: Editions Salama, 1991).

Katzenstein, Peter & Byrnes, Tim. (eds.) *Religion in an Expanding Europe* (Cambridge: Cambridge University Press, 2006).

Kelsay, John. *Islam and War* (Louisville/KY: John Knox Press, 1993).

Kenny, Sue; Mansouri, Fethi & Spratt, P. *Arabic Communities and Well-Being: Supports and Barriers to Social Connectedness* (Melbourne: Deakin University, Centre for Citizenship and Human Rights, 2005).

Kenny, Sue. 'Reconstruction in Aceh: Building whose capacity?', *Community Development Journal, An International Forum*, vol. 40, no. 3., (2005).

Kepel, Gilles. *Jihad-Expansion et le Déclin de l'Islamisme* (Paris: Gallimard, 2000).

Kepel, Gilles. *Jihad: The Trail Political Islam* (Cambridge: Harvard University Press, 2002).

Khadduri, Majid. *War and Peace in the Law of Islam* (Baltimore: The Johns Hopkins Press, 1955).

Khan, Ismail. 'Militants were paid to repay Al Qaeda debt', *Dawn*, Karachi, 9 February, (2005), www.dawn.com/2005/02/09/top1.htm.

Khoury Philip S. & Kostiner, Joseph. (eds.) *Tribes and State Formation in the Middle East* (Berkeley: University of California Press, 1990).

Kinzer, Stephen. *All the Shah's Men: An American Coup and the Roots of Middle East Terror* (New Jersey: Wiley, 2003).

Klein, Naomi. 'The Rise of Disaster Capitalism', *The Nation*, 23 May, (2005).

Korten, D *Globalizing Civil Society: Reclaiming our Right to Power*,(New York Seven Stories Press, 1998).

Kull, Ann. *Piety and Politics. Nurcholish Madjid and His Interpretation of Islam in Modern Indonesia* (Lund: Lund Studies in History of Religions, 2005).

Kuran, Timur. *Islam and Mammon: The Economic Predicaments of Islamism*, (Princeton: Princeton University Press: 2004).

Kymlicka, William. *Multicultural Citizenship* (Oxford: Clarendon Press, 1995).

Lahoud, Nelly. *Political Thought in Islam: A Study in Intellectual Boundaries* (London: Routledge, 2005).

Lane, Ann. *Yugoslavia, When Ideals Collide* (London: Palgrave, 2004).

Lapidus, Ira M. *A History of Islamic Societies* (Cambridge: Cambridge University Press, 2001).

Lash, Scott & Featherstone, Mike. (eds.) *Recognition and Difference: politics, identity, multiculturalism* (London: Sage, 2002).

Levy, Jacob. *The Multiculturalism of Fear* (Oxford: Oxford University Press, 2000).

Lewis, Bernard. *What Went Wrong? Western Impact and Middle Eastern Response* (Oxford: Oxford University Press, 2001).

Lewis, Bernard. *The Crisis of Islam: Holy War and Unholy Terror* (London: Weidenfeld & Nicolson, 2003).

Lincoln, Bruce. *Holy Terrors. Thinking about Religion after September 11* (Chicago: University of Chicago Press, 2003).

Lipson, Leslie. *The Ethical Crisis of Civilizations* (London: Sage, 1993).

Lobe, Jim. 'Gap Grows Between U.S., World Public Opinion' *Inter-Press Service*, 16 March, (2004).

Lupton, D. *Risk* (London: Routledge, 1999).

Lyon, D. *Surveillance after September 11* (Cambridge: Polity Press, 2003).

Lyons, Gene. M. & Mastanduno Michael. (eds.) *Beyond Westphalia* (Baltimore: John Hopkins University Press, 1995).

Lyotard, Jean-François. *The Postmodern Condition: A Report on Knowledge*, (Minnesota: University of Minnesota Press, 1985).

MacFarquhar, Neil. 'Muslim Scholars Increasingly Debate Unholy War', *The New York Times*, 10 December, (2004).

Mandaville, Peter. *Transnational Muslim Politics* (London: Routledge, 2004).

Mann, Michael. *Incoherent Empire* (London: Verso: 2003).

Martin, Leonore. (ed.) *New Frontiers in Middle Eastern Security* (New York: St. Martin's Press, 1999).

Marty, Martin & Appleby, Scott. (eds.) *The Fundamentalism Project* (Chicago: Chicago University Press, 1991–1995).

Mayer, Jean-François. 'Hizb ut-Tahrir – The Next al-Qaida, Really?', *PSIO Occasional Paper*, Federal Department of Foreign Affairs, Switzerland, April, (2004).

Mazzetti, Mark. 'Spy Agencies Say Iraq War Worsens Terrorist Threat', *New York Times*, 24 September, (2006), www.nytimes.com/2006/09/24/world/middleeast/24terror.html?pagewanted=1&_r=1.

Meijer, Roel. 'Jihadi Opposition in Saudi Arabia' *ISIM Review*, vol. 15, spring, (2005).

Miller, Lynne. *Global Order* (Boulder: Westview, 1990)

Mitchell, Richard. *The Society of the Muslim Brothers* (London: Oxford University Press, 1969).

Montgomery, John D. & Glazer, Nathan. (eds) *Sovereignty under Challenge. How Governments Respond* (New Brunswick: Transaction, 2002).

Muenkler, Herfried. (2005) *The New Wars* (Cambridge: Polity Press, 2004).

Mulkhan, Abdul Munir. *Dari Semar ke Sufi. Kesalehan Multikultural Sebagai Solusi Islam di Tengah Tragedi Keagamaan Umat Manusia* (Kalasan, Sleman, Yogyakarta : Al-Ghiyats, 2003).

Mythen, G. *Ulrich Beck. A Critical Introduction to the Risk Society.* (London: Pluto Press, 2004).

Napoleoni, Loretta. *Modern Jihad: Tracing the Dollars Behind the Terror Networks* (London: Pluto Press, 2003).

Nardin, Terry. (ed.) *The Ethics of War and Peace* (Princeton: Princeton University Press, 1996).

Noer, Kautsar Ashari. *Tasawuf Perenial. Kearifan Kritis Kaum Sufi* (Jakarta: Serambi, 2002).

Noor, Farish. 'Mapping out the Political Topography of Political Islam in Malaysia: Actors, Agents and Currents of Thought and Ideas' CSCAP General Conference, Jakarta, 4 December, (2003).

Novikov, Evgenii. 'The Recruiting and Organizational Structure of Hizb ut-Tahrir', *Terrorism Monitor,* The Jamestown Foundation, March (2004), jamestown.org/publications_details.php?volume_id=400&issue_id_3 148, accessed 6

Nugent David & Vincent Joan. (eds.) *A Companion to the Anthropology of Politics* (Oxford: Blackwell, 2004).

Nye, Joseph. *Bound to Lead. The Changing Nature of American Power* (New York: Basic Books, 1990).

Ong, Aihwa. *Flexible Citizenship: The Cultural Logics of Transnationality* (Durham: Duke University Press, 1999).

Osborne, D. & Gaebler, T. *Reinventing Government: How the Entrepreneurial Spirit is Transforming the Public Sector* (New York: Plume, 1993).

Page, Susan. 'Poll: Muslim Countries, Europe Question U.S. Motives' *USA Today*, 24 June, (2004).

Papastergiadis, Nikos. *The Turbulance of Migration* (Cambridge: Polity Press, 2000).

Peters, Rudolph. *Islam and Colonialism* (The Hague: Mouton Publishers, 1979).

Peters, F.E. *Islam: A Guide for Jews and Christians* (Princeton: Princeton University Press, 2003).

Philipott, Daniel. 'The Challenge of September 11 to Secularism in International Relations' *World Politics*, vol. 55, no. 1, (2002), pp. 66–95.

Pillar, Paul R. *Terrorism and US Foreign Policy* (Washington/DC: Brookings Institute, 2001).

Joshi, Pooja. *Jama'at-i Islami: The Catalyst for Islamicization in Pakistan* (Karachi: Kalinga Publications, 2003).

Popper, Karl. *The Open Society and its Enemies* (London: Routledge, 1945).

Powers, Roger & Vogele, William B. (eds.) *Protest, Power and Change: An Encyclopedia of Nonviolent Action* (New York: Garland Publishers, 1997).

Putnam, Robert D. Bowling Alone: The Collapse and Revival of American Community (New York: Simon & Schuster, 2000).

Qutb, Sayyid. *Ma'alim fi al-tariq/ Signs along the Road* (Cairo: Dar al-shuruq, 1989).

Qutb, Sayyid. *al-salam al-alami wa al-Islam/ World Peace and Islam* (Cairo: Dar al-shuruq, 1992).

Rahman, Fazlur. *Islam* (London: Weidenfeld and Nicolson, 1966).

Rahman, Fazlur. *Islam and Modernity: Transformation of Intellectual Tradition* (Chicago: Chicago University Press, 1982).

Rahman, Fazlur. *The Major Themes of the Quran* (Minneapolis: Bibiotheca Islamica, 1994).

Ramakrishna, Kumar. 'Jemaah Islamiah: Aims, Motivations and Possible Counter Strategies', (2002), www.ntu.edu.sg/idss/Perspectives/research_050221.htm.

Rana, M. *A to Z of Jehadi Organizations in Pakistan* (Lahore: Mashal Books, 2004).

Rashid, Ahmad. *Jihad: The Rise of Militant Islam in Central Asia* (Lahore: Vanguard, 2002).

Revel, Jean-François. *Democracy against itself* (New York: Free Press, 1993).

Riddell, Peter. *Islam and the Malay-Indonesian World, Transmission and Responses* (Honolulu: University of Hawaii Press, 2001).

Roberts, Les 'Morality Before and After the 2003 Invasion of Iraq: Cluster Sample Survey' *The Lancet*, 29 October, (2004).

Robertson, Roland. *Globalization, Social Theory and Global Culture* (London: Sage, 1992).

Rosaldo, Renato. *Culture and Truth* (Boston: Beacon Press, 1989).

Roy, Olivier. *The Failure of Political Islam* (Cambridge: Harvard University Press, 1994).

Roy, Olivier. *Globalised Islam: the search for the new ummah* (London: C.Hurst & Co., 2004).

Roy, Olivier. 'Europe's Response to Radical Islam', *Current History,* Vol. 104, No. 685 (2005),

Roy, Olivier. 'A Clash of Cultures or a Debate on Europe's Values? *ISIM REVIEW*, vol. 15, spring, (2005), pp. 6–7.

Russet, Bruce. *Grasping Democratic Peace* (Princeton/NJ: Princeton University Press, 1993).

Saad, Wissam. 'Alternate Australian Muslim Religious Leadership', *The Religion Report,* 20 October, (2004), www.abc.net.au/rn/talks/8.30/relrpt/stories/s1223296.htm.

Sadiki, Larbi. *The Search for Arab Democracy Discourses and Counter-Discourses.* (New York: Columbia University Press, 2004).

Sageman, Marc. *Understanding Terror Networks* (Philadelphia: University of Pennsylvania Press, 2004).

Said, Edward. *Orientalism* (New York: Pantheon, 1978).

Saikal, Amin. *The Rise and Fall of the Shah* (Princeton: Princeton University Press, 1980).

Saikal, Amin. *Islam and the West: Conflict or Cooperation?* (London: Palgrave, 2003).

Saikal, Amin. 'Securing Afghanistan's Border' *Survival* vol. 48, no. 1 (2006).

Salamon, L.; Anheier, H.; List, R.; Toepler, S. & Sokolowski, S. *Global Civil Society. Dimensions of the Non-Profit Sector* (Baltimore: The Johns Hopkins Centre for Civil Society Studies, 1999).

Salim, Agus. 'The Rise of Hizbut Tahrir Indonesia (1982–2004): It's Political Opportunity Structure, Resource Mobilization, and Collective Action Frames', MA Thesis, Syarif Hidayatullah State Islamic University, Jakarta, (2005).

Sarat, Austin. (ed.) *The Blackwell Companion to Law and Society* (Oxford: Blackwell, 2004).

Sassen, Saskia. *Guests and Aliens* (New York : New York Press, 1999).

Satori, G. Pluralismo, multiculturalismo e estranei (Milano: Rizzoli, 2000).

Sayad, A. *The Suffering of the Immigrant* (Cambridge: Polity Press, 2004).

Sayyid, Bobby S. A Fundamental Fear: Eurocentrism and the Emergence of Islamism, (London: Zed Books, 1997).

Schmiegelow, Michèle. (ed.) *Democracy in Asia* (New York: St. Martin's Press, 1997).

Schmitt, Carl & Schwab, George. *The Concept of the Political* (Chicago: University of Chicago Press, 1976).

Schwartz, Stephen. *Democracy and Islam After September 11, The case for optimism. The Weekly Standard,* paper offered at the 23rd annual convention of the Assembly of Turkish–American Associations, as part of a panel discussion titled 'Reevaluating Democracy and Islam after September 11', 16 December, (2002), www.frontpagemag.com/Articles/ReadArticle.asp?ID=5102

Schwartz, Stephen. *The Two Faces of Islam: The House of Sa'ud from Tradition to Terror* (New York: Doubleday, 2002).

Schwartz, Stephen. 'Islamic Fundamentalism in the Balkans' *Partisan Review*, summer, 21 November, (2000), www.bu.edu/partisanreview/archive/2000/3/schwartz.

Schwedler, Jillian. (ed.) *Toward Civil Society in the Middle East?* (Boulder: Lynne Rienner, 1995).

Scruton, Roger. *The West and the Rest: Globalization and the Terrorist Threat* (Wilmington, Delaware: ISI-books, 2002).

Seremetakis, C. Nadia. (ed.) *The Senses Still: Perception and Memory as Material Culture in Modernity* (Chicago: The University of Chicago Press, 1996).

Shahrani, Nazif M. 'War, Factionalism and the State in Afghanistan', *American Anthropologist*, vol. 104, no. 3, (2002), pp. 715–722.

Shklar, Judith N.; Hoffman, Stanley & Thomson, Dennis F. *Redeeming American Political Thought* (Chicago: University of Chicago Press, 1998).

Siegel, James T. 'Images and Odors in Javanese Practices Surrounding Death', *Indonesia*, vol. 3, no. 6, (1983), pp. 1–14.

Slovic, P.; Lichtenstein, S. & Fischhoff, B. 'Perceived Risk: Psychological Factors and Social Implications', *Proceedings of the Royal Society*, (1981), pp. 17–34.

Smart, B. (ed.) *Resisting Modernization* (London: Sage, London, 1999).

Snyder, Robert S. 'Hating America: Bin Laden as a Civilizational Revolutionary', *The Review of Politics*, vol. 65, no. 4, (2003), pp. 325–350.

Starr, Joel. 'How to Outflank al Qaeda in the Balkans', *European Affairs*, fall, (2004).

Stern, Jessica. 'Pakistan's Jihad Culture', *Foreign Affairs*, vol, 79, no.6 (2000).

Strauss, Leo. *Natural Right and History* (Chicago: University of Chicago Press, 1950).

Swick, Sarah. *From London to Andijan: The rising global influence of Hizb-ut-Tahrir among Muslim Youth*, Minaret of Freedom Institute, 18 November, (2005), www.minaret.org/hisb%20at-tahrir.pdf.

Taji-Farouki, Suha. *A Fundamental Quest: Hizb al-Tahrir and the Search for the Islamic Caliphate* (Grey Seal, London, 1996).

Taji-Farouki, Suha., 'Islamists and the threat of *Jihad*: Hizb al-Tahrir and al-Muhajiroun on Israel and the Jews', *Middle Eastern Studies*, vol. 36, no. 4, October, (2000), pp. 21–46.

Takeyh, Ray. 'Iran: from Reform to Revolution?', *Survival*, vol. 46, no. 1, (2004), pp. 131–143.

Tan, Merlyna. Islamic Radicalism and Anti-Americanism in Indonesia: The Role of the Internet, *Policy Studies, vol. 18*, East–West Center, Washington, (2005).

Taylor, C. *Hegel* (Cambridge: Cambridge University Press, 1975).

Taylor, C. (ed.) *Multiculturalism: Examining the Politics of Recognition* (Princeton: Princeton University Press, 1994).

Telhami, Shibley. 'Arab Public Opinion: A Survey in Six Countries' *San Jose Mercury*, 16 March (2003).

Peerenboom, Rajenthran. (ed.) *Asian Discourses of Rule of Law* (London: Routledge, 2004).

Tibi, Bassam. *The Crisis of Modern Islam* (Salt Lake City: Utah University Press, 1988).

Tibi, Bassam. *Islam and the Cultural Accommodation of Social Change* (Boulder: Westview Press, 1990).

Tibi, Bassam. 'Islamic Law/Shari'a, Human Rights, Universal Morality and International Relations' *Human Rights Quarterly*, vol. 16, no. 2, (1994), pp. 277–299.

Tibi, Bassam. *Conflict and War in the Middle East. From Interstate War to New Security* (New York: St. Martin's Press, 1997).

Tibi, Bassam. *The Challenge of Fundamentalism: Political Islam and the New World Disorder* (Berkeley: University of California Press, 1998).

Tibi, Bassam. *Krieg der Zivilisationen. Politik und Religion zwischen Vernunft und Fundamentalismus* (Munich: Heyne Verlag, 1998).

Tibi, Bassam. *Fundamentalismus im Islam. Eine Gefahr für den Weltfrieden* (Darmstadt: Wissenschaftliche Buchgesellschaft 2000)

Tibi, Bassam. 'Post-Bipolar Order in Crisis: The Challenge of Politicized Islam' *Millennium, Journal of International Affairs*, vol. 29, no. 3, (2000), pp. 843–859.

Tibi, Bassam. 'Secularization and Desecularization in Modern Islam' *Religion, Staat, Gesellschaft* vol. 1, no. 1, (2000), pp. 95–117.

Tibi, Bassam. 'Habermas and the Return of the Sacred. Is it a Religious Renaissance? Political Religion as a New Totalitarianism' *Religion, Staat, Gesellschaft* vol. 3, no. 2, (2002), pp. 265–296.

Tibi, Bassam. *Der neue Totalitarismus* (Darmstadt: Primus, 2004).

Tibi, Bassam. *Islam between Culture and Politics* (New York: Palgrave, 2005).

Tibi, Bassam. 'From Islamist Jihadism to Democratic Peace? Islam at the Crossroads in Post-Bipolar International Politics' *Ankara Paper 16* (London: Taylor & Francis, 2005), pp. 1–41.

Touraine, A. *Can We Live Together? Equality and Difference* (Cambridge: Polity. Cambridge, 2000).

Toynbee, Arnold. *The Study of History* (New York: Oxford University Press, 1947).

Turner, Brian. S. 'The erosion of citizenship' *The British Journal of Sociology*, vol. 52, no. 2, (2001), pp. 189–209.

Turner, Brian S. 'Cosmopolitan virtue, globalization and patriotism' *Theory Culture & Society*, vol. 19, no. 1–2, (2002), pp. 45–63.

Turner, Brain S. 'Warrior charisma and the spiritualization of violence' *Body & Society*, vol. 9, no. 4, (2004), pp. 93–108.

Twining, W. *Globalisation & Legal Theory* (London: Butterworths, 2000).

Ulfkotte, Udo. *Der Krieg in unseren Städte. Wie radikale Islamisten Deutschland unterwandern* (Frankfurt: Fischer, 2004).

van Bruinessen, Martin. *Kitab Kuning, Pesantren dan Tarekat, Tradisi-tradisi Islam di Indonesia* (Bandung: Mizan, 1995).

van Bruinessen, Martin & Howell, Julia. *Sufism and the 'Modern' in Islam* (London: IB Tauris, Forthcoming).

van Creveld, Martin. *The Transformation of War* (New York: The Free Press, 1991).

van Creveld, Martin & von Knop, Katharina. (eds.) *Countering Modern Terrorism* (Bielefeld: Bertelsmann, 2005).

van der Laue, Theodore. *The World Revolution of Westernization* (New York: Oxford University Press, 1987).

van Rooy, A. *Global Legitimacy Game. Civil Society, Globalization and Protest* (London: Palgrave, 2004).

von Clauswitz, Carl. *On War* (London: Pelican, 1968).

von Pilar, Ulrike. 'Humanitarian Aid across Borders: Activities and Experiences of Médecins sans Frontières', *Workshop Strausberg*, vol. 17, 18 June, (1998).

Watt, William M. *Islamic Fundamentalism and Modernity* (London: Routledge, 1988).

West, C. *Matters Matters* (New York: Vintage Books, 1993).

Whittacker, David J. (ed.) *The Terrorism Reader* (London: Routledge, 2001).

Wiktorowicz, Quintan. (ed.) *Islamic Activism: A Social Movement Theory Approach* (Bloomington: Indiana University Press, 2004).

Wikan, Unni. *Managing Turbulent Hearts, A Balinese Formula for Living* (Chicago: University of Chicago Press, 1990).

Wilkinson, I. *Anxiety in a Risk Society* (London: Routledge, 2001).

Wilkinson, M; Davies, Anne & Clennell, Andrew. 'Muslims unite – it's time to disown terror', *Sydney Morning Herald*, 26 July, (2005).

Wordlaw, Grant. *Political Terrorism* (Cambridge: Cambridge University Press, 1982).

Wuthnow, Robert. (ed.) *Encyclopaedia of Politics and Religion* (Washington, D.C: Congressional Quarterly Inc., 1998).

Ye'or, Bat. *Islam and Dhimmitude* (Cransbury: Associated University Presses, 2002).

Zohar, Danah & Marshall, Ian. *SQ: Spiritual Intelligence, The Ultimate Intelligence* (London: Bloomsbury, 2000).

NAME INDEX

SUBJECT INDEX